CITIZEN POWER

Senator Mike Gravel

CITIZEN POWER

A People's Platform

Holt, Rinehart and Winston

New York   Chicago   San Francisco

To RITA
and our children,
MARTIN *and* LYNNE,
with love
and hope for the future

Contents

Preface

As BOTH an elected public official and a private citizen, I have become increasingly distressed over the continuing exclusion of the people from any meaningful role in our governmental, economic, and social power structures. At the same time, I have become acutely aware of the rising dissatisfaction and crumbling patience among citizens constantly frustrated in efforts to participate in decision-making processes which directly impinge on their lives.

Everywhere I go, people ask the same questions: "How can we change things?" and "What can ordinary people do to beat the system?" They want to know: "Why doesn't anyone listen to us? *Really* listen, so they can find out what we want and need, not what 'they' (the entrenched establishments) say we want or think we need." Most of all, they ask: "What can I do?" or "When do *we* (the people) get a chance to run things?"

This book is an attempt to answer some of those questions and to say that some of us are listening. Some of the proposals to be presented here are my own, drawn from my own experience and what I perceive to be the common views of vast numbers of Americans. Some ideas have been adapted from the thinking and writing of individuals or groups. All are included, however, with but one objective in mind: to help chart a course of action that will enable people to gain a greater measure of control over their lives.

Such a program, or what I prefer to call "a people's platform," is needed if only to start thinking about how to attack our social problems. We Americans have become a people without apparent purpose, permitting ourselves to sink into a morass of self-defeating disputes at home and self-defacing involvements abroad. The results have served to magnify our problems, obstruct our progress, and severely strain our national fiber.

"What has happened to America?" The world wonders and we, ourselves, wonder. What, indeed, has happened? Have its goals changed, its dreams vanished, its promise been expended? And as an extraordinary human force, are we on the downhill side of the mountain?

I do not believe it. I refuse to believe it. The goals remain; the promise is yet to be fulfilled for all. But the dreams of our founders, dreams of a land characterized by individual freedom and economic well being that did not sacrifice human values, have been compromised. The concept of a nation bound together by wisely crafted laws, rather than corruptible men, has remained unperfected. A sense of self-righteousness, born of newly acquired and immense state power, too often has supplanted a sense of what is right. America's greatest gift to the world—the idea of a government "of the people, by the people, and for the people" has been perverted.

This has not been the people's doing. To the contrary, it has happened because of the very lack of their ability to do, to participate in or to control the actions of either their government or their society.

This is not to say that many citizens haven't been trying to improve our country and haven't been making progress. In the past decade there has been an awakening, especially among the young, to a need to do something personally in the civil rights and peace movements and now the consumer and environmental movements. Although these movements have had varying degrees of success, I know that today many of the people who have worked hard in them are discouraged. They feel that while they have made an impact, it isn't big enough.

Nonetheless, to have reached this point to me is very exciting, not cause for dismay. We should not turn away from what has been accomplished, but build upon it. It seems to me we need to regroup and find a new starting point. Citizen movements have been making a frontal assault on the system. Now I believe it is time to seize the tools of power from within. We need to change the Constitution and the laws of the land and change our political and social institutions to meet today's realities. Our founding fathers believed in this. Indeed, in the Declaration of Independence they said accommodating institutions to change is a permanent, perpetual duty of free men.

In setting down here what could be the nucleus of a people's platform, I am in effect only reiterating the belief that America is still open to revision—not by just some of the people, the activists and radicals, but by *all* the people. To make our government truly responsive and our society truly democratic we need the will and the efforts of every citizen.

A people's platform is a prerequisite if we are to realize the democratic ideals of public participation and public control. Such a platform, I hope, will become a sweeping citizen challenge to the overpowering, existing establishments to change our failing political institutions and repressive economic relationships.

It is an American trait to pursue an ideal, not abstractly, but as a direct confrontation with reality—to believe, in short, that ideals *can* be achieved. What this means in a people's platform is that our system is not hopeless, that it must not be rejected. American pragmatism is open-ended, leaving no questions unasked and no solutions unsuggested. Every idea (or plank) I outline here, however radical it at first seems in the context of today's politics, is basic to our spirit and consistent with our history. These portions of a people's platform are but a continuation of the Declaration of Independence (see Appendix A). They represent elements of the same platform, brought up to date, that the Populists put forward at Omaha in 1892 (see Appendix C), when they sought "to restore the government of the Republic to the hands of 'the plain people,' with whose class it originated."

Surely there is nothing strange or new or threatening about such a platform. It will distress only those who have the essentially un-American view that change itself is frightening and should be avoided at all costs. But change, after all, is only a grindstone for honing our society so we can diminish the bad and sharpen the good.

My purpose, then, is to present what I suggest would be part of an appropriate 1972 version of the traditional American people's platform—a populism of substance more than style. A *new* populism wherein the individual can acquire the tools to contribute in the management of his government and his society.

The place to begin, and the place where we become most aware of the appropriateness and necessity of the task, is the Constitution. The immediate crises faced by the framers of the Constitution included representation of majority and minority interests and the basis for taxation. Today, these two questions rise again to crisis proportion and we are confronted, on the one hand, with huge groups of unrepresented people and, on the other, with a tax structure that, as a product of the vested interests, saddles the middle class and the poor, while it rewards the rich and near-rich. In addition, we face two major difficulties not even dealt with in the Constitution: how to utilize our resources responsibly and fairly and how to guarantee the free flow of government information to the public. These problems demand entirely new approaches or representation and new checks and balances within both government and society.

Yet within the present context of two-party politics, no one is really suggesting any new models; in fact, within conventional politics, few dare ask the important questions in the first place. No wonder people are politically "apathetic." Politically, nothing important has been happening.

What I am saying is that there *are* solutions to our problems. They need to be talked about, debated, and tried. I believe in the great American experiment of self-government. Our political system need not remain stagnant. It can be changed; the people can do it. In fact, they are the *only* ones who can do it.

Acknowledgments

BOOKS SELDOM ARE WRITTEN without a great deal of assistance and encouragement from friends and associates. This book is no exception.

My thanks to the wonderful women on my staff, whose abilities and efficiency made it possible for me to find the time to write a book without diminishing the effectiveness of my office: Flora Bergman, Dianne Church, Susan Gordon, Roselynn Heath, Marcia Miller, Bea Oertel, Elisabeth Romayko, Betsy Schoenfeld, Alice Slater, Jill Smythe, and Kathy Morgan.

My appreciation for the thoughtfulness of those who so generously gave of their hospitality and logistical support: Mr. and Mrs. James T. Barnes, Mr. and Mrs. Rafael Ramos Cobián, Henry Dormann, Mark Fleischman, Walter R. Schoenknecht, Ivan Orlandi, and Gustavo Agrait, and my good friend Charles Hamel.

My gratitude to those who contributed many of the thoughts and writings from which much of the finished product was drawn: Dr. Len Rodberg, Dr. Douglas Jones, Dr. Tom Lantos, Bill Hoffman, Egan O'Connor, Arlie Schardt, Joe Rothstein, Karl Hess, Marcus Raskin, Charles Fishman, Bernard Poirier, Tom Smythe, Ted Johnson, Tom Reeves, and Michael Rowan. Also to the many others, too numerous to list here, who offered helpful suggestions and thoughtful comments.

My recognition of the important roles played by my literary agent, David Obst, and by Aaron Asher and Sig Moglen of Holt, Rinehart and Winston, Inc.

Finally, a special acknowledgment and deep personal gratitude to the two men who served as my chief editorial consultants and advisers throughout the compilation and the preparation of this work: Bill Howard and my administrative assistant, Marty Wolf.

CITIZEN POWER

1

Now It's the Citizen's Turn

*There can be no democracy unless
it is a dynamic democracy. When
our people cease to participate—
to have a place in the sun—
then all of us will wither in the
darkness of decadence.*

—*Saul D. Alinsky*

"BULLSHIT, Senator. It won't work."

"Why not?"

"Because you're talking about something that doesn't exist, man, that's why. There's no such thing as 'citizen power.' Not for people like us." The black youth tilted his chair back against the wall and regarded me with open skepticism, challenging me to prove him wrong. The others nodded their agreement.

It was a hot summer afternoon in mid-1970, and I was in a Harlem storefront street academy, rapping with a group of social and educational drop-outs—the ones polite society paternalistically refers to as "the disadvantaged." I had scheduled the visit when I arrived in New York earlier in the day and learned I had some free time available before my evening speaking engagement. The street academy program was get-

1

ting some good reviews. I wanted to see one for myself, and I wanted to talk with the students.

For months now I had sensed a "happening" taking place in America. Everywhere I traveled, I saw growing public dissatisfaction, frustration, and anger. This was no *silent* majority I was witnessing. This was the people articulating in both words and deeds that they wanted something more out of life than they were receiving. They were demanding more economic security, more benefits and safeguards, more personal freedom, and more control over the decision-making process.

The demands were not particularly new, but there was something significantly different about the manner in which they were being presented. Instead of complaining and demonstrating individually, citizens were joining together and forming powerful public-interest constituencies: blacks, Spanish surnamed Americans, peace groups, young, the aged, women, homosexuals, environmentalists, welfare mothers, consumers—each with its own specific objectives and proposals, yet all sharing the common bond of seeking to change the status quo in America, to improve it, to have some impact on society.

Out of the seeds of despair and conflict and alienation, I detected, and probably others have also, that the embryo of a new people's platform was taking shape—a program for change struggling to achieve life. A new force was emerging upon the American scene: citizen power. All that was needed, I felt, was for the people to become aware of the power and to reach out and assume it.

But sitting in that Harlem street academy in the middle of neglected America, I could readily understand why the idea of "citizen power" was greeted with contempt when I raised the subject. What did that mean to these alienated young men and women? They had only to look out the window to see a street—their street—littered with debris, where crime and poverty were daily facts of life. They had no jobs, no money, nothing to call their own. What little they received from government was doled out as a privilege not as a right. Maybe if I had talked about the possibility of getting some extra money to buy some clothes or get a car or rent a better apartment, they would have responded more enthusiastically. But citizen power? What was in it for them?

"Hell, man, there's no such thing as citizens around here, much less citizen power," the boy seated next to me argued. "There's just people. The only citizen I know is the Dude in the White House and, I guess, maybe the fat cats that get all the money. They're the ones who call it their way. The rest of us, we got no say. We just got to cut it our own way."

"Look around you," I said. "How do you think this academy got here. It wasn't the government. A bunch of citizens joined with the Urban League to set up this academy, because so many of you were dropping out from the public school system. They couldn't get the government or the schools to come up with any solutions to the problem, so they raised the money, rented the buildings, hired the teachers, and started doing something about it on their own. I'm not saying it's going to be easy. For example, I understand the street academy program is in trouble because the private money sources are drying up and the government refuses to fill the breach by pumping in sufficient funds needed to keep it alive. That's a real shame. The fact remains, however, that the people are trying to bring about a change through their own efforts. They might not succeed this time, or even the next time. But their actions put the type of pressure on government that, if applied often enough, will force it to respond. What has to be done is to get more people involved and raise the level of demand until the problem becomes such a visible issue that the government will not be able to ignore it any longer. That's what I mean by citizen power. And it all starts right here at the neighborhood level."

"I guess you're right," the boy grudgingly admitted, "but that's not it, man. I mean, I'm not talking about street academies. I'm talking about the big things. You know, like going to Vietnam, or a good job, or more money. We don't have any say in those kind of things."

He was right, of course. The "common man" has been precluded from the decision-making process. The balance of power rests in the hands of the government, business, and organized labor—the triumvirate leadership of an eco-political society.

"Wouldn't you like to change that?" I asked. "Be a *part* of government instead of just under it? Have enough control and enough influence so it has to listen to you when you need or want something?"

"Sure I would," he conceded, "but it can't be done. You've got to have a lot of clout to do that, and we don't have it."

"Yes you do," I countered. "How do you think business or labor or the corporations or farmers are able to make government pass the laws they want and give them the help they need? They do it by presenting united fronts at all levels of government and applying pressure at the polls from the neighborhood right up to the White House. You've got the numbers to do it, if you will just stick together."

"What good does that do? They all promise us everything around election time, but they never deliver."

"Make them. Tell them what you want and if you don't get it, vote them out of office. Don't take any excuses."

"But how do we let them know what we want or what we need," a voice on my left asked.

"You get together and make up a program—that's all a people's platform is—and then you present it to all the candidates running for office or those who are now in office, no matter what political party they're in, and you tell them that either they support *it* or you won't support *them*."

"Do you really think something like that would ever work?" a girl asked. She hadn't seemed very interested until now.

"I think it can," I said. "It has to. It's worked for others in this country. The only way you can beat the system is *to use it.*"

"Yeah, but someone has to start putting it all together, man," an angry voice shouted from across the room.

"That's really what I feel is happening throughout the country right now," I answered. "People like yourselves are starting to make their demands known, loudly and clearly, and that's how a platform is created. It's on the way. But you've got to be a part of it. That's what I mean by citizen power."

"Right on, man, right on!"

Now, nearly two years later, I believe more than ever that the time for citizen power is at hand. By their actions and in their demands, the people, perhaps unknowingly, have been assembling a platform to change America; a program that is neither conservative nor liberal, but presents a citizen-oriented plan for bold action to end the severe social troubles we all experience daily; a program which puts people ahead of politics and enables them to participate in the decisions and share in the control of the policies and actions which shape their destinies and determine their lives.

The people are tired of liberal "promises" and conservative "game plans" which offer the rhetoric of hope but, in reality, merely protect and perpetuate the status quo. Conservatism in America has too often meant reaction, racism, and support for the wealthy against the poor. Liberalism, on the other hand, has relied too heavily on the power of the state to solve problems, while failing to assure continued popular participation and control. The liberals have not attacked the increase and centralization of wealth and power; they have abetted it. What astounds and irritates so many of the people is that the liberals, of both Democrat and Republican varieties, have been in power for nearly forty years. Yet, they have not made good on their promises. Liberals have given some band-aid emergency measures to the poor, but their programs have been paid for by the little man and their policies have often benefited the rich and the powerful. To achieve "security" they built a mighty military machine, and a world empire to go with it. The conservatives advanced and perpetuated it. Liberals also built a confusing bureaucratic structure of anti-poverty and welfare programs which rob the middle class of their money and the poor of their incentive and integrity. These programs are but a hodge-podge of patchwork solutions applied sporadically to meet emergencies.

Indeed, the programs have not even been able to meet the emergencies. In the first place, the real money has gone for war preparation and war making. In the second place, the liberals have left the basic economic structure of the country untouched. The tax system continues to rest heavily on the middle class, and even on the poor, while it practically exempts the rich and near rich. The liberal programs fostered not only great industrial growth, but also allowed the growth of poverty, alienation, and urban blight.

Now the people want a platform of their own—a platform which strongly supports the old liberal notions of increasing the public sector and increasing the public responsibility in all areas of life, including business and work, but which also supports the traditional conservative notions of the freedom to be left alone and of the necessity of strong protection of the individual against the state. Such a people's platform will go beyond the authentic forms of liberalism and conservatism in the tasks it sets for itself. First, it will seek to change the present tremendous concentration of wealth and power in America. Second, it will carve out new areas of autonomous public interests and form highly visible and active citizen constituencies capable of fracturing the existing power structure.

A people's platform will demand a balance of power between the citizen and the state and between the executive and Congress. People want the state as an instrument for protection and action on their behalf, but as their servant rather than their master.

But governmental reform is not enough. A people's platform must also address itself to those forces in society whose power now blocks both responsible government and needed social and economic change. It must be made clear, however, who and what is being attacked. When we assail military spending, we are assailing the idea of a system which values building missiles for overkill more than correcting social ills. When we criticize business or industry, we are criticizing the notion that any part of the American economy can be run for private profit alone without regard for the public's interests.

Most Americans today are dissatisfied. They are told by everyone that they are "the richest people in the world" and "the world's freest nation." Yet, they see poverty in the midst of plenty and an eroding of civil liberties. With national security as practically the only primary concern of the state for the last twenty years, enormous portions of our wealth and our human resources have been poured into military programs, while desperate human needs lie neglected in every corner of our nation.

"Today," James B. Conant points out, "we all realize that democracy is not a self-perpetuating virus adapted to any body politic—that was the assumption of a previous generation. Democracy we now know to be a special type of organism requiring specific nutriment materials—some economic, some social and cultural." Recognizing this to be true, a people's platform must inject the healing properties of citizen participation and control into the mainstream of American life. The people must be permitted to assume the responsibility necessary to preserve their own freedoms and solve society's problems. Such responsible participation requires an open adversary environment of controversy, in keeping with the original design of American government, which generated a built-in arena of conflict through the devices of checks and balances and separation of powers. Rather than minimize conflict, therefore, a people's platform will encourage it in the belief that it is in the tension between competing interest constituencies that we can best serve the needs of total society. The growing constituency of consumerism, for example, has repeatedly demonstrated how a public-interest constituency can successfully challenge the power of long-entrenched private-interest constituencies once it becomes sufficiently visible. Spearheaded by activist Ralph Nader, consumers have been able to bring their new-found power to bear upon government and win legislation forcing needed improvements in areas such as product safety and quality standards. In my own state of Alaska the environmentalist constituency has served as adversary to the oil companies in an attempt to ensure that construction of the proposed trans-Alaska pipeline will not do excessive damage to the ecology. A poorly constructed pipeline would not only endanger the environment, it also would tend to raise the end cost of oil to the consumer. The nation's energy consumers need Alaska's oil, but no one wants a *bad* pipeline.

The recent surge of viable public-interest constituencies upon the national scene has prompted a flurry of new public-interest legislation and executive orders in response to their demands and in recognition of their rising political power. These new laws provide citizens with heretofore unavailable recourse through the courts and can be used as tools to check many private and government acts and policies which run counter to the public's best interests. Nader, for example, has used the government's own information, pried loose under provisions of the Freedom of Information Act, to expose instances when our hard-earned taxpayer dollars have been wasted. In Alaska, conservationists used the 102 Statement of the National Environmental Protection Act to block construction of the oil pipeline by court injunction, until the project could be proven environmentally safe. There are many other such laws now available to the citizen, of which the reader may not be aware, and I have compiled a list of some of them in the back of this book (see Appendix F, Laws for Citizens to Make Waves By). These laws represent real citizen power, power that should be used.

A people's platform, however, must not rely only on the public for help in reaching its goals. It must speak to the private interests as well. While private interests must be reminded that nothing private can be allowed to control an entire segment of the economy or affect the lives of millions of people, the creative talents and the efficiency of the business-corporate constituencies should be enlisted in the fight against social and economic injustice.

Although a people's platform must set forth broad goals and general principles, it must not hesitate to make specific proposals, whenever possible, for attaining its stated objectives. Nor can it be timid in breaking fresh ground or searching out new ways to solve old problems. If it is to succeed, it will follow the advice of city planner C. A. Doxiadis: "People must learn to recognize that they must be very conservative when dealing with men, and very revolutionary when dealing with new systems and networks." In this way, a people's platform will become one of substance rather than simply of style.

What follows, then, is an attempt to recap some of the major problems besetting the American citizen today and to offer some innovative solutions. Most of the problems it attacks have already been identified and are known to all. Some of the stated objectives and principles, but not all, have been articulated. A few of the suggested solutions have been proposed elsewhere, but many have not. Hopefully, the end product contains at least some of the ingredients needed to make a people's platform effective. Someone, as that angry young black in the Harlem street academy recognized, "has to start putting it all together."

2

Who Stole the American Dream?

*The present state of things
is the consequence of the past;
and it is natural to inquire as
to the sources of the good we
enjoy or the evils we suffer.*

—*Samuel Johnson*

UNLIKE MOST PEOPLES, Americans have always had a platform, a dream of a free nation in which the people would have some control over their own government and society. Conceived by men and women who had endured the inequities and repressions of autocratic governments, the platform was forged in the American Revolution to become the ideal of the world's most ambitious experiment in self-government.

It was a great and visionary dream. But many feel that at some point in time, between the stirring principles and bright promises enunciated in the Declaration of Independence, the Constitution, and the Bill of Rights and the widespread alienation, frustration, and disenchantment of today, the American dream was lost or, even more reprehensible, stolen—stolen by big government, stolen by big business. I contend that it was

10

not stolen, but given away. The people gave it away. The Congress gave it away.

The dream disappeared a little bit at a time in the evolving struggle for power that has shaped our political history. At the beginning, the people's platform of our founders envisioned a pluralistic, not a monolithic, society. Checks and balances were carefully constructed in the political framework so that the interests of all the many constituencies composing society, of business, and of the government would be furthered while preserving the freedom of the people. Under the guiding hands of such masterful planners as Jefferson and Madison, the framework was structured in a manner designed to make government not an instrument of control, but a tool for protecting the rights of all.

Even at the beginning, however, the dream was tarnished by our founders' failure to recognize the rights of two of history's most suppressed constituencies: blacks and women. Compounding this original sin of omission was the fact that some constituencies would later discover how to use government to their advantage better than others. Experience has shown the constituencies which succeeded were those strong enough and smart enough to petition government effectively to get the laws and backing needed to serve their particular interests and further their own objectives.

The first of these politically aware constituencies were the landed gentry—the farmers, the slave-owners, the growers of cotton and tobacco—and the always powerful banking interests. As America expanded geographically and prospered materially, new constituencies rose to the fore as the wielders of governmental influence—the producers of goods, the merchants, the traders—and they, too, shrewdly utilized government to their own best advantage.

The "common man," the basically apolitical American, lulled by a new sense of freedom and later a steadily rising standard of living, was content to forego the search for influence. The average citizen developed a reliance on government and the special-interest constituency of a growing business-oriented economy to insure his security and promote his well being. Certainly, it should not be too surprising that government and business, two of the major structures for human endeavor, were more than willing to assume the control that the populace seemed so willing to relinquish. It was not that government necessarily thirsted for power or that business was basically "bad" (anymore than it is inherently "good"), but it was merely the instinctive reaction of these forces in our competitive society to seize the opportunity thrust upon them by an apathetic citizenry. The result was that the balance of power, so laboriously, albeit imperfectly, established by our founding fathers, was tilted away from the people and toward those politically alert constituencies which rushed to fill the power vacuum.

THE FRAMERS of the Constitution sought not only a balance of power within the federal government and among the states, but a healthy balance of power against the state in the form of strong, competing public and private interests (constituencies). This was all the more remarkable because the founders were themselves members of powerful private interest constituencies—New England bankers, frontier land speculators, Virginia plantation owners, Pennsylvania yeoman farmers, etc. Later they encompassed a wider range of public constituencies in the various regions of the expanding nation. At the same time, some of the people had organized into their own powerful pressure groups and even built revolutionary local government organs, under a radical structure of popular ad-hoc committees. The government responded to a network of conflicting private and public interest group pressures.

It was James Madison who saw the value of encouraging development of a wide variety of public and private constituencies to guard against the concentration of too much power in too few hands. He pointed out that religious freedom had been best served in America because there had been such a variety of religious interests (denominations), and he feared that their consolidation into "only a few, strong and regional religions" would eventually lead to the domination of one church over the others. Similarly, he thought it important to increase the representation of some interest groups (in small states) so as to guarantee that "no faction shall combine with another to lord it over the rest." This could be assured, however, only if the method of representation varied in different branches of the government and if the executive were chosen by a method clearly different from the legislature.

The President was intended, through the device of the Electoral College, to be chosen by the established and conservative elites of the various states. But he could make no claim to rule unchecked. An independent Congress, chosen in other ways, would limit the President's powers.

Congress also would be free of the domineering trait so familiar to Americans in the English system of parliamentary government, simply because it would not rule at all. There was to be no privy council (cabinet of ministers) chosen from Congress and the President was not answerable to it as its prime minister. The point was to set the people's representatives outside of government, as it were, in order that they be adversaries for the people. Separation of the Congress from virtually all executive authority meant that neither the "people" under some tyrant, nor one coalition of interests under a regional oligarchy, could capture the government and rule alone. In a sense this creative American Congress, whether captured by private wealth or publicly supported demagogues or spokesmen for well-defined and powerful interest constituencies, would provide the counterbalance for a too-powerful state.

Almost immediately after the Constitution was written, two developments occurred which polarized the various interests in the private sector of society. First the party system developed, initially Federalist and Republican, to unite moderate libertarians with national commercial interests on the one side and radical reformers and agrarian rebels with local, especially southern, landed interests on the other. The second development was the enthronement of cotton in the southern economy. As a result the private interests in our fledgling nation divided themselves into "nationalist" and "regionalist" groups. The division of private interests was the basis of the two-party system, which was really nothing more than two coalitions of many regional private interests.

At first the two parties identified with a division in public interests, primarily along the lines of urban and rural, seacoast and frontier. However, soon these public groupings became more and more simply the fronts for individual private interests. Both parties and their internal private interests exploited what Madison called the "inevitable extension of suffrage" with regard to presidential elections. The forces determining the election of the President came to rest with the parties' elites and not the state-based electoral colleges. Then, in order to satisfy the proliferation of private interests, the scope and range of government grew, in the person of the President, his cabinet, and the total executive establishment. This occurred to a degree not called for nor envisioned by the Constitution. Such growth took place under Jefferson and again, more rapidly, under Jackson—and this despite the philosophies of both presidents against a strong, arbitrary national bureaucracy.

After Jackson, a badly divided private sector feared too strong a government and most presidents until the Civil War were "know-nothings" regardless of their party. The division of private interests deepened and agitation for abolition of slavery by northern interests insured eventual open conflict. In the aftermath of the Civil War the people demanded reform and, especially, radical reconstruction in the South. These demands, if met, would have meant the creation of a more powerful federal government. Such a prospect was far too frightening for the private northern interests who promptly deserted the cause of radicals and Negroes alike.

THE HAYES-TILDEN AGREEMENT in the 1870s temporarily ended any threat of a strong federal government. In this agreement the "nationalists" decided it was better to allow the South and other "regionalist" private interests to continue in power in some areas, while they proceeded to build the fabled "integrated corporation" which reached its zenith in the giant monopoly complex of modern American business.

Although reduced to its lowest level of prestige and power, the federal government provided plenty of sport for private interests as they united and centralized themselves within corporate structures and bilked millions of small landholders out of their property. Political power came to be derived almost solely from the private resources of increasingly fewer persons who used their power to influence the government to promote popular acquiescence in private interest goals and to discourage resistance by oppressed constituencies.

In the late 1800s, following the Civil War, new blood was injected into American life. Waves of immigrants from Europe filled the cities and spread over the countryside. Farmers came into the cities as well and brought new life and vision with them. Whole new professions and industries created new opportunities. Enthusiasm for the great American experiment was renewed.

The people's platform of the time was the populist vision. Workers and farmers joined together to build a national and radical movement. It was the first such labor-farmers thrust in the world. The populists were from the poor and middle classes, from both educated and uneducated masses. They felt themselves intimidated, oppressed, and ostracized and, together with the dreamers and the idealists of the day, they organized into the People's Party of the United States.

The party was formed in 1891 and at its convention in
Omaha in 1892 it adopted an agrarian reform platform—a
people's platform (see Appendix D)—which was a statement
of what they believed America was meant to be. Like many
today they wanted to establish control over their own lives.
The objectives of the Populists were to keep faith with the
original people's platform, to destroy unjust wealth, to curb
corrupt power, and to bring America under control of the
people.

In the election of 1892, the Populists received 1,040,886
popular votes and garnered all or part of the electoral votes
from six Western states for a total of 22 votes in the Electoral
College.

The Populists scored well in the congressional elections of
1894 and looked forward with great optimism to the presidential election of 1896 with their own candidate. At the
Democratic convention of 1896, William Jennings Bryan delivered his famous "Cross of Gold" speech and swung the
delegates behind the policies advocated by the Populists, who,
at their own convention later in the summer, also nominated
Bryan for the presidency. However, Bryan lost to Republican
William McKinley in November in one of the most expensive
presidential campaigns in the history of our nation. The business-corporate establishment was under assault and poured
out the wealth of its treasuries to meet the challenge posed
by the people's platform.

The decision to join with the Democrats in 1896 and an
over-reliance on people alone without forming stronger constituencies more organized for action was the beginning of the
end for the Populists. The movement disappeared after the
election of 1908. According to Arthur M. Schlesinger, Sr.,

. . . Populists had fallen upon evil days since they had chosen
Bryan and silver over Henry Demarest Lloyd and radical reform
in 1895–96. Prosperity had quieted the chant for silver, the Negro
question had forced many southern Populists back into the Demo-

cratic fold, the fusion in the West had often resulted in Democrats swallowing up Populists, and many of the more radical Populists believed Bryan was interested in political opportunism rather than in socio-economic change.

The Populist party, like other third parties in American history, served to alert the major parties to discontent within the electorate. And, like most other third parties, it saw its most popular issues preempted by the major parties. This took place to such an extent that the party lost its major attraction for voters, who always have been reluctant to abandon traditional party allegiances in the absence of an overriding issue.

The "progressivism" of Theodore Roosevelt rendered the Populists harmless, and, at the same time, covered up burgeoning national imperialism. Such activity required a stronger government, and the federal executive renewed its growth under Roosevelt and continued at a fever pitch into World War I. War has always been the great stimulus for government growth. Woodrow Wilson said, "I tremble to think what influence at home will be wrought by the power we now build to do battle abroad."

After World War I the popular fear that government would outgrow constituency control or that business-corporate interests were not yet united enough to take command demanded a virtual dismantlement of the federal apparatus. Oddly, the isolationist business interests joined antiwar radicals in the successful antigovernment and anti-internationalist coalition, which, among other things, kept the United States out of the League of Nations.

The stock market crash of 1929 signaled the end of the last serious effort to control the growth of government. The excesses of freewheeling business enterprise had brought our society to the brink of chaos. The business-corporate interests were still fifteen years away from realizing that a partnership with big government offered stability and in the long run

greater and more sophisticated profits than an unregulated
society with a benign small government.

THE NEW DEAL of Franklin Roosevelt, speaking with the
rhetoric of populism, saved capitalism and continued the
power of the business-corporate constituency. His policy of
shoring up private business enterprise with government aid and
regulation prevented a more radical turn.

The major accomplishment of the New Deal was permitting
the working-man constituency to wedge itself between the
business-government power broker partnerships. Unionism,
with its host of social goals, finally became the legitimate
countervailing force to the excesses of the unchecked profiteers
operating in the business-corporate constituency.

Labor learned, after its crushing defeats in association with
the Populists at the turn of the century, that, like business, it
could accomplish its goals better by using its power to influence government to pass laws for its advantage than it could
through conflict-ridden confrontations with the scions of industry. To get its "piece of the action" the labor movement
found a home in the Democratic party. With the assumption
of this political base, it became part of society's new power
triumvirate—business-corporation (enthroned in the Republican party), labor, and government.

One might have hoped the formation of this triumvirate
would have established a new balance of power. But it didn't
work out that way. With World War II and the onset of the
cold war, the interests of business, labor, and government
merged. They found a common ground in the nation's obses-
sion to stop the spread of communism with the expansion of
our military power and influence abroad. The missile race
began and with it came the rise of the military-industrial complex, a power center which was to dominate the direction of
social policy. With the force-feeding of defense contracts, the
wars in Korea and Indochina, and the program for landing a
man on the moon, big business and big government and big

labor flourished. Ever-increasing economic stimulation brought rewards for the triumvirate's constituencies—stock ownership appreciated with high returns, federal bureaucracies proliferated, and there was ready employment for the working man. The benefits of a permanent wartime economy seemed unlimited, until one perceived how true social progress was being starved to feed the military machine.

In this period of widening involvement abroad big business underwent a transformation. It became internationalized and the last vestiges of cherished isolationist and regional private interest were left behind. Business discovered a new benefit under the umbrella of American strategic military policy—the ability to develop markets in many other countries through the device of the multinational corporate structure. And there were side benefits to be had here, too, in gaining bigger leverage in domestic labor and financial marts.

Government, abetted by big business and big labor, also developed a philosophy to sustain their advantage. As government adopted a paternalistic role as "Big Brother" or "Big Daddy," it attempted to project an image of itself as the nation's only legitimate problem solver. The Congress abandoned its adversary role during the war years, abdicating its crucial powers to the executive. First, it abrogated the principle of voluntarism in use of military manpower. Second, it denied our defense budgets intelligent scrutiny and criticism so vitally needed in a democracy. Congress merely reacted to the wishes of the major private power constituencies. Elements in Congress which could have offered criticism were no match for a society that regarded defense as the basis of the main eco-philosophy of produce, grow, and prosper.

The people had no representation. Congress in its abdication retreated to pontificating principles and allowed the executive to pass itself off as the true representative of all the people. The last four presidents (Eisenhower, Kennedy, Johnson, and Nixon) have all used the phrase "all the people" when speaking of their constituencies.

So the cycle turns. The first presidents were elected by elites of the states, then by elites of parties. Now they are elected by the elites of three powerful national constituencies which are also the forces which control the membership of Congress and hold sway over the priorities of American society.

The people acquiesced to an expanded government-military bureaucracy because most Americans have been enjoying a better way of life than the world has ever known. In point of fact, the people welcome the growth and pervasiveness of the state, though it continues to finance its operations by taxing the poor and middle class while granting privilege to the powerful and the rich. They still look to the state as the protector of their welfare against predatory private interests.

Voluntary patriotic obeisance to constituted authority, though responsible for our national stability, is a flaw in our efforts at self-government. Only time will tell if it is the major flaw. In his book, *American Credos,* Stuart Chase summarizes the problem:

> When the country is prosperous, the voter finds little reason to connect this happy condition with the party in power. When the country goes into a business slump, the voter begins to think it is time to throw the rascals out. Homo Americanus . . . is not a political animal. (His interest in an election is primarily "who's going to win," on all fours with his interest in the World Series, the Kentucky Derby, and the annual Rose Bowl football game.)

THERE IS A BREAKING POINT, however, in the tolerance level of the masses. Even an apolitical public can and does challenge the power structure when abuses become intensely personalized. Those challenges come during times of depression, when inequities in the distribution of wealth are apparent to all; during a criminal war like Vietnam, when men are killed in the heat of false patriotism; and during periods of excessive repression as in reactions against the civil rights movement and the black revolution, when the civil liberties of all individuals are threatened.

Today, the noncohesive constituencies of blacks, Chicanos, poor, young, old, and women must realize they can get a "piece of the action" only if their constituency becomes viable enough and angry enough to threaten the establishment. As Bernard Rapaport, a Texas insurance executive, suggests, "People have to once again become visible"—visible and viable through their voluntarily selected constituencies.

For people long deprived of meaningful determination in the activities affecting their lives, the concept of simple populism is appealing indeed. After all, it promises them the control they seek. But the populism conjured up by ambitious politicians is rarely fulfilled. It has been used as a catch-all phrase by Republicans, Progressives, and liberal Democrats bent on increasing the power of the existing leadership of the triumvirate in society. No real changes in the justice or the controls of society are made. From Theodore Roosevelt until, and including, Richard Nixon, the formula has remained the same: speak loudly about reform and at times improve conditions for some people, but kowtow to the power of the big constituencies.

There are zealots today who, using their political charisma and popular style, pretend to carry the banner of populism into the political fray. They offer the nation scapegoats in the form of "big business" and "big government" and promise "power to the people." But at the same time they advocate the destruction of the very tools of power by means of which the people could attain their goals.

Such destruction can lead only to a state of anarchy. Destruction is not the answer. What is needed instead is a restructuring, a check and balance of powers in our society as called for in the Constitution. We must reconcile all major interests of the public, as well as those of private minorities, in the context of today's complete dominance by the business-labor-government triumvirate.

The Achilles' heel of all populist movements to date has been the over-reliance by its self-appointed spokesmen on spontaneous action by the "people" and their utter disdain of the government and business-corporate constituencies. They would totally emasculate government and business rather than utilize their strengths for the total good. The business corporation developed after all, because it proved to be the most efficient method for meeting the changing demands of a surging technological economy. The way to correct its shortcomings is not to destroy it, but to make it more responsive, through public and governmental accountability, to the needs of total society. Similarly, government is still the only practical instrument for serving and protecting broad private and public national interests. The challenge is to ensure that no one segment of our society can attain a position of unchecked power where it can further its own goals at the expense or to the exclusion of the others. A truly democratic people's platform, therefore, should seek not greater concentration of power, but an equitable distribution of power among all constituencies.

How far we have strayed from the road of balanced political power in America becomes obvious if we but recall that when Alexander Hamilton proposed to George Washington and the first federal Congress that "a national park for industry" be set up in New Jersey, his idea was never fully implemented because it was too radical. Yet all he wanted was a few thousand acres and a few thousand dollars to promote specifically American business in fields of endeavor not yet developed in this country. Today, however, we have the wholesale underwriting of private corporations in fields as varied as missiles and railroads. George Washington's desperate call for conscription during the Revolution was likewise rejected as "a monstrous tyranny." Yet, Congress now docilely ignores the public will and permits the executive to continue drafting the youth of our nation to sustain policies the people oppose. We should seek to reduce the scope of government over various areas of activity and limit its power over the lives of people.

For the last fifty years everybody has seen the state as a

potential friend, an easy touch. As noted earlier, big business began speaking of "cooperation" and "partnership" with big government during the profitable World War II and has been addicted to big government money ever since. Labor unions, educators, urban politicians, liberals seeking redress of grievances against the states, minority groups—all turn to the federal government and that, in turn, has made the executive bureaucracy only more powerful and more responsive to the most powerful constituencies.

It seems to me that the citizen can best be assisted in regaining his dignity in America and with it his basis for political power and freedom by encouraging him in autonomous, nonregulated activities. If we encourage free men to build powerful, free constituencies based on the important work and social relationships in their lives, these relationships will become humanizing activities. They will become the basis for a renewed democratic republic, the balancing of state power, and the checking of the exaggerated powerful private interests.

Our founding fathers, the aristocrats of their time, did not have to share the control of government, but they endorsed the principle of self-government and purposefully promoted the development of a broad middle class to share in the control and benefits of a democratic society. Through their generosity, great numbers of the people have been able to prosper and progress. Many segments of our society, however, were, and still remain, excluded. Now, it is time to pass that gift along, ensuring that *all* the people can share in the fulfillment of America's promise.

This is not an impossible dream.

3

Revitalizing the Governmental Process

They have gambled me all
around, bought and sold me
a hundred times. I cannot
begin to fill the pledges
made in my name.

—*Abraham Lincoln*

THE FIRST STEP in returning control of the government to the public is to stop the selling of our elections to the highest private bidders.

Let's face it. The public simply is not going to receive the attention and responsiveness it wants from government until political candidates are freed both from the necessity of turning to wealthy private sources for the financing needed to win office and from the pressures of having to stay in good favor with those same monied interests if they are to remain in office.

A people's platform, therefore, must insist on the public financing of elections to help ensure that our elected officials are not unduly inhibited or excessively influenced by the real and imagined obligations which accompany large private campaign contributions. Only in this way can public officeholders

24

be made responsible to the majority of citizens they supposedly represent.

It will not, however, be an easy task. Those in office understandably have little incentive to alter the election process which put them there in the first place, and which in an overwhelmingly large number of the cases returns them there election after election. Since 1954 incumbents in the House who have run for reelection have won 92 percent of the time, incumbents in the Senate 85 percent. Such remarkable success is attributable primarily to the present method of financing election campaigns. The reliance on personal fortunes or massive contributions from one or more special interest groups naturally tends to perpetuate in power those who are allied with corporate and other big-money interests. To appreciate this fact fully, it is important to understand its direct relationship to the already high and steadily increasing cost of campaigning in the electronic era.

The cost of conducting a political campaign increased 100 percent over the past 15 years and skyrocketed 50 percent in just the years between 1964 and 1968. Spending for candidates at all levels of government, from city council to President, amounted to at least $200 million in 1964, but was up to $300 million for the 1968 contests. Of this sum, one-half was spent on campaigns for federal office, $50 million going to congressional candidates and $100 million, or one-third of the total 1968 costs, to presidential candidates. It is not uncommon for a House seat to cost a single candidate $100,000, and expenditures in a Senate race sometimes exceed $1 million for each contender.

An immense and rapidly increasing portion of campaign expenditures goes into broadcasting, and these big outlays for television and radio advertising explain much of the runaway costs of conducting a political campaign. The broadcasting industry reported charges of nearly $59 million for political broadcasting activities in the 1968 elections, a 70 percent jump over the 1964 figures. Within this same time span the use of spot announcements increased from 81 percent to 91 percent of all political broadcasting, and the rate for spot advertisements rose more than 30 percent. Expenditures for professional pollsters, managers, public relations firms, and advertising companies boost the costs related to modern communications techniques even higher. An estimated $6 million was spent on private public opinion polls alone in 1968.

Under the present system of financing campaigns exclusively from private funds, the candidate who does not have great personal wealth must raise the large sums required for a successful campaign by relying on large contributions or loans from a monied elite composed of corporate executives and directors, financiers, professional entertainers, labor leaders, and individuals with family and inherited wealth. An analysis of contributions to all the major campaign committees in 1968, for instance, reveals that Republicans received 47 percent and Democrats 61 percent of their funds from gifts of $500 or over. Moreover, some $12 million, or 42 percent, of these $500 and over contributions came from individuals who gave $10,000 or more. The economic associations of those individuals who account for the largest dollar percentages in the $10,000 and over category are investment banking and brokerage, insurance, the legal profession, publishing and editing, real estate, oil, chemicals and pharmaceuticals, electronics and computers, entertainment, and family and inherited wealth.

There could hardly be a clearer demonstration of the muscle of corporate wealth in American campaign finance. Obviously, these generous contributors expect something in return for their investment. What they want, and what they usually get, are elected officials who are beholden to them and inclined to be sympathetic and responsive to their interests and needs.

The people should have the same motivation in seeking public financing of elections. Until this fundamental change is made, the monied interests will always be served ahead of the public interest, except when a public issue receives enough visibility to threaten the politician with a substantial loss of votes if he fails to side with the people. The principle of visibility is that the more visible an issue between the public and private interests becomes, the more likely it is to be decided in favor of the public. Unfortunately, most of the time public visibility of issues is low enough that the politician can respond to the needs of his big campaign contributors without losing too many votes. Knowing this, he usually comes down on the side of the private interests.

We have to democratize our elections, and we can do this only if we provide federal subsidies for both presidential and congressional election campaigns. This, of course, would establish an independence from big contributors and simultaneously create a financial bond between the citizens and their elected officials. The same approach eventually should be used to finance elections at the municipal level as well. Hopefully, the change to public financing in federal contests would prompt early reform by state and local governments.

Public subsidy of campaigns, although never actually tried in the United States, is not a new idea. In 1907 President Theodore Roosevelt, responding to the controversy over the influence of corporate contributions in the 1904 presidential campaign, recommended that political campaigns be paid for by public rather than private funds. His proposal was rejected in favor of a limitation and disclosure approach, which was essentially an earlier form of the legislation adopted by the Congress a few months ago when it finally repealed the inadequate 1925 Corrupt Practices Act in favor of the more comprehensive Federal Election Campaign Act of 1971. As important as they are, however, limitation and disclosure are not sufficient by themselves. They may help control campaign costs and reveal where the money is raised, but they in no way address the more critical problems of who puts up the money, what the contributor's pay off will be, and who does and does not get the money.

Since Roosevelt's original proposal, the idea of public subsidy has gradually received an increasing amount of attention. In 1966 it was even passed into law in so far as presidential campaigns are concerned, only to be voted inoperative in 1967. In December of 1971 the Congress once again enacted legislation providing public subsidies to presidential campaigns. This time, in the face of intense Republican opposition and the threat of a veto by President Nixon, it was decided the provisions of the act would not take effect until January 1, 1973. This, of course, means no campaigns will be subsidized until at least 1976. The prognosis for achieving the goal even then is not particularly good. Five years provide more than ample time for the Congress to have second thoughts and to reverse itself, as it did in 1967. Moreover, the Presidential Election Campaign Fund Act of 1971 requires a new appropriation bill before each presidential election for candidates to receive any public funds. This is a particularly crippling provision. The probability is high that, in the heated months before a presidential election, one party or the other will see federal subsidies to the opposition party as a disadvantage not to be tolerated and will attempt to sabotage the appropriation bill either in Congress or by presidential veto. Indeed, if President Nixon still occupies the White House in 1975, a veto would appear to be a virtual certainty, since he was prepared to risk the wrath of an outraged public in order to veto the public subsidy provision, even when it was attached to his economic program. We can hardly expect him to have greater qualms as a lame duck president if he believes a veto of the appropriation bill might ensure Republican success in 1976 by keeping the Democratic coffers empty.

Should the 1971 act somehow survive, it still would require extensive overhaul to be an effective vehicle for delivering power to the people. Most noticeably, it must be expanded to include congressional as well as presidential campaigns. Secondly, the method by which funds are made available to candidates should be altered. The present law stipulates that each taxpayer, by checking a special box on his income tax return, either may direct one tax dollar into a fund for financing presidential campaigns for the party of his choice, or designate that his tax dollar be set aside in a nonpartisan general fund to be distributed among all eligible candidates. This so-called check-off system has several liabilities, the most basic being the uncertainty as to whether enough money would come into the fund to allow significant subsidies to the eligible candidates. If not enough people "check off"—and interest in campaigns is not particularly high at income tax time—it would still be necessary to rely almost wholly on private funding, and the purpose of the federal subsidy would be defeated.

Proponents of the check-off approach usually fend off this criticism by arguing that it alone of all the federal subsidy plans preserves the American tradition of voluntarism in election campaign finance. The individual citizen, so the argument goes, is left free either to check off or not to check off, and in this way indicates his approval or disapproval of a specific party or candidate. But the voluntarism argument is specious. The individual who decides not to check off still foots the bill equally with the individual who does check off, since creation of the fund produces a revenue loss paid equally by all taxpayers. What, in effect, the check-off would do is allow a portion of the people (perhaps a minority) to authorize the expenditure of public monies—a task properly reserved to the Congress. More generally, the voluntarism argument is misleading because, under present arrangements, the majority of the people do not exercise enough control over campaign funding to affect candidates one way or the other via their financial approval or disapproval.

THE REALISTIC ALTERNATIVE to the check-off is public funding by direct appropriation. Under this method money would simply be appropriated to both a presidential and congressional campaign fund on a permanent basis, and each qualified candidate would be paid, without regard to party, from the appropriate fund at a specified rate, for example, 25¢ times the number of eligible voters in a candidate's district in a House race.

In addition to the voluntarism argument, two objections are generally raised to federal subsidies to finance political campaigns. The first contends that to pay large sums directly to candidates will weaken the two-party system by cutting the financial bond which ties the individual to his party. This may be so. Nonetheless, this is precisely what is required if the government is to be wrested from the hands of a corporate elite and returned to the people.

Perhaps the most frequently heard criticism of federal campaign subsidies is that they are merely devices for lining the politician's own pockets. This was the major argument made by the Senate Republican leadership during the December, 1971, debate on presidential election financing. Senator Hugh Scott claimed the Presidential Election Campaign Fund Act amounted to the creation of a huge "slush fund," and characterized it as a raid on the people's treasury. In reality, it is the present method of campaign finance which permits a raid on the public treasury—a raid by the special interests which have for years benefited at the expense of the ordinary citizen. Of course, such a fund could be used to personal advantage if not closely monitored, but with well-written disclosure laws it should not be particularly difficult to prevent abuses. An excellent proposal which would assure public confidence in this regard has been offered by author and philanthropist Philip M. Stern. He suggests that federal assistance be given in such a way that the candidate never sees any actual money. Assistance would be in the form of drawing accounts in the federal treasury. The candidate would simply send to the treasury invoices for goods or services furnished him in connection with his campaign, and the treasury would then send the funds directly to the purveyor of the goods and services, not to the candidate. Stiff penalties against "kickbacks" would further minimize the possibility of corruption.

Even more important than how a candidate gets paid from the campaign fund is who gets paid and how much. This has always been one of the thorniest problems associated with public subsidies to campaigns. Although the issue has been approached from many different angles, it has almost always been resolved in favor of the candidates of the two major parties. For instance, the Presidential Election Campaign Fund Act provides major party candidates with payments at the rate of 15¢ times the number of eligible voters in the United States. However, minor party candidates (defined as those candidates whose party received more than 5 percent but less than 25 percent of the popular vote in the last presidential election) receive payments equal only to that percentage of the major party allotment which corresponds to the ratio of their own popular vote to the average of the popular votes of the major parties. For example, if one major party received 30 percent of the vote, the other major party 50 percent of the vote, and a minor party 20 percent of the vote, the ratio of minor party popular votes to the average of major party popular votes is 1 to 2 (20 percent for the minor party; 40 percent average of major party votes). The minor party would therefore be entitled to only 50 percent of the amount allotted each of the major parties.

While it may at first seem eminently fair and reasonable that a candidate whose party receives only 20 percent of the votes should also receive only half as much money, upon reflection this method of allocation appears a great deal less just. In the first place, this criterion is not applied to the major parties at all; they receive equal funding even though their vote percentages may be quite different. The implicit assumption is that major parties are somehow more worthy than minor parties. Secondly, this way of distributing funds suggests that minor parties are being rewarded according to whether they win, place, or show. The purpose of federal subsidies should not be to reward those who succeed, but to encourage political dialogue and participation in order to assure the people a voice in the government. If it serves the public interest to subsidize a candidate, then it serves that interest best to subsidize him equally with all other candidates. To persist in according special advantages to major parties will only perpetuate their unresponsiveness to the needs of the people.

The decision as to the point at which the public interest ceases best to be served by expending federal funds in support of a candidate must be partially subjective. It must be sufficiently low to allow, in fact, to promote, the expression of a great variety of political views, and yet it must be high enough to avoid wasting taxpayers' dollars on the expression of opinions which only a handful can embrace. An equitable compromise can perhaps be struck by providing federal subsidies in general elections to those candidates who present petitions signed by a number of voters equal to 1.5 percent of the total number of votes cast in the last election for the office sought. For primary elections the required signatures could be reduced to 1 percent of this number, but by no means should primary campaigns be ineligible to receive subsidies. In states dominated by one of the major parties success in the primary is tantamount to election. The only way to open up political dialogue is to provide a financial base for challenges at that point.

THE ACTUAL AMOUNT of the subsidies to be made available to candidates in both general and primary elections is also somewhat of an arbitrary decision, at least within certain limits. The primary goal should be to provide "floors" upon which candidates can then build their election campaigns. Subsidy levels should not be designed to serve as ceilings on campaign expenditures, as in the Presidential Election Campaign Fund Act, primarily because no enforceable limits can be placed on overall campaign spending. Limits are useful and desirable when imposed on policeable areas such as broadcasting, billboards, newspapers, and telephone service, but become counterproductive and invite evasion if extended to items not easily monitored. Moreover, campaigns vary a great deal from locale to locale, and it is virtually impossible to take all the differences into account when establishing equitable and practicable formulas for subsidies.

The cost of providing public subsidies for all federal offices is actually remarkably low for the returns it would bring. If federal funds were paid at the rate of 15¢ per eligible voter for presidential elections and 25¢ per voter for congressional and senatorial elections, and, if it were assumed that the availability of public financing would increase the number of candidates for each presidential election to five contestants, each congressional election also to five, and each senatorial election to four, the total bill for general election campaigns would be only $547 million every four years. This figure is almost $200 million less than the amount the United States has spent over the past four years on Operation Phoenix, the unsuccessful CIA program designed to wipe out the Viet Cong's political infrastructure. It is a sad commentary on this nation's priorities that it spends millions of dollars to destroy another country's political structures and not one cent to preserve or develop its own.

THE WILLINGNESS of elected officials to blur the public-private distinction, as they have become increasingly dependent upon corporate and other monied interests to finance their election campaigns, has led to the sacrifice of the public good and the best interests of the majority of the people. The education budget is cut, but the ABM program is expanded. There is an increase in the maritime subsidy, but new restrictions are imposed on payments to welfare recipients. The public is warned of 300,000 deaths annually from cigarette smoking, but the government pays $80 million annually in subsidies to tobacco growers. Corporate executives write off their lunches as a business expense, but more restrictive regulations are issued to limit participation in the school lunch program. The list could go on and on.

The line between public and private has been, for all practical purposes, wholly obliterated. Public functions such as defense construction, procurement of health services, the provision of transportation facilities, and now even policy formulation are contracted for in the private sector, and at the same time government spends millions of dollars for research and development of direct benefit to private industry, subsidizes huge farm conglomerates, bails out billion-dollar aerospace companies faced with bankruptcy, and insulates big business from the vagaries of a free market by creating so-called regulatory agencies. Perhaps of even greater significance, there now exists a revolving door relationship between the men who fill government's top policy-making positions and those who fill the upper echelons of the country's biggest corporations: a retiring general takes an important executive post in the automotive industry, a New York financier becomes the President's chief economic advisor, a deputy secretary of defense returns to his managerial role with one of the nation's prime defense contractors, a senior corporate lawyer is nominated to be secretary of state.

The political parties, whose organizations might once have provided the structures within which citizens could organize to formulate their opinions and to act as a unit sufficiently powerful to halt the prostitution of public interest to private advantage, have now become hollow sounding boards used by status quo candidates to sell their wares rather than to bridge the gap between the people and their government. Debate of genuinely alternative policies, which is the lifeblood of any political order, has been replaced by the quadrennial rite of contriving vacuous party platforms in an effort to disguise the truth that both major parties offer voters the same tasteless fare.

We all recognize that a free election in which there is but one candidate is a contradiction in terms. Yet the practice which prevails in the United States today is not much better, because our elections more often than not provide the electorate with only the marginal choice between the Democratic and the Republican contenders. A recent survey of voters conducted by the *Washington Post* reveals that many people think both major parties are equally out of touch with the people and no basic change in social policy may be expected to emerge regardless of who is in power. When asked which party would do a better job at handling ten basic social problems, those polled frequently replied it would make no difference. The percentages of those who felt this way are as follows:

Controlling inflation	50%
Keeping the peace	56%
Helping poor people	35%
Helping blacks	40%
Helping the working man	32%
Doing more for business	30%
Preserving law and order	73%
Holding down unemployment	47%
Cutting down drug usage	87%
Stilling campus unrest	75%

Of course, some of the respondents did perceive important differences between the parties in certain select areas. The Democrats received far more credit for helping the poor, the blacks, the working man, and holding down unemployment, whereas it was generally recognized that the Republicans do the most for business. But the fact of overriding importance is that on the average more than half the people see no difference between the two parties.

FROM THEIR INCEPTION political parties have been dedicated first of all to getting votes and winning offices, both integral parts of their function of providing the people with an organizational base from which to control their government. But as the forces of industrialism became dominant in the parties and used their economic leverage to displace the representation of agrarian and working-man interests, great numbers of people were left without influence in the political process. This led to abuses and loss of individual rights, the gravest of which was the outright denial of the franchise to vast numbers of people.

Beginning in the last decade of the nineteenth century and continuing into the early decades of the twentieth, numerous "undesirables" were simply eliminated from the body politic by restrictive voter laws, laws which for the most part have persisted to the present and were still operative in the 1968 presidential election. Their perverse variety has been catalogued by William Crotly, former staff director of the Freedom to Vote Task Force of the Democratic National Committee. Every state had some type of residency requirement in effect in 1968, ranging in severity from the minimum 90-day period for presidential elections in New York and Pennsylvania to 1 year in 33 other states. Twenty states had in effect some form of literacy requirement, and in all cases these were more stringent than the U.S. Census definition of literacy. A number of states still required the satisfactory interpretation of state or federal constitutions, although South Carolina would waive the limitation if a prospective voter owned $300 of assessed property. Loyalty oaths were still law in six states, and a number of others included "good character" provisions in their voting laws. All the states prohibited prison inmates from voting and most deny it to exfelons. Nine states did not permit paupers to vote, although Massachusetts, in a burst of patriotic zeal, excluded veterans from this provision. One or more states barred those convicted of improper lobbying practices or some form of election abuse, those receiving dishonorable military discharges, those not paying taxes, those who defraud the government, those convicted of subversive activities, and so on. Louisiana excluded for varying periods inmates of charitable institutions, deserters, those living in "common law" marriages, and parents of illegitimate children. Idaho prohibited from the vote prostitutes, persons who frequent houses of ill fame or who lewdly cohabit together, bigamists, polygamists, those in "patriarchal, plural or celestial marriages," those who teach state laws are not supreme, and those of Chinese or Mongolian descent.

These obstructions to full democratic participation—together with more infamous ones such as grandfather clauses, white primaries, and the poll tax—are the institutional descendents of good intentions turned to bad purposes. With the ascendency of the powerful new economic interests after the Civil War there emerged all the abuses of urban machine politics, and toward the end of the nineteenth century reformers began to score success as state after state adopted voter registration laws aimed at curtailing the most flagrant practices. But party bosses and other politicians with special interests to serve were quick to turn the new legislation to their own advantage by excluding minority and low-income groups from the democratic process. By 1924 the participation in the presidential election, at 48.9 percent for the nation as a whole, was the lowest it had been in 100 years, having averaged 77 percent in the 60 years from 1840 to 1900. Voter turnout was lowest in South Carolina, where only 6.4 percent of the citizens went to the polls, but it was also low in the northern industrial states. Sample figures are New York, 56.3 percent; Ohio, 57.8 percent; Pennsylvania, 45.8 percent; Illinois, 64.1 percent; and Connecticut, 57.9 percent. In 1888, before any of the registration restrictions were imposed, these same five states had voter participation of 92.3 percent, 91.9 percent, 83 percent, 82.9 percent, and 85.5 percent, respectively.

Although voter participation in presidential elections has picked up somewhat since 1924, the national average of about 60 percent for the years 1900 to the present is still quite unimpressive, particularly when compared to the figures for other modern democracies such as Denmark, Germany, and Sweden, which show voter turnout percentages in the upper 80s. The fact that voter participation continued to hover around 60 percent during the past two decades (it was only 60.6 percent in 1968) in spite of the repeal of some of the worst restrictions, e.g., the poll tax, provides concrete evidence that the malaise in our political life runs deeper than externally imposed barriers to political participation such as voter registration requirements. Of far greater significance is the people's inner alienation from a political process which they sense they could not control even if there were no obstructions whatsoever to voting. Implicitly they recognize that political institutions such as elections have been debased to the status of annual rituals used to reaffirm the people's faith in democratic procedures which in reality long since have ceased to be honored.

Nonetheless, the presence of the larger problem hardly justifies inaction on the voter registration front, which, no doubt, has been a contributing factor to the general political disaffection. The solution which has been proposed, in a variety of forms, is a system of national voter registration for elections to federal office either to replace or supplement the present state systems. The merit of this approach is that by aggressive national campaigns to register as many duly qualified citizens as possible, local registration laws and procedures which effectively keep voters off the rolls could be circumvented. The prerogative of Congress to legislate in this area is clear, so theoretically it is quite possible simply to wipe away lengthy residency requirements, loyalty oaths, "good character" clauses, and all the rest, where they are applied to elections for federal office. Unfortunately, all such proposals for national registration have one basic liability: it will never be possible to register everyone, and on election day some citizens who are otherwise qualified will not be able to vote simply because they will not be registered. The answer is to abolish registration altogether as a precondition of voting.

The case for not ending voter registration rests on one contention, namely, that massive election fraud would result. Several considerations seriously call that proposition into question. First of all, in sparsely populated areas of the country registration never was required; many states were merely swept up in the registration crusade which was aimed at urban abuses. Secondly, voter registration never did score great successes in making elections more honest, but it did keep many honest people from taking part in elections. Thirdly, the experience of North Dakota, which now has preserved its electoral integrity for 20 years without voter registration, proves the feasibility of abolition. Lastly, abolishing registration as a precondition of voting does not entail discontinuing registration.

If voter registration were abolished as a prerequisite to voting, the states would nonetheless continue to enroll voters just as they now do, conceivably with the cooperation of a nationally administered program. However, if for one reason or another an individual should fail to register before election day, he could present himself at the polling place, sign an affidavit swearing he is a qualified voter in the precinct and that he has not voted elsewhere in the same election. He then would be allowed to vote, unless either the election officials or the party watchers had reason to doubt his sworn statement. In that instance the voter would be required to cast a challenged ballot and, before that ballot was counted, the same checks could be made as are used under present registration systems.

There are many other systems which could be set up to guard against a person attempting to vote more than once in the same election. For example, a mark which shows up under ultraviolet light might be stamped on each voter's hand as he leaves the voting booth. Whenever there is any doubt as to whether a person may have voted previously, his hand could be checked to see if such a mark appears. This system, of course, is similar to the one used by amusement parks and others to identify patrons who wish to return through the admission gate once they leave. Any such procedure could enfranchise 46 million Americans for the 1972 presidential election—a full one-third of the eligible voters.

In addition to abolishing voter registration requirements, election day should be declared a national holiday to solemnize the occasion and to give each citizen an opportunity to exercise his right of suffrage. This, too, undoubtedly would increase voter participation significantly.

Citizen participation in the political process could be enhanced still further by abolishing the electoral college system of selecting a President in favor of direct popular election. The arguments of those guardians of the status quo, who are opposed to replacing the electoral college, only reveal the extent to which political equilibrium has become the fundamental value in our political system. Warning of ideological fragmentation and purist candidates "animated by the demands of conscience," they prophesy catastrophe for the two-party system which, according to their analyses, is underpinned by the regional bias perpetuated in the electoral college structure. They see the end of the electoral college as heralding the demise of moderate governments achieved by the politics of coalition and consensus, and they imagine their replacement by transitory compromises and partial alliances hammered out between competing factions.

While it may be doubted that the disappearance of the electoral college system could prompt such profound rearrangements in the furniture of the American electoral process, such rearrangements, if they were accomplished, could be regarded only as a positive improvement. The much-touted interest in preserving the impregnability of consensus politics cannot be squared with the people's interest in free and public debate of genuinely alternative government actions. Bipartisanship in public policy, while no doubt commendable during the war years when it had its start, long ago ceased to be justifiable. Now it is nothing but a congressional "cop out" to the executive in power. The people need representatives in the Congress who will speak up for them in an adversary fashion against the executive government, instead of politicians who subscribe to the philosophy of not rocking the boat in order to preserve their own positions of power among the ruling elite. The best way to stay in office may be never to do anything different or innovative and to try to be all things to all people. But going along just to get along hardly serves the public need for constructive political dialogue.

THE MOST IMPORTANT SINGLE DOCUMENT affecting the people of this nation is the Constitution. It is the basis for our laws, the guarantor of our rights, the protector of our liberties. It is the symbol of a free people, and yet the people are not permitted to amend this document directly. It can be changed only by agreement of the Congress and the state legislatures. However, Congress and state legislatures do not always represent the majority view of their constituents. I therefore propose the adoption of a constitutional amendment that would give the people the power of initiative, whereby the voters themselves could propose statutes and amendments to the Constitution and would adopt or reject them in a general or special election. An initiative measure could be proposed by a relatively small number of the country's eligible voters, perhaps 3 percent in the case of a statute and 6 percent in the case of an amendment to the Constitution. If a majority of those casting their ballots then voted to accept the proposed law or constitutional amendment, it would therewith be adopted and would not be subject to veto or congressional repeal. (See Appendix F for a model constitutional amendment to give the people the power of initiative.)

The federal government must be able to respond to the desires of the people more quickly than it has in the past. The time-consuming procedure of obtaining the approval of 38 state legislatures for a constitutional amendment is unnecessary, and the failure of these bodies to act can be very unrepresentative. What reason, for example, is there to delay granting equal rights to the women of this nation when the issue could be resolved quickly and democratically by a direct vote of the people on a constitutional amendment? Likewise, a constitutional amendment or a law to institute a single tax as proposed in Chapter 8 could be passed by a vote of all the people, if it were blocked in Congress by the elected elite (see Appendixes F and G).

The people should also reserve to themselves the power of referendum, under which they would be able to order a vote against any general act or any item of an appropriation bill or any other measure passed by the Congress. The procedure would be the same as under the initiative. By a petition of 3 percent of the voters a statute or appropriation bill could be challenged and submitted to the people for their decision. Think, for example, what this power of the people could accomplish in regard to the Vietnam war. The 70 or 80 percent of the American people who oppose the continuation of this tragic war could simply vote down the appropriations which allow it to go on.

Of course, the people should also have the powers of initiative and referendum in their states. A few already do. California, Arkansas, and Missouri are model cases in point. In fact, 20 of the 50 states have some type of provision which allows the people to alter the state constitution without recourse to the state legislature. Unfortunately, in the majority of instances, the procedures are so restrictive as to be almost useless. And then, there are 30 states in which the people have no direct control whatsoever over the content of their state charters. This must be changed by winning constitutional amendments in all states to reserve to the citizens themselves the power of initiative and referendum.

The laws of this nation and of the individual states are made to serve the people and to protect them. How ridiculous it is not to permit the public to have a voice in establishing the criteria and determining those laws for themselves.

THERE IS A LOT of unnecessary waste and inefficiency in America today simply because we are so timid about attacking regional problems on a regional level. With few exceptions we try to handle such area-wide problems either too broadly with national programs or too narrowly with state-by-state projects. Neither approach has proved to be effective, and a new formula must be developed if we are to find the needed solutions.

The United States has a host of easily defined regional constituencies, such as New England, the Great Lakes area, Appalachia, the Gulf Coast, and the Pacific Northwest. Each region has its own problems. Some have shortages of water or inadequate transportation. Others have polluted streams or excessive smog. Still others—such as Alaska, which is a state so large and isolated as to be considered a region all by itself—suffer from a lack of adequate communications. Obviously, these problems could best be solved at the regional level through coordinated planning, funding, and implementation. Some attempts have been made to find solutions, with limited success, through the formation of regional compacts or commissions for a specific purpose, such as fighting poverty in Appalachia. However, as a rule such attempts are hampered by a lack of funds, their limited scope, and disputed authority. Generally, the states must fend for themselves, wasting money and duplicating efforts.

The only workable answer, I believe, is to be found in the establishment of permanent, regional governmental units designed and funded to deal with all the shared needs of citizens in areas which, though overlapping state boundaries, have a bond of common problems and objectives. These units would be comprised of a representative of the federal government, appointed by Congress, and a member of each member state, appointed by the governor or state legislature. Funding would be provided by a share of the federal distribution of the single-tax revenues as detailed in Chapter 8. The states working with one another to overcome their mutual problems and coordinating their efforts with the rest of the nation, through the federal representative to the regional unit, could provide services and programs for the entire region at less cost and with greater efficiency than the individual states could ever hope to achieve.

CONGRESS NEEDS HELP if it is to perform its adversary function assigned by our forefathers. An Office of Scientific Assessment (OSA) should be established which would equip the Congress with an impressive array of scientists, engineers, and other specialists with the expertise to make independent scientific and technical inquiries and to examine whether or not the advice provided to Congress by the executive departments is politically self-serving, incomplete, or otherwise biased and unscientific.

Congress has no scientists at its own command and is, therefore, at a great disadvantage whenever it attempts to question the administration's scientific advice. Small wonder, then, that it almost always caves in to administration ideas, no matter how bad. Of course, congressional committees do hear testimony from so-called "independent witnesses," but these experts are often not truly independent, because their "private" scientific research is funded by government grants administered by executive agencies. Obviously, these scientists do not fail to notice which side their bread is buttered on. Moreover, the diverse opinions of a few scattered scientists are no competition for the well-coordinated research and investigation of large teams of specialists available in the administrative agencies and departments. Clearly, what Congress needs is its own stable of independent scientists and engineers who can evaluate whether or not a scientific art has been developed to the point of justifying public support, calculate the costs of applying the art, and estimate scientifically the public good which could be achieved by its implementation. Independent advice of this sort, before the money is spent, would help, for example, eradicate most of the cost overruns which scandalize the American public. Of course, an elected official looks good bird-dogging agencies and exposing cost overruns, but I feel an elected official should eliminate the problem ahead of time if he can see it. My goal is to siphon out the surprises before the money is spent, not afterwards. We have repeatedly seen enough examples, including the mammoth C-5 overruns, to know it is time to act. With billions of dollars at stake each year Congress should have the appropriate tools to assure the people the job is being done right to begin with.

In addition to injecting new life into the adversary function of the Congress, we need to create a public adversary system which will provide a check and balance to the whole of big government, including Congress. The explicit responsibility of such a system would be the development and presentation of an effective adversary position on each project or activity funded by the Congress, to assess it for fidelity to the public interest. Duties would include effective investigation into sloppy bureaucratic management to force a corrective procedure, independent assessment of the benefit-cost ratio of new programs, ferreting out hidden expenditures, conducting audits of authorized projects to see how public monies are being spent, and evaluation of general effectiveness. The adversary system would also be charged with questioning the need for every program, developing alternative ideas and approaches, and setting up mechanisms for the constructive evaluation of the pros and cons of each issue.

Funding for this adversary system could be based on a simple formula: 1 percent of the total amount appropriated for any given project would go to evaluate and challenge that project. Thus, if project A were funded $500 million for FY 1973, $5 million of that amount would be appropriated for adversary purposes. The nation's 50-member Governors Conference might be an appropriate body to review the adversary projects and to contract with nongovernmental groups, such as universities, private corporations, and public institutes, to establish a project team or task force to serve as a counteragent vis-à-vis the executive agency or department administering the project. I have always felt that the Governors Conference should be given a stronger voice in matters concerning the national economy, since it represents one of the most significant links existing between the federal government and the people at the local level where the ultimate effects of those activities are felt most personally.

Vast amounts of public funds undoubtedly would be saved through increased governmental efficiency brought about by the discipline of having an alert adversary monitoring spending practices. At the same time, cumbersome government bureaucracies which, in accordance with Parkinson's Law, usually expand at a rate wholly unrelated to the tasks to be performed, would have their unnecessary, even oppressive, growth checked, again resulting in savings to the taxpayer.

To avoid the development of its own internal bureaucracy and the establishment of a symbiotic relationship between it and its assigned agency, each adversary project team should have its contract terminated and its functions wholly abolished after three years of operation. Records would, of course, be preserved and made available for congressional and public use at any time. A different project team then would be formed to assess and criticize the project for the next three-year period. This periodic changing of the guards, so to speak, would be repeated for each governmental program or activity for the lifetime of the project.

The implications for democratic government of the failure to preserve the adversary function in society were well understood by James Madison who, in the famous tenth paper of *The Federalist,* noted that when a faction or single group of people with common interests becomes a majority in the government, then "the form of popular government . . . enables it to sacrifice to its ruling passion or interest both the public good and the rights of other citizens." Madison further observed that it is in vain to suppose that clashing interests will always be resolved by enlightened statesmen, who will render them all subservient to the public good. "Enlightened statesmen will not always be at the helm: nor, in many cases, can such an adjustment be made at all, without taking into view indirect and remote considerations, which will rarely prevail over the immediate interest which one party may find in disregarding the rights of another, or the good of the whole."

WE ARE AT A CROSSROADS. We can either seize the opportunity of revitalizing the governmental process in the United States or we can consciously allow the dangerous trend of the alienation of citizens from our political system to gain added momentum. The growing disaffection with the political process can be traced directly to the powerlessness of our people, the unresponsiveness of our parties, and the increasing control of our lives by a monied elite. Immediate action to remedy the failings and weaknesses of our electoral system is urgently needed. Reform in many areas is called for, but most importantly we must make fundamental changes in how our public officials are nominated and elected by removing the influence of special interest money from our campaign process and replacing it with public subsidies which will create a financial bond directly between the people and their representatives. This goal can be brought to realization, of course, only by the people themselves through their citizen constituencies. Congress will not act by itself, and no other group will lobby against arrangements which serve its own vested interests. It is a people's problem, and the people must solve it.

4

Toward a New Internationalism

More than an end to war, we want
an end to the beginnings of all
wars—yes, an end to this brutal,
inhuman and thoroughly impractical
method of settling the differences
between governments.

—*Franklin D. Roosevelt*

THE AMERICAN PEOPLE are experiencing a profound loss of faith in their nation's purposes in the world. They see their leaders unable to deal effectively with the problems which face the nation, either domestically or on the foreign scene. They have realized that their government is unable to protect its people from total destruction in the event of war; it cannot promote economic development, either overseas in the under-developed nations or in the underdeveloped regions and the ghettoes of our own country; and it cannot work its will on small but stubborn countries halfway around the world—or 90 miles off our shore. Americans ask for guidance. Are our purposes faulty? Is there conspiracy abroad or in high places? Are our institutions incapable of responding to the contemporary situation?

In the eyes of the rest of the world, this country has shown itself to be not, as it likes to view itself, the preserver of world order, but one of the major problems of world order. Our desire to use our power where and when we please has made us one of the world's most dangerous nations. I am not saying that other nations are necessarily more peace-loving than we or that they are less willing than we to use force, when they are able, to enforce their will. It is only that we have the power to be a danger to world peace, with no constraints on our nation's leaders but their own moral judgment—and we have learned in Vietnam, to our horror, how shockingly weak that can be—and, ultimately, the voice of the American people as expressed at the polls or in the streets.

In Vietnam we have seen that it is we who create the threats to our own security, through our own actions and the commitments our leaders make. By no stretch of the imagination could the type of government in power in the southern half of a tiny country halfway around the world affect the security of the United States or any of its vital interests. But we have been, in William Fulbright's words, "in thrall to fear." By losing sight of the negligible risks to ourselves, by permitting commitments to be made in our name, we became militarily involved. We were, in short, our own worst enemy, and we have paid dearly for our blunder, not only in loss of life but in loss of faith among our own people in the wisdom and purposes of our own government. This is the ultimate threat to the security of a nation, when its own people no longer have confidence in its government.

Our people have also seen the precious resources of this nation squandered on wasteful and obsolete armaments. Fully two-thirds of the "controllable" funds, those over which the Congress has some discretion, go each year to the Pentagon. But it is not only the money poured into the military budget which is draining our society; it is the sense of human and material waste through reactionary and often illegal military interventions and the loss of national purpose, as we get bogged down in futile and meaningless wars, that are destroying the nation's spirit.

America has a long anticolonial tradition, going back to its beginnings. The recognition that we have become an imperial power has not been a pleasant one for the American people, and we have attempted to shield ourselves from it by pretending that our kind of empire was somehow different from those that preceded us. It is true that we did not want to colonize the land ourselves, but we did want to determine the type of government the people could have. We did want them to join us in military alliance and to permit us to base our armed forces and intelligence services on their soil, and we did want the right to invest in, and thus to exploit, the natural resources of their land. We have played exactly the same role in the underdeveloped world as the British, the French, the Dutch, and the Germans before us.

Out of the caldron of Vietnam we have learned that our dreams of benevolent empire are destined to be, in the end, no more than the unreal imaginings of a goodhearted but naïve people. We cannot mold societies so different from our own to our liking, but must allow them to develop in their own way.

They will work out their own fates, true to the character of their internal societies. Our attempts to "modernize" them, that is, to mold them in our image, inflict far more destruction on these societies, because of the massive and indiscriminate nature of our weaponry, than they would ever inflict themselves, if left to their own, less "modern" devices.

The global crisis brought on by nuclear weapons, assaults on the environment, population growth, and the advance of technology demands from us higher standards of humanity and wisdom than ever before. But the nation-state has shown itself unable to respond to this challenge. America is only the most powerful example; it is not alone in its inability to respond to the needs of this epoch. While people everywhere are searching for a style of life and a set of institutions which will promote a passably humane life, the nation-state continues to pursue the course of death and to use its most advanced talents to magnify still further its ability to inflict destruction on an already suffering populace. As Richard Barnet of the Institute for Policy Studies, Washington, D.C., has observed, the state may still have the sheer power to govern, but it can no longer claim to exercise legitimate authority over its people.

WE HAVE WITNESSED in the United States, during the past quarter century, a growing separation of the state apparatus—including the presidency, the Department of Defense, the CIA, FBI, the Department of State, and associated agencies—from the people it is supposed to be protecting. It is axiomatic that the custodians of the state will attempt to preserve it and to advance its interests. But when the state surrounds itself with the structures of secrecy, creates a loyalty system to ensure that those who serve it possess its values, and maintains a surveillance network to detect and apprehend citizens who oppose its purposes, then we are far along toward a 1984-style state system which suppresses its citizens and serves only its own interests.

In such a state system, policy-makers act on the international scene to advance their own interests and those of the state, rather than those of the citizens they are supposed to represent or the people in other lands affected by their policies. In Vietnam, Laos, Cambodia, and elsewhere we have seen our leaders decimate whole countries and destroy the societies of those countries, simply to preserve their own reputations for toughness and determination. Indeed, one high policy-maker described our purposes in Vietnam as 70 percent to preserve "our reputation as a guarantor," 20 percent to keep the territory from "Chinese hands," and only 10 percent to "permit the people of South Vietnam to enjoy a better, freer way of life."

Such leaders want to increase their power and that of the state they control. In the case of the United States, our leaders have wanted to keep America "first," even though that meant maintaining the world's largest arsenal of destruction: we

would be first in death, even if we could not be first in life—
in health care, in quality of education, in concern for the aged
and the underprivileged, in support for culture, and in all the
activities that make life worth living.

As economist Robert Heilbroner has written, "It is the fear
of losing our place in the sun, of finding ourselves at bay, that
motivates a great deal of the anti-Communism on which so
much of American foreign policy seems to be founded." Our
actions have seldom been taken in response to the requests of
other nations for our help—those requests are usually engi-
neered by our representatives in the nation or, as in Vietnam,
they are frequently not bothered with at all. Thus our apparent
altruism has too often masked actions intended to expand
American influence or satisfy our nation's ego. It is, indeed,
our lack of confidence on the world scene that has made us so
dominating.

While we begin to recognize our limitations, both of understanding and resources, we must gain the confidence to relate
to other nations on the same basis as lesser powers have for
centuries—using negotiation, peaceful contacts, and trade, ex-
pecting to win some contests and lose others, but retaining a
belief in our ability to participate productively on the world
scene in a peaceful and cooperative fashion.

The Nixon administration has declared its intention to alter
the way America has pursued its state interests, but it has not
redefined those interests. It wants to rely more on foreign
troops ("change the color of the bodies," as our ambassador
to South Vietnam so graphically put it) and to back up the
"natives" with American technology. As foreign policy analyst
and the author of *In Peace with China* Earl Ravenal has
written, the Nixon administration's policies "support the same
level of potential involvement with smaller conventional
forces. The specter of intervention will remain, but the risk
of defeat or stalemate will be greater; or the nuclear threshold
will be lower. The fundamental issues of interests, commitments, and alliances are not resolved."

The Nixon policy has retained the same attitudes, the same military bases, the same covert interventions, which in the past have led us to intervene with American military force an average of once every eighteen months since World War II, and there is no reason to believe that he, or one of his successors, will be any more willing to yield in a conflict before introducing American ground troops. As long as we insist on remaining "first," rather than appear to be a "pitiful, helpless giant," we will find ourselves militarily engaged around the globe, ceaselessly trying to prove we're the "big boy on the block."

President Nixon asserts that the "most prevalent Communist threats now are not massive military invasions." They are, he argues, "a more subtle mix of military, psychological, and political pressures." However, in spite of this changed assessment, his administration continues to maintain ground, air, and naval forces ready for instant action in any part of the globe, as if there were immediate danger of a major war. And we continue, year after year, to spend half of all appropriated federal funds on the defense establishment. And, in spite of our protestations to the contrary, we continue to behave as the policeman for the world, ready to employ our nuclear carriers, our helicopter gunships, our antipersonnel bombs, and our people-sniffers whenever some client state claims it is being threatened by "Communists."

It is time we recognized that the old cold war is passing. There is no communist conspiracy bent on world conquest. Russia and China have split, and the smaller communist nations are becoming much more independent, pursuing their own national interests even when they conflict with those of the Russian superpower. But we maintain the outworn myths and institutions of another era, killing communists in Vietnam even as we aid them in Yugoslavia and feast with them in Peking.

Simultaneously, our own NATO alliance has come asunder, as the threat which brought it together has appeared less real and less immediate. Our European allies have lived in proximity with Russia for centuries, and they no longer feel the need to accept long-term subordination to the United States in order to live with what is, after all, just a modern, nuclearized version of an ancient condition.

Many factors point to a new era in world relations. Europe, both East and West, is demonstrating renewed self-confidence and vitality, suggesting the ability to determine its own defense needs and to meet them through its own, not inconsiderable resources, based on its own perceptions of the threats it faces. Western Europe's GNP is fully 80 percent of our own, and it is quite capable of meeting its own defense requirements. At the same time, the Soviet Union has developed its military might to the point where it is now roughly comparable to our own. Thus, our military forces are not as badly needed by our allies as they once might have been, and we can no longer use them with the freedom that we once could, without fear of response from the Soviet Union.

Our assessment of the Soviet Union is changing as well. In the past we often attributed a high degree of rationality and purposiveness to Soviet policy. More sophisticated studies of recent years now suggest that, like policy-making here in the United States, Soviet policy is a mixture of a general, long-term design for the advancement of its economic system, an interplay of bureaucratic pressures and interests, a reaction to the policies of others, and a response to opportunities that arise without prior planning. And any aggressive plans the Soviets might wish to implement would first have to deal with the continuing unrest in eastern Europe, the persistent conflict with China, and bureaucratic rigidities within the Soviet system that inhibit any change in policy. The Soviet Union, in short, is another nation-state pursuing its national interests, and we are going to have to learn to deal with her on that basis.

IN DEALING WITH THE THIRD WORLD, we must recognize that most of the existing governments are composed of conservative elites which hold onto their positions of power and privilege by force of arms (usually purchased or borrowed from the United States). If all the people of these nations are to benefit from the modernization of their lands, there is going to have to be a revolutionary struggle in which political control is wrested from the traditional ruling classes and a program of land reform, education, and economic development having mass support is instituted. The United States may want to resist this development, but the pressures from the unhappy masses are overwhelming. In the end we will find ourselves shut out of these countries entirely, if we do not alter our view of what constitutes beneficial changes in these lands.

We must recognize that there are real limits to what we can achieve through our influence upon another country. Foreign affairs analyst and author of *The Politics of Hysteria* William Pfaff has wisely written that "foreign policy is fundamentally a means by which the American nation is protected, and it is not an appropriate vehicle for reform or revolution of foreign societies." We need only reflect on our inability to solve the problems we have within our own country to recognize the far greater limitations that act on us when we attempt to introduce change in other nations. Nor can our military power be applied successfully to enforce our will. With the rise of sophisticated techniques of guerrilla warfare and new means of communicating ideas—and, hence, of arousing latent national feelings and welding popular movements together—great powers, regardless of the military force they deploy, can no longer exert control over territory not occupied by their own citizens.

We must learn that revolutions in far off, or even in nearby, countries do not necessarily threaten our own interests. The Soviet Union has discovered, just as we have, that it is no easy matter to control another country. As Richard Barnet has observed, every revolutionary government that has come to power without the Red Army has turned out to be ambivalent, cool, or even hostile toward the Soviet Union—Yugoslavia, Albania, North Vietnam, China, and Cuba. In each case the relationship is complex, but does not make the USSR stronger or more of a threat to the United States. And so a revolution, even if it takes a socialist or communist course, does not necessarily represent a loss to us; indeed, if it should result in a government which has greater acceptance among its people, it can work toward our own interests of maintaining peace and improving the human condition. And, as we have now found in Algeria, it need not even shut off opportunities for investment, provided we tailor our demands to the legitimate needs of the people in these developing countries. Instead of viewing international relations as a "game" which some win and others lose, we should view it as a process of building a world society, of learning to live with each other in an increasingly interconnected world, of aiding each other to develop to the maximum of our capacities and resources, and of avoiding the deadly conflicts which have come to characterize this most destructive of centuries.

Our present interventionism must be seen as merely another form of our old isolationism. Now, instead of retreating into our shell and ignoring the world, we reach out to the four corners of the globe for unilateral influence and power, but still ignore the opinion and the desires of the rest of the world. We are as isolated as before from the influence and the good offices of other nations; only our power is engaged, not we as a people, interacting for mutual benefit, receiving as well as giving assistance.

THE OPPOSITE of our present interventionism is not isolationism, but a new internationalism which embodies the same kind of participation as other, smaller nations have engaged in for decades—diplomatic discourse, active cooperation and assistance through the United Nations, trade and travel, and other forms of cooperation and participation in the family of nations. But it would forswear the unilateral resort to force which has characterized American policy during the last 25 years. Ironically, it has been the so-called "internationalists" who have isolated the American people from much of the world, deciding for our allies what their military postures should be, without even a pretense at consultation, setting up and toppling non-conforming client states, and forbidding travel, trade, and even diplomatic representation with many of the communist countries of the world.

The United States cannot, and must not, withdraw from the world. Technology and communications have multiplied the international contacts in which we all participate, and these will expand with time. But we must realize that our country cannot attempt to take on the tasks of a UN to manage political and economic change around the world, to police a stable international order. Its people can only assist, with their extraordinary wealth and industrial capacity, as young countries attempt to find their own ways toward a better life. And we must become, again, the champion of revolutionary change and of decolonization.

I believe we are moving, slowly but steadily, toward a new type of international relations, in which relations between groups of people—scientists, trade unions, students—and economic units—multinational corporations and enterprises—supplant the traditional relations between states. We already see minority groups expressing their sense of identity with people of the same racial character in other nations, and we see cities providing each other with mutual aid in times of natural disaster or economic deprivation. Should we not recognize that nations themselves are transient, that transnational structures may be as real and as enduring as national loyalties, which are sometimes capricious and force-grown?

The new internationalism will incorporate military nonintervention, the tolerance of revolutionary politics, and a reassessment of the inequalities of enjoyment of the planet's resources, which are so vastly, and precariously, in our favor for this fleeting historical moment. Most important, we must

demonstrate a renewed respect for international law and international institutions, as our best hope for creating the conditions for peace and the resolution of conflict.

It is fashionable to ridicule the United Nations as a peace-
keeping body. But, as William Fulbright has observed, those
of us who believe in international institutions "do not think
the United Nations is a failure; we think it has never been
tried."

Over the years, our country like some others has systematically undercut the power of the UN and used it for our own
purposes. Twenty years ago we usurped the UN's name. We
used our great influence to secure a UN cover for our intervention in Korea. In this last decade we deliberately ignored
efforts by the UN to produce a peaceful settlement in Vietnam
while we prosecuted and expanded our private war with the
communists. As the Pentagon Papers show, we deliberately
avoided negotiations with "the other side," in spite of our
obligations under Article 33 of the United Nations Charter
always to seek to settle disputes by "negotiation, inquiry,
mediation, conciliation, arbitration, judicial settlement, resort
to regional agencies or arrangements, or other peaceful means
of their own choice."

The United States, as the most powerful country on earth,
must now lead the way in building up the power and capacity
of the UN to act effectively in areas of possible conflict. As
Philip Jessup, a former American representative to the UN,
has written, "One has hoped that the disastrous policies of the
United States in Vietnam would have convinced this Administration that one cannot solve by unilateral measures the problems of a multilateral international community and that the
channel for multilateral diplomacy is through the United Nations." As he so cogently observed, "The United Nations can
hardly be strengthened if the United States continues to treat
it with contemptuous indifference."

In the long run, I believe the UN must develop into the
primary peace-keeping force on earth, and we should be tak-

ing the lead in aiding this development. This is most difficult to achieve, of course, in a period of revolutionary change such as we are now living through. On the one hand, there are powerful nation-states, such as our own, who are jealous of their ability to use armed might wherever they wish and who fear the constraints that a world body would impose on them. On the other hand, there are incipient revolutionary movements throughout the Third World which we would not want to strangle by imposing a world order which denied their legitimate aspirations for independence and freedom, in the name of a mythical and oppressive "stability."

A more powerful UN must then grow slowly, applying its influence and power initially in regions where the conflicts of interest are limited and where the parties involved want to avoid war and to seek a peaceful settlement. Beyond this, it can apply sanctions in cases of colonial oppression to permit independence movements to achieve their legitimate ends. And it can maintain a permanent stand-by peace force, to serve as a visible UN presence whenever armed conflict threatens.

However, if the UN is to play a more vital role in keeping the peace, its membership will have to be expanded and its structure improved. If we are going to have a union of the nations of the world, all nations should be represented within the organization. This country should support the principle of universal membership in the United Nations; in particular, the divided countries which emerged from World War II—China and Taiwan, East and West Germany, North and South Korea, North and South Vietnam—should all be represented. Each is the focus of active present-day conflict, and their absence prevents the UN from playing an effective role in ameliorating and, eventually, resolving these conflicts. With representation, these countries could have a chance to face each other across desks rather than across armed barricades. As the UN moves in this direction, both it and the United States in supporting it would be attaining a new level of maturity on the world scene.

But inviting all nations to participate in the UN is not

enough. The unrepresentative nature of existing UN bodies—
with tiny islands having the same voting power as continent-
size great powers—has served as an excuse for failing to use
the UN. The operations and voting procedures of the UN must
allocate to each nation a degree of influence proportionate with
its size, population, economic resources, military power, and
so on. It has become manifest that a body such as the General
Assembly, in which every country is accorded one vote, regardless of how small or how large it is, does not have the
capacity to take effective actions in times of crisis. We have
seen in too many cases how the Security Council has been ham-
strung by the big-power veto in attempting to resolve world
crises. While recognizing that this is an exceedingly complex
matter, we must work toward developing new arrangements
for the UN that could multiply its effectiveness as a peace-
keeping body.

One arrangement that I believe could be most fruitful would
be the development of regional subdivisions of the UN. Under
Article 52 of the UN Charter, the nations in each region of the
world would work together, under the aegis of the UN, to
maintain peace in their area. Parts of Africa, the Caribbean,
and the Pacific Islands might be suitable regions to begin. It
might be appropriate in these regional bodies to experiment
with new forms of representation, such as giving each nation
a voting strength proportionate to its population. Having seen
the dangers of making the great powers the policemen for the
world, we should now turn more energetically to the concept
of regional peace-keeping and even federation, under the overall umbrella of the United Nations.

At the same time, the United States should be leading the
way in the development of new norms of international law,
appropriate to an age of economic and military interdependence. With the 3-mile limit now having only a historic connection to the realities of naval life (it was the range of shore-
based artillery), with the multinational corporation operating
beyond the confines of any national legal structure, and with

the deadly character of modern weaponry having made the resort to arms the ultimate folly, it is essential that we give renewed attention to updating and then to enforcing the body of international law. Burdensome as we may at times find the restrictions of law, they are the only means we have to restrain the brute power of arms and to bring order into an anarchic world of contending nation-states.

William Fulbright has observed that "the essence of any community—local, national, or international—is some degree of acceptance of the principle that the good of the whole must take precedence over the good of the parts." Just as we believe in the supremacy of law over might in relations within our nation, we must begin to apply these same standards in our dealings with other nations. I believe that only when we recognize this and begin to take international institutions seriously will we at last be on the road to workable arrangements for preserving the peace. Our world leadership should be exercised, not through might as in the past, but through moral example, economic aid, and support for international law and institutions.

No more than any other has our country kept its treaty commitments, when our leaders deemed it in our interests to violate them. We interpreted our treaty commitments to allow our intervention in Vietnam, even as we systematically violated the Geneva Accord, which we had agreed not to resist, and we violated our solemn treaty obligations in Latin America by our invasion of the Dominican Republic.

In pursuing what our leaders have deemed to be our "national interest," we have too often flouted international law and prior international agreements and, by this action, reduced the effectiveness of these restraints for maintaining world peace. Our policy should be intended instead to strengthen the institutions and conventions of international law and international cooperation. It must bolster at every occasion our respect for and reliance upon international law and cooperation as peaceful means of settlement, rather than insisting on an American solution that leans heavily on the decisive and lonely use of force.

A NEW INTERNATIONALISM will have profound tangible effects on military planning, military strategies, the American presence abroad, our support for military clients, our alliances, our budgets, our weapons systems, and the role of the military in American society.

The postwar period has witnessed the diminishing utility of military power for achieving national objectives. Despite its possession of the most powerful military arsenal in history, American society would be utterly destroyed should it become involved in a nuclear war. And, despite the expenditure of nearly $200 billion in Vietnam, we have been unable to achieve our political objectives there. The same paradox applies to the Soviet Union. Even with its military power at a peak, its own sense of security is diminishing. Increasingly, when great powers resort to military operations, they reveal their weakness rather than their strength.

As we reexamine our interests in Europe, Asia, and Latin America, we must determine whether they require that we continue to maintain forces in readiness to intervene in these areas. President Nixon has not proposed reexamining any of our commitments; he has suggested only that we attempt to meet them by supplying money and weapons instead of American troops—even as the Armed Services redesign their forces so they can be deployed anywhere in the world, on C-5A aircraft and special new military ships, in spite of the President's announced position. We have seen in the case of Vietnam how the ready availability of a capacity to intervene leads to the decision to send in our troops, even when all the advice of experienced military men is strongly against such an act.

We must close out the cold war period, begin to withdraw from our wide-ranging commitments, bring our troops home, and deactivate them. This will be in our own interest as well as in the interest of those to whom we made commitments.

The place to begin, of course, is with a prompt pull-out of all our forces in Vietnam. But there are other areas where our troops are maintained out of an unwillingness to respond to the new circumstances of the present era.

First, there is Europe. Surely there will be no lasting security on that divided continent until the natural aspirations of the peoples of eastern Europe are fulfilled. This does not mean, however, that we can have a direct hand in removing the heavy yoke that holds them down. All we can do, and what we must do now, is to create a political climate in which no nation, including especially the Soviet Union, would feel threatened by the growth of freedom in another. That cannot be achieved by maintaining a high level of armaments, but requires instead that the military confrontation be eased by the removal of forces facing each other and by other acts of conciliation.

There are few people indeed who have ever believed in the likelihood of a massive Russian invasion of western Europe. Given the terrible risk of nuclear war which this would provide, it is hard to visualize any vital Russian interests that could compel such an attack. Our troops can then be withdrawn as a part of a process of creating the climate in which freedom and reconciliation can come to all of Europe. World War II is over, and the subsequent occupation should come to an end.

We have allowed ourselves to become deeply enmeshed in the inner workings of western European defense planning, even though both geography and politics enforce a wide disparity in our interests. With our overwhelming military power we have dominated the NATO alliance, forcing our allies to adopt our all-too-rigid anticommunism and picking up the largest share of the tab for their defense.

George Kennan, the architect of our policy of containment, has argued that NATO violated the essential principles of valid relations between nations with such divergent interests "that they set up their own organizations and that we appear as their great and good friend, but not participating member of what they had set up." It is time to move back to that realistic basis for a long-term relationship between us, allowing the Europeans to define their own defense needs and to support them, as they see fit, without having our world-view forced down their throats. We should invite the Europeans to replace Americans in positions of military leadership in the alliance. We would remain in the alliance, but the primary initiative for European defense would lie with the Europeans, in a way that it has not for the past twenty years.

A small number of our troops might remain in Europe, but they are not essential. The balance of forces in central Europe would not be unfavorable to the Western alliance even if all American troops were withdrawn. West Germany, France, and Great Britain can field almost 1.4 million men. The 300,-000 Russian troops in that region can be supplemented only by the unreliable—from the Russian point of view—forces of the eastern European countries or by a massive troop build-up from the Soviet Union, which would be clearly visible from the start and would, if it were to occur, certainly produce substantial reactions from both the western European countries and from us. Our troops should not be held as military hostages nor the American taxpayers as economic hostages to that occurrence.

The thousands of nuclear weapons we retain in western Europe should also be withdrawn. A purely conventional communist attack with existing forces could be contained by the present conventional forces of the Western alliance, and any massive Russian mobilization could still be met by the introduction of nuclear weapons by air, if that dreadful eventuality were thought to be desirable.

Our forces are arrayed all along the periphery of Asia: air force personnel in Thailand and Laos, support and headquarters units in Japan, bombing squadrons in Okinawa, ground troops and tactical nuclear weapons forces in South Korea, refueling and intelligence units in Taiwan, Southeast Asian support units in the Philippines, and on and on. We must begin to withdraw both our excessive military presence and our concomitant support for the military regimes in the area that exist only by virtue of our money and military supplies.

Such a policy of nonintervention in Asia could be justified on many grounds: a clearer perception of China's limited expansive intent; the restricted American interest in Asian real estate or natural resources; the lack of any true American interest in the stability of any particular government around the rim of China or in the success of any particular ruling group or transient political formula; the remoteness of any threat from that region to our security; a desire to see the emerging powers of east Asia work out a new relationship without American intervention; and a desire to reestablish working relations with China. All of these factors suggest a limited American interest and a skepticism about the possible productivity of any American military effort. But, of course, it does not necessarily imply diplomatic, economic, or cultural remoteness. On the contrary, we might be able to involve ourselves far more successfully if our military presence were not such a dominant factor in our relationship with Asia today.

Elsewhere in the world a similar policy should be adopted. In some cases, like that of Israel and, should they be threatened, the countries of western Europe and Japan, we have the opportunity to provide a defense back-up to nations which have democratic governments, whose people support them, and who might be subject to foreign attack. There are many other cases, however, where the threat to the "security" of these countries is from their own people, who want desperately to rid themselves of oppressive, dictatorial regimes. In too many cases today we find ourselves expending money and, in the case of Vietnam, precious American lives to preserve such unworthy regimes. The foreign policy which led to this, the blind support of any country willing to call itself "anticommunist" and to accept our arms, must be reversed.

Equally, our subversive activities must be curtailed, in order that our presence can be a legitimate one and that the small entanglements which lead to big wars can be avoided. The CIA and our other intelligence agencies serve as a direct arm of our interventionist policy, providing the information on which military preparations are based, subverting revolutionary governments, and, at times, organizing and leading covert armies. We need to know something about potential adversaries, but essential information can be provided today by reconnaissance satellites and by reading published information. The clandestine activities in which our government engages today do not truly defend our nation. They serve only to allow the executive branch to project itself overseas, to create and preserve client regimes, to overthrow obstreperous regimes that refuse to kowtow to America, to advance American business interests by bribing friendly government officials and defaming the opposition, and to otherwise engage in the kind of improper and, at times, illegal activities which most Americans would object to if any country but their own were engaged in them.

THE COMPLEXITY AND REMOTENESS of international affairs seem to suggest that effective citizen action is impossible. How can the lone citizen have an influence on these issues? It isn't as hard as it sometimes seems. First, he should see that he and other members of his community are informed. Local organizations such as world affairs councils, UN support groups, World Federalist chapters, SANE, Women Strike for Peace, and others all provide the means for citizens to gather their strength together and to inform themselves. But, then, to be effective, they must be heard. The active citizens must see that influential segments of their communities are informed on critical international issues. They must raise issues of foreign policy in their local congressional and senatorial elections and, equally important, see that their elected officials are held accountable for the positions they adopt once they are elected.

On many issues an informed portion of our citizens already have at least as good a grasp on foreign affairs as their elected representatives in Congress. For instance, every year 25,000 Americans travel in the Soviet Union and get a clearer mental picture of that country than most of our political leaders. Not all of what these travelers learn is good, but all of it is real. A picture is worth a thousand words. A visit is a million pictures. No one can be sure, using words alone, that his judgment on Soviet policy is sound. Consider what state of affairs now exists. Since World War II a trillion dollars has been spent for our defense, principally against the Soviet Union. Yet only 35 percent of the members of the Senate and only 15 percent of the members of the House who cast their votes for these appropriations have ever been there. Citizens are, therefore, no less capable of making informed decisions on the monumental questions of national defense than their Senators and Congressmen.

5

The Warfare State

Of all the evils to public liberty,
war is perhaps the most to be dreaded,
because it comprises and develops
every other. War is the parent of
armies; from those proceed debts
and taxes. And armies and debts,
and taxes, are the known instruments
for bringing the many under the dom-
ination of the few. In war, too, the
discretionary power of the executive
is extended; its influence in dealing
out offices, honors, and emoluments
is multiplied; and all the means of
seducing the minds are added to those
of subduing the force of the people!

—James Madison

IN THE AFTERMATH of World War II, several changes of enormous significance were made in American domestic and foreign policy. It was decided to keep the draft in peacetime, despite a 175-year tradition in America against all forms of conscription. Massive espionage and secret police organs, developed in the pressure of World War II, were kept and expanded. After the troop reduction at the end of the war, a great military build-up was begun, with increasing military budgets for increasingly costly and fancier weapon systems. The first two-million-man standing army in America's peacetime history and an economy anxious for the presumed stability that comes from "defense expenditures" required the construction of a "warfare state" capable of garrisoning the world.

The establishment of The National Security Council, the Truman Doctrine which made America the world's policeman (a policy carried on to this day), the abdication from foreign affairs of the Congress—all these meant no questions were to be asked of the military. The result was the continued "bipartisanship" of the war which thwarted any constructive analysis and criticism of our postwar foreign activities. Having a "warfare state" also meant that grievous problems at home were unattended to and domestic priorities were given last place—attitudes which continue to haunt us today.

This institutional attitudinal transformation was achieved without a change in the written Constitution. It was achieved largely without public debate and with little public notice. It amounted to a *coup d'état* that has already changed America, and not in attractive ways. No major elections were won or lost on these issues, no extensive debate was carried on in Congress, but the institutions of the cold war changed the focus of American power and the American political structures that surround it.

Side by side with this change in government came a great increase in the centralized power of the corporate structure and the beginnings of a truly worldwide American empire. America set up military bases around the world, and the corporations followed the flag.

Domestically, senior military men, defense bureaucrats, defense industry executives, retired officers in and out of Congress, and the scholars paid by defense contracts worked together in a climate of shared interests in weapons, standing forces, real or imagined threats, and protracted conflict. They have now become an interlocking self-serving directorate for American militarism as they replace each other at the top of the hierarchies of power. Their prophecies of conflict become self-fulfilling as they induce the very international maneuvers which feed their power positions. Just as an unchecked rivalry in arms led directly to World War I, so there is a large element of truth in C. Wright Mills' statement that the "immediate cause of World War III is the preparation for it."

Although there has been corruption in this military-industrial complex, it is not the corruption that frightens one as much as the built-in lobby for war, for preparations for war, and against domestic priorities. As the constituency dependent on the military-industrial complex is broadened, the critical faculties of the citizenry are dulled, neutralizing one of the key checks on the power and growth of that complex. The great constitutional checks and balances of states against federal government or Congress against executive or a critical citizenry against both have all been eroded by this great change in the American political and economic power constellation.

IN HIS OFTEN-QUOTED (and rather astonishing) farewell address, President Eisenhower called attention to "the conjunction of an immense military establishment and a large arms industry" and warned the nation to "guard against the acquisition of unwarranted influence, whether sought or unsought, by the military-industrial complex. The potential for the disastrous rise of misplaced power exists and will persist." We failed to heed his admonition and the dimensions of our warfare state are now appalling.

The raw size of the "defense" budget is a large part of the problem. Between 10 and 15 percent of the federal budget during the 1930s went for national defense; in the 1960s the range was 55 to 65 percent, in spite of a great expansion of social progress in the intervening years. This reflected an increase in annual outlays from $750 million in the early 1930s to $1 billion in 1939 to $77 billion in 1970. We spend on the defense establishment $400 for every man, woman, and child in America. By comparison, the Soviet Union spends only $230 (in equivalent purchasing power per capita); Great Britain, $100; France, $123; West Germany, $103; and the People's Republic of China, $9! We are indeed Number One —first in overkill, first in wasteful extravagance, and first in irrational fear of foreign enemies.

All this is no accident. These huge sums not only make possible the continuation of a runaway warfare state, but they also serve an important economic function that wins them the support of the business-corporate constituency. Most advanced private enterprise economies now require a large public sector for the stabilization of aggregate demand, and in the United States this has been most easily achieved through a large defense sector. Once the mechanism is used, of course, it becomes in the interest of all those in the defense sector that there be an uninterrupted, and preferably expanding, flow of public money into it. Policies, programs, and attitudes that support and reinforce that flow are looked upon as good in themselves, and those that don't are strenuously opposed. The momentum is great and the constituency large.

Businessmen and chambers of commerce who regularly rant against the dangers of socialism and a large public sector regularly exclude all defense spending from their condemnation. Yet it is this category of government spending that has increased most markedly in the past forty years.

It is not surprising that supervision of expenditures has been woefully deficient in the defense industry. Uniformed military on duty as plant representatives in defense enterprises soon become captive of the very firms they are supposed to oversee. Retired officers people the executive halls of the defense corporations with non-jobs that have more to do with whom they still know on active duty or in public office than with any particular "technical expertise" they might bring to the firm. A congressional study several years ago found that some 2000 retired military officers of the rank of colonel or Navy captain and above were employed by the 100 largest defense contractors holding two-thirds of the contracts. Almost one fourth of this number (465) were former military officers employed by the nine major contractors involved in the ABM system—a formidable lobby indeed.

Contracts are written to be as risk free as possible for the corporation, with government bearing the burden of cost overruns, of design deficiencies, and often furnishing plant and equipment. The defense market is made secure and stable, negotiated rather than competitive bidding is too often the practice, and profits are allowed which are frequently far out of proportion to the minimal risks incurred.

In 1971 an independent analysis by the General Accounting Office of $4.3 billion worth of defense business found the average rate of return on investment to be 56 percent. Yet in the face of this the Secretary of Defense announced that new procurement policies would allow even higher profits in the future.

When the government changes its mind about a contractor, it pays cancellation penalties; when a project goes sour, the contractor is given another so he can keep his "management team intact"; when, through gross mismanagement, a firm gets in trouble, the government bails it out; and when the whole aerospace industry feels the pinch, a new round of weapons is the government's response.

Although the avowed public policy favors competition, the structure of the defense sector involves practices such as "weapon system managers," subcontracting, and "single source procurement" which foster collusion and concentration and do away with the market mechanism. It is ironic that an industry whose purpose is supposedly to defend the free enterprise system is one in which competition is the exception (only

12 percent of Pentagon procurement for FY 1971 was made through open, competitive bidding).

TWENTY-FIVE YEARS AGO the first Secretary of Defense, James Forrestal, told the graduating class of the Armed Forces Information School, "It is your responsibility to make citizens aware of their responsibility to the services." They, and many like them since, have done their job well. The all-pervasive public relations campaign carried out by the military and its industrial allies, coupled with the popular propensity to venerate the man in uniform and his commander in chief, has produced a mood of public acquiescence in whatever the Pentagon wants. Those of us who oppose the warfare state face a formidable task indeed.

Every element of American society is marshaled to support the warfare state. Everyone loves a parade and the military goes all out to show its stuff before the home folk. Armed Forces Day ceremonies throughout the land typically draw large crowds to nearby military bases (and surprising numbers of them are nearby). Children are especially welcome, for it is important that the image-making begin early in shaping a favorable view of the military. Community leaders are placed on advisory panels of various sorts, flown to firepower demonstrations, and hosted at military installations. Even though military men are supposed to execute policy, not make it or propagandize for it, teams of officers conduct indoctrination seminars on world affairs and national security, frequently sponsored by the local chamber of commerce.

Propaganda which relates military values to manliness is persistent and widespread. Even as we attempt to improve our relations with communist nations, the military distributes films portraying the crude stereotypes of the cold war period and attempts to stir up the syndrome of fear and hate that gripped us in the 1950s. They are playing to the darker instincts in each of us in a barely subliminal theme. The military needs an enemy to justify its huge budget, and it uses all the media at its disposal to convince us that the threats are dire and the danger imminent.

The Department of Defense itself spends nearly $50 million annually on lobbying efforts and indoctrination of the public under the guise of information programs. Yet it is outraged when a solitary television documentary attempts to expose the peddling of the Pentagon. Defense contractors spend huge sums (reimbursed, of course, as a "normal business expense") on romanticizing of airplanes, missiles, ships, and guns.

All of the propaganda has created a great reservoir of favorable support which has paid off handsomely for the military and its industrial associates by providing a barrier to criticism that is hard to penetrate. However bad the product or mismanaged the weapons program, no major contractor is really called to account for his failures. No generals or admirals are ever fired, however gross their performances, whether it be the sinking of a submarine in drydock, the Tet offensive, machines and weapons that don't work, or My Lai.

It is important that citizens resist the military line. When the Pentagon's cold war films are shown in their local communities, they should protest the showings and arrange to present speakers and documentaries portraying the true dimensions of American militarism and questioning the accuracy of the information fed to them by the Pentagon. Foreign officials and citizens can be invited to speak to local clubs and citizen groups. Regional conferences can be organized, bringing together experts and citizens to explore the issues of foreign policy and defense. The American people are beginning to realize that they have been the victims of a bald misrepresentation about the threats we face and the defense we need, and they will respond to the truth when it is brought before them.

NIKITA KHRUSHCHEV tells in his memoirs of a conversation he had with President Eisenhower at Camp David. The President asked him how he decided on funds for military expenses, but then added, "Perhaps first I should tell you how it is with us . . . My military leaders say, 'Mr. President, we need such and such a sum for such and such a program.' I say, 'Sorry, we don't have the funds.' They say, 'We have reliable information that the Soviet Union has already allocated funds for their own such program.' So I give in . . . Now tell me, how is it with you?"

And Khrushchev replied, "It's just the same. Some people say, 'Comrade Khrushchev, look at this! The Americans are developing such and such a system.' I tell them there's no money. So we discuss it some more, and I end up by giving them the money they ask for."

Neither in Russia nor America does the political leadership seem capable of resisting the persistent pressures from the military-industrial complex for ever-advancing weapons technologies. In the absence of such independent political judgments, military procurement in both countries comes to be determined by interservice and interagency competition, aided and abetted by the two largest private constituencies in our society, the business-corporate constituency and labor, augmented by the patriotic feelings of the people which all military leaders call upon at budget time.

I believe we are going to need a combination of new political leadership, which will apply a firm brake on military spending, and a series of understandings with the Soviet Union that will forestall the continuation of this kind of senseless competition. Both will be needed. Without some agreement with the Russians, the pressures from military-industrial complex for new arms will be irresistible; but the difficulties and delays of negotiation are so great that such agreements alone will never go far enough to put a sufficient curb on military spending.

President Nixon has admitted that "we and our NATO allies do not believe that war is imminent in Europe," but, he asserts, "we must face the possibility that it could occur." Of course, war could occur—anything could occur—but the sane man prepares for the most likely and realistic contingencies. And it is time, after twenty-five years, we re-examined whether or not we have become the victims of our own paranoic fears. Are we wasting our treasure and depleting our domestic society in preparing for a war which the other side is not, and never has been, planning?

Have we, in fact, been increasing the chances of such a war through the rising level of armaments and the increasing tension, hostility, and chance of miscalculation which can in themselves be the cause of a war which no one wants? Because of the vivid memory of World War II, we have maintained a high level of armaments in order to deter the aggression that might come if we were unprepared. Perhaps we should recall instead the situation which brought on World War I, when nations faced each other armed to the teeth, none wanting war, but each fearful of attack, until the war erupted out of the mutual fears the arms race had created.

Furthermore, in this nuclear era no level of defense spending can guarantee security against attack. We can never hope to prevent truly staggering losses to our country in a nuclear war, regardless of the level of arms we maintain. Our only hope of survival is to prevent the outbreak of war, and this can be achieved in less expensive and more effective ways than by continuously building up our weapons arsenal. Through wise negotiations, through sensitive attention to the fears of other nations, through personal contacts at the governmental and private levels, through the good offices of international organizations, we can strengthen the barriers to war.

This country has been maintaining its military forces on a wartime basis since the late 1940s. Our overseas forces are supposed to be ready to move instantly to repel an attack, and the "strategic reserves" maintained within the continental United States are supposed to be ready for deployment overseas within thirty days. The difficulty with this set of contingency plans is that neither we nor our allies believe a war is imminent. Neither Russia nor China nor, indeed, any other country is preparing to launch an attack on that assemblage of democracies, totalitarian states, and military dictatorships which we so brazenly call the "free world." Because no one believes in the likelihood of the contingency for which we are preparing, our ability to maintain those armed forces in such a state of readiness is steadily waning.

Those who refuse to reexamine our purposes in keeping this vast army deployed around the world must accept responsibility for the snowballing disintegration of our armed forces. Any group of human beings will begin to come apart once their reason for coming together has disappeared. An army is not a machine that can sit on the shelf, waiting to be used with a simple injection of fuel. It is a body of men motivated by ideas and images of their role, and it is starting to come unstuck.

We see the signs of disintegration most strikingly at our overseas bases, where our men and their families find themselves in a strange land with an undefined, meaningless job. The inevitable result is rising internal dissension, refusal to obey the orders of superior officers, cynicism, and a general decay of both the quality of our armed forces and the belief of the men in the honorable purposes of their own land.

At the same time, we have the top officers in our armed forces appearing every year before the Congress to report that they cannot do their job with the money that we make available to them. Of course they can't! They have been asked to achieve a high state of readiness for a war in which the rest of us do not believe and for which we are therefore not willing to pay. As large as our military budget is, it cannot provide the capability to fight a major war at any spot on the globe with ready forces. Since our people do not believe such a war is imminent, they are not going to provide those funds. High as defense is on the government's scale of priorities, it is low on the priorities of our people as compared to the other pressing demands for their financial resources.

I believe that our military budget need be only half as large as it is to achieve the valid purposes for which we need military force today. Decisions concerning purposes are political matters, not strictly military questions or matters of expert estimate. They are questions that can be decided by the Congress and the people in order to return this country to a sane defense program and a realistic world posture.

Admiral Thomas Moorer, the Chairman of the Joint Chiefs of Staff, has admitted that, even if the Soviet Union were to achieve a "clearly evident overall strategic superiority"—a most unlikely possibility, in view of our continuing rate of expenditures and on-going weapons deployments—this might have "no practical effect" on the outcome of a major war. However, he suggests, it would diminish the "effectiveness of our diplomacy." If the military balance has now, even in his view, reached the point where military judgments give way to political ones, then our political leaders, the American people, and their representatives are as able to judge the need for new arms as is the military.

We need to ask what is the nature of the threat, not in terms of mere numbers of missiles, aircraft, tanks, and ships, but in terms of the purposes of those forces and the dangers they actually pose to the United States and its friends. The mere possession of military forces by any nation, even one whose social system we may abhor, does not, by itself, pose a threat to us. Those forces become a threat only if they are directed toward infringing on our rights or the rights of some nation of concern to us. Our own arsenal, the largest on earth, does not, in our eyes, constitute a threat to any nation. Undoubtedly, though, Soviet military men see it as a threat to Russia, just as ours see Russian forces as a threat to us. The U.S. Navy points to the growing Soviet Navy as a justification for its multibillion dollar shipbuilding program. However, the purpose of the Soviet build-up may simply be, like our own, to be prepared to defend the interests of their country and to balance the U.S. fleets that have been deployed on their borders for twenty years.

The fact that the Russians have a large army and a growing navy is not sufficient to prove that they are a threat to the security of this nation. Whether we like it or not, the Soviet Union is a great power, with a large population, the world's second largest industrial capacity, and extensive borders to defend. It has always had and continues to maintain, a large standing military establishment. But these facts alone do not mean that we have to see this as an imminent threat to our security.

When the possession of arms itself is perceived as a threat, an arms race results, as each side tries to close any "gaps" and match the capabilities of the other. The greatest military danger to the United States and to the world today lies in that arms race, not in any intentional decision to attack. As the strongest military power on earth, we must assume the responsibility for diminishing that danger by slowing down or eliminating the arms race.

We must remember that in a nuclear age no government, no matter how powerful, can protect its people from ultimate destruction. There is, in President Eisenhower's words, no alternative to peace. And so we must halt the continuing expansion of our nuclear arsenal, which is bringing us not protection, but only the threat of ever greater destruction.

THE MILITARY should have to provide for the country's defense within a limited budget. It should be the function of the Congress to relate the military budget to other expenditures of the federal government, while it leaves some of the technical decisions for allocation within the Defense Department to the technical specialists themselves. Furthermore, the Defense Department should be required to present the budget in terms of the capabilities it provides to meet certain foreign policy objectives, so that the Congress and the American people can effectively deal with those objectives and examine whether it indeed wants to pursue certain foreign policy goals. Defense and security are too important to be left in the hands of anyone but the people.

Congress must develop the same kind of questioning attitude toward defense funding as it has toward the much smaller sums involved in domestic programs. It must recognize that the Pentagon is an entrenched bureaucracy and, as such, one of its primary functions is to obtain additional funds for its programs. Congress must, in other words, remove the "sacred cow" image which the military has managed to acquire since World War II. The adversary studies, proposed in chapter 3, would aid the Congress in developing a critical judgment on military programs.

While it may be that the citizen cannot judge the technical efficacy of particular weapons systems, he is quite capable of judging whether or not the United States should exercise its military muscle throughout the world. If the military budget were presented to him in terms which made clear its relation to foreign policy goals, and if much more information were made available to him, he would then be equipped to exercise overall political and civilian control of our military spending.

There is inadequate public supervision today of the appropriations process when defense spending is involved. There is an unwillingness to question defense expenditures (as compared to the way domestic expenditures are scrutinized). There is a tendency to accept the recommendations of the military man without questioning very deeply the reasoning behind these recommendations or the motivations which might be leading to them. The military man is assumed to have only the best interests of his country at heart and, beyond that, to have special expertise which qualifies him to make recommendations which mere civilians can question only at their peril.

However, the military man today is dealing with weapons which, until Vietnam, he had never used in practice. Too often his viewpoint has been a direct extrapolation from World War II or Korean War experience. In making such an extension, his judgment may be no better than that of a concerned civilian and, indeed, it may be worse because of his inability, or unwillingness, to see factors other than past experience. (The Allies became painfully aware of this in World War I when what was to have been a rapidly concluded conflict degenerated into an endless, enormously lethal war, and in World War II when the most secure and carefully developed fortifications were swiftly overcome.)

In considering motivations, we often fail to recognize that the military man behind his desk is like any other man, subject to the same kinds of bureaucratic pressures and subject to the tendency to identify his special interests with the general welfare. Men easily come to believe that what is good for them is good for their country, and military men are not immune to this disease of the bureaucrat. We must, then, question the opinions of a man in the military just as much as we question the opinions of a man in business. Each is concerned for his country, but each develops special viewpoints which may blind him to some important aspects of the national interest.

I don't believe the Congress can effectively conduct a line-by-line critique of the defense budget or successfully confront the military on the choice of individual weapons systems. But Congress does have a unique responsibility, and a special vantage point, for determining what the priorities of this nation should be and what the nation should be spending to address the various problems it faces. From that point of view, it should be the responsibility of Congress to establish strict budget ceilings on the military. Because this has not been done in the past, the nation is now faced with a ravenous military machine that gobbles up every spare dollar in the federal treasury. We must curb its appetite, or it will devour us as well.

THE ACTUAL DEFENSE of the United States takes only a small portion of what is called the "defense" budget. Because of our geography and the excellent relations we have with our immediate neighbors, we are in the fortunate position of requiring almost no defense at all from conventional attack on our shores. Only the strategic nuclear forces, the missiles and bombers which deter nuclear attack, and the antisubmarine forces which guard our shores are actually defending our country from attack. And these consume less than $20 billion out of the total of $75–$80 billion which we spend every year on our armed forces. All the rest is used to "project our forces," to provide a capacity for intervening in overseas conflicts—some of which may conceivably affect our vital interests, but many of which may be only remotely related to the lives of our citizens.

The cost of operating our strategic forces can and should be drastically reduced. Today half our expenditures on these forces are used to purchase new weapons including MIRV warheads for missiles (a response to an ABM system which the Russians never built) and the Safeguard ABM system (now admitted even by the Defense Department to be inadequate to do the job).

We will soon have the capacity to deliver more than 500 warheads, each capable of destroying a city, on every major city in the Soviet Union. Even the most dedicated military enthusiast should be able to see the absurdity of spending more money to expand that overkill capacity. Our Polaris submarine forces alone, which are still completely invulnerable to enemy attack, will soon be able to deliver more than 200 warheads on every major Soviet city.

If we were to call a halt to the mad momentum of this absurd and deadly race, phase out the expensive and obsolete manned bomber force, negotiate the removal of all land-based missiles, and take other steps to reduce nonessential spending in the strategic area, we could cut the costs of our deterrent forces to less than $10 billion a year.

The remainder of our forces serve, not for defense, but for intervention. As Secretary of Defense McNamara once observed, "The overall requirement for General Purpose (ground, air and naval) Forces is related not so much to the defense of our own territory as it is to the support of our commitments to other nations." It is those "commitments," whether formal or informal, whether the result of congressional action or executive fiat, to at least 45 countries, that keep our defense budget so high and our military forces so dispersed around the world.

By conjuring up the image of another "conventional" war in Europe or elsewhere, on the scale of World War II, the military can create endless "requirements" for more men, tanks, aircraft, and the entire panoply of nonnuclear armament. Retired Marine Corps Colonel James Donovan has described World War II as the Golden Age of the American military establishment. In their weapons "wish lists" for today, the Army has a new tank for a replay of the glorious tank battles of the 1940s, the Air Force is purchasing new fighter planes to repeat the epic dogfights of that era, the Navy is preparing to "control the sea lanes" as it did when the U-boats were trailing the Liberty Ships, and the Marines are preparing to assault the Pacific Beaches again. Presumably because they would find their roles diminished if they were to recognize the truth, none of them admit that those days are gone forever. The destruction of German and Japanese militarism and, most of all, the advent of the nuclear weapons have eliminated all of that.

New thinking is required for a new era. Unfortunately, it does not appear we are going to get it from our armed services, as they are presently constituted. They must, first and foremost, defend their budgets against the onslaught of those like myself who believe our nation's priorities are dangerously askew. Since, in their view, more weapons are always better than less and "what is good for the (insert the service of your choice) is good for the country," the necessary rethinking is not going to come from them.

I must emphasize that I do not mean to disparage either

their courage on the battlefield or their dedication to the country. They serve to the best of their ability both on the battlefield and behind a desk. But, as the brilliant French statesman Talleyrand said, "War is much too serious a matter to be left to military men," and, we might add, to military institutions which always prepare for the last war they fought.

One reason the Army wants so badly to keep its forces in Europe is that it is the one place where a World War II-style conventional war could be fought. Nowhere else is there either the terrain or the assemblage of industrialized countries capable of sustaining such a conflict for very long.

Similarly, the Air Force needs the manned bomber and the fighter plane simply to justify its existence. The control of its missiles could be turned over to a separate missile corps, which might even be civilian, and the Air Force's close support role for the Army could be turned over to the Army it is supposed to support. But the maintenance of an institution, even one with as proud a record in its short history as the U.S. Air Force, is not reason enough for the extraordinary expenditures which the Air Force has brought us in recent times.

In an era when surface ships can be sunk by cheap but effective antiship missiles, the obsolescence of the Navy is clear to everyone but the most dedicated "carrier admiral." Nevertheless, the U.S. Navy is now beginning a massive shipbuilding program, constructing an entire new fleet of ships. These will be just as vulnerable to the new antiship missiles or to nuclear weapons as were the older ships they replace.

The Navy is neither small nor depleted, but, as Colonel Donovan has pointed out, it needs a rest. The demand for aircraft carriers at Yankee and Dixie stations off Vietnam, for carrier task forces in the China Sea, for a massive fleet in the Mediterranean—all have tended to wear down the ships, the aircraft, and the crews. We have learned that we do not need to keep large fleets constantly on patrol in foreign waters; the mere presence of our fleet will not forestall either revolution or aggression, and ships can move quickly to "show the flag," if that does prove to be desirable. So we should bring a large portion of the Navy home, let families be reunited, reduce the problems of retaining young men in the service, and we will end up with a stronger Navy for it.

The same reasoning applies to the Army. Keeping large numbers of American troops in Vietnam, Korea, and Germany has done nothing but breed discontent, cynicism, and the drift to drugs among our soldiers. Without a meaningful role, the Army is disintegrating. Bringing these troops home and reducing the Army to a size consistent with its role as the nucleus for any national emergency would go far toward reestablishing the pride and character of the Army.

If we looked realistically at today's needs for "conventional," that is, nonnuclear, forces, I believe we would find that our present expenditure for such forces of over $55 billion per year could be reduced to below $30 billion. At the same time, troop levels should be reduced from their present 2.5 million men to a level of no more than 1.5 million men. If this were done, the military draft could be eliminated without the need for excessive expenditures to support a high level of volunteers. The professional quality of the armed forces could be restored, and our forces-in-being would, for the first time in a generation, bear a clear relation to our true security needs.

For me, the strongest argument against the continuance of the draft is that it has allowed the President to take from Congress its constitutional control over the making of war. By providing the President with the power, whenever he wishes, to expand the size of the armed forces, it permits him to exercise total control over the use of our armed forces. He need not come to Congress to provide the manpower he needs to undertake any foreign adventure.

But even when no crisis is present, the draft allows the President to maintain a large enough army to keep our forces stationed around the world, even when the sentiment of the American people has turned against that kind of imperial presence. Without the draft, the President would find it much more difficult to carry out a policy which did not have the strong support of the American people, for he would not be able to find the soldiers to man the bases. If he must rely on volunteers, he will automatically be constrained by the mood of the people whose lives he is committing to military adventures.

Some may say this "ties his hands" and "reduces his flexibility," but we have to tie his hands. Even good presidents have misused America's military might. We have seen too many instances in history, culminating in the catastrophe of Vietnam, where the concentration of military power in one man has led to disaster, and I, for one, fear the expansion of this power, with nuclear weapons and all that modern technology can make available, far more than I fear the effects of imposing democratic constraints upon the President of all the people.

To limit the now enormous power of the President in foreign policy and military intervention, what we need is not new legislation on his war powers, but exercise by the Congress of its existing powers over money and military force levels. It is the Congress which has the sole authority "to raise and support armies," and all we need do is reclaim that power in order to reassert the democratic basis for our foreign policy.

We have seen over the years the gradual and regrettable eroding of the exercise of this authority, both through presidential usurpation and congressional abdication. Despite the widespread observation that the honeymoon is finally over for the military, real evidence of this is hard to find. In over two years in the Senate, I have not seen the Department of Defense lose on any issue on which it really wanted to prevail. Some of us in the Senate have tried cutting out duplicate and useless weapons with no success. We have tried overall expenditure cutbacks with no success. We have tried merely to improve information systems in order to know more about what was

and will be requested with no success. We have tried simply
to strengthen the comptroller general's role in overseeing defense expenditures with no success.

Now it is time for the voice of the people to be heard, demanding that Congress again play its constitutional role as
watchdog of the military and guardian of civilian control.
Only the people can make the Congress assert its judgment
on the defense budget.

The defense posture I have outlined is consonant with this
country's tradition. It is a return, after the aberration of the
past quarter century, to the mainstream of our wise traditions.
We would be returning to a level of military manpower that
could easily be provided by volunteers in a voluntary society.
We would have another opportunity to reconstruct the kind
of dedicated military force that would be a respected contributor to the total aims of our society.

Only in the context of a new internationalism can it make
sense to contemplate defense budgets of $40 billion or less
each year. These figures need not be a mark of naïveté, fool-
ishness, or even negligence and irresponsibility, but the evidence of a return to rational security planning for America.

IT IS GENERALLY AGREED that the underlying basis of our national security is the strength of our national economy. The
continued soundness of that economy, taken together with our
national unity and an able military, is our real line of defense.

Apologists for the military argue that massive defense
spending is a boon to the U.S. economy. This is false. Although the direct beneficiaries of military spending form a
powerful constituency in favor of it, the U.S. economy as a
whole would be far healthier with a much smaller defense
budget. The substitution of other types of expenditures, creating goods and services that the society needs, would over a
relatively short period create much more income and employment than would be lost through cutbacks in military spend-

ing. Protection money, whether paid in Old Chicago or Modern America, benefits no one but the "protector" whose pocket gets lined.

There would be some problems associated with any substantial shift away from defense. Some workers would be laid off, and particular regions of the country would be hard hit. There would be rapid depreciation of specialized skills and equipment. There might be some temporary falling off of total demand and economic momentum, but the real pain for individuals could be eased by compensatory measures or even eliminated by the adoption of the Citizen's Wage (proposed and discussed in chapter 6).

Because the Pentagon shopping list is very different from the private citizen's, a cutback in defense spending would produce demand increases in some industries and markets while others slacked off. Measures to ease the transition for workers, such as vocational reeducation and relocation allowances, could easily be instituted.

After the initial dislocations I believe we would have a far healthier economy. The funds released from the military budget could be used to finance the rebuilding of our cities, the provision of decent housing for all our citizens, the cleaning up of our environment, and the many other improvements which our financially starved "infrastructure" so badly needs. In purely economic terms, past experience suggests that the economy will grow more rapidly with a higher proportion of civilian spending. This was the case after World War II and the Korean War as the economy rather painlessly converted to peacetime production.

The production of goods and services usable in the broad nondefense sectors of the economy propels our economy forward at a far better pace than does devoting unusually large amounts of resources to the defense sector. Moreover, the distortions of the economy—inflationary and otherwise—that come from disproportionately high levels of spending on the military are avoided.

A special issue is the probable impact of defense cutbacks on the research and development industry. The Department of Defense supports more than half the R & D performed in the high technology industries, such as aircraft, electrical equipment, and communications, and, as an occupational group, scientists and engineers will suffer proportionately greater job layoffs than any other group, when defense spending is cut. They also will experience special problems of adjustment, if they have to move out of the defense industry, since the level of technology is generally lower and the demands of the market are so different in the nondefense sector of the economy.

At the same time, however, there are forces at work to assist their adjustment. These include increased demand for technical means of combating the deterioration of our environment and for ways to solve the numerous problems of our cities. Using the financial security provided by the Citizen's Wage and expanded unemployment insurance, technologists will be able to acquire new skills which will allow them to contribute in these fields. Many others will have to switch to entirely new fields, as the demand for new types of workers is created by a shift in our national priorities.

In bringing about defense cutbacks we can expect resistance from communities that would be hit hard by reductions. Their concern is the impact on local economies through the loss of jobs and this is a legitimate worry when a military base or defense contractor is the town's main industry. We must provide assistance in the form of financial aid and relocation of new industries to these communities to help them through their readjustment period. In doing this, we should remember that the military holds an enormous amount of valuable real estate that could be converted to recreational use, to industrial parks, schools, and to home building sites. Intelligently redeveloped, these installations could become the nucleus for a rejuvenation of many towns and cities on a solid peacetime economy. It can be done; it only takes the will and the awareness of the citizen that in the long run his future will be more secure than forever dangling at the mercy of the defense budget cutters.

In sum, there is a way of bringing the runaway warfare state under control. Many have already tried to do it, but the Executive has managed to discredit them as alarmists, and the citizenry generally has remained apathetic on the issue, so deeply has the militarist indoctrination penetrated. For these reasons, it is of crucial importance that those of us who think another way continue to be heard. We must persist in our call for a return to reason until the people see clearly what we have become and are becoming, as a nation, and say, "No more! Enough!"

6

Work and the Work Place

It violates right order
whenever capital so employs
the working or wage-earning
classes as to divert business
and economic activity entirely
to its own arbitrary will and
advantage without any regard to
the human dignity of the workers,
the social character of economic
life, social justice, and the
common good.

—*Pope Pius XI*

FOR A NATION supposedly devoted to the ideas of democracy, it is a curious fact that the most important aspect of daily life in America—the aspect of work—is almost totally removed from any association with democracy.

While most of our great debates have been fought publicly over the issue of whether the government is democratic or whether it is becoming authoritarian, there has been virtually no public discussion of the need for democracy in our economic life, in our working lives.

Democratic participation in work must take many forms.

91

The working population of America must have available to it the widest possible choice of jobs, unrestricted by accident of birth—race, sex, or location—or by the education one may have received as a child. We should make it possible for an individual to acquire the skills he will need for any job in which he has an interest and for which he has the necessary talent. This should apply to his first job, if he is attempting to gain the skills which others may have acquired through the advantages of a superior education, or to a new career he is seeking after outgrowing or being laid off from an old job. The circumstances of a man's early childhood and then the financial obligations he incurs in later life are restricted. Many people are not afforded the opportunity to make new choices as they grow and develop throughout their active life. By making the necessary educational opportunities available and by providing the necessary economic security. I believe we can greatly expand the freedom of occupational choice for all Americans.

However, this is not enough. Once an American has a job, he or she, together with co-workers, must be able to share in decisions on how the work is to be done. This has not traditionally been permitted to our workers, and the result has been a latent dissatisfaction with the work place expressed in wildcat strikes, local job actions, and outright sabotage of the product and the tools to make it. We must seek imaginative and creative new ways to involve workers in the conduct of this major and productive portion of their lives. I believe this can be done without sacrificing the many advantages of America's productive and innovative free enterprise system.

It is imperative, first, that we embrace a new principle that the control of the wealth of this nation and of its means of production, the machines and processes upon which our modern life style depends, must be fractionalized and redistributed basically and absolutely. This must be done so that the people have democratic access to the control, to the purposes, to the products, to the economic proceeds of it all.

This will mean allowing customers and producers to share, along with owners and managers, in the basic decision-making privileges of business and industry. It will mean the gradual divesting of that control from the few who now exercise it or mandate it.

Our objective must be to return the meaning and fruits of work to the people who work, in addition to those people who simply own.

This philosophical change should be undertaken by a declaration—perhaps written into our Constitution—that every American *owns* a share of the country automatically at birth, and is thereby entitled to participate directly in the nation's present and future affluence. Unless we adopt this fundamental principle, there will never be any true meaning in work for the majority of the people nor any democracy in the work place.

THE QUESTION a people's platform must address is *how* every one of the 205 million Americans living today can participate in the economy and obtain from it the basic financial security which is their share of this material affluence. I believe it should be done through a Citizen's Wage, to which everyone is entitled at birth and which is available to the worker and the poor alike. The Citizen's Wage should be seen as a dividend from the nation's total affluence and as a reflection of each person's right to economic security. The amount paid to the individual should not be restricted to a token share, but should be geared realistically to the nation's total productivity and to the level of income needed to maintain a minimum, decent standard of living. The Citizen's Wage should also become an effective tool for the long-run economic improvement of our entire society.

Here is how I visualize the Citizen's Wage at work in today's economy. The basic Citizen's Wage would be $5,000 a year for a family of four and $1,500 for the single individual. Every family and every individual earning up to $3,500 a year would be eligible to receive a graduated portion of the Citizen's Wage in addition to his earnings.

Under the proposed formula, the Citizen's Wage for a man with an income would be reduced by an amount equal to half his earnings. A family man with no other income would receive the full Citizen's Wage of $5,000. A family man earning $4,000 a year would have $2,000 subtracted from his Citizen's Wage, for a total income of $7,000; the man making $8,000 would wind up with a total income of $9,000. Anyone earning more than $10,000 would no longer receive the Citizen's Wage.

The intent of this plan is plain: to banish poverty and financial insecurity. I have chosen the $5,000 minimum because that is the Department of Labor's estimate of what a family of four needs, after deduction of taxes, to get by in a city without privation. Under the tax proposals which I make in chapter 8, the tax burden falling on those earning less than $10,000 would be drastically reduced, enabling a family to meet its basic needs at the proposed level of the Citizen's Wage.

It is possible and perhaps desirable to establish regional councils to determine what the basic Citizen's Wage should be for a given area, and it could be adjusted up or down according to the cost of living in a particular locale.

One could say that this plan comes down to a form of guaranteed income. While this is obviously the case, there are important differences from other such proposals made before now. The most important difference is the number of people who would receive some benefits—some 120 million Americans, including more than half of all families. It is a rather sad measure of our democracy that this many people are presently denied financial security—particularly when it can be had for so little.

Presently we are spending $50 billion a year on welfare and Social Security programs which are totally inadequate. The Citizen's Wage would cost only an additional $15 billion, a small sum indeed to provide real economic security for all. The whole program is 1.5 percent of our GNP.

The low cost of the program can be realized if the establishment of the Citizen's Wage is combined with a drastic reduction in the tax burden that falls on those who earn less than $10,000 per year. Under the present inequitable tax structure, the Citizen's Wage would have to be $6,500. (In my view, the citizen should be required to pay taxes on all of his income, regardless of whether it comes from a job or from his Citizen's Wage, in order that every citizen will share in supporting necessary public services.) The circulatory impact of this wage or dividend on our economy could cause us to explode into a new era of prosperity and production. Then as we come into new and greater affluence we could recalculate and increase the wage as our national wealth permits.

We are inevitably going in the direction of financial security for all whether we like it or not. The shame is that we do not acknowledge it, so we can guide this trend with intelligent planning.

Practically nothing has been projected about what true security for all would mean to the economy and the country as a whole. Consider what would happen if additional money were put into the hands of millions of people and fed directly back into the economy in the purchase of goods and services, for all the recipients of the Citizen's Wage would be consumers. Our economy is suffering today from a lack of consumer demand. An increase in the number of consumers and the amount of capital available to them would give the economy a tremendous boost, creating more demand for goods and more jobs. This effect has been totally ignored by those who claim that a substantial attack on poverty would bankrupt the country.

Nor has a great deal been said about how the quality of life in this country might be improved through an equitable distribution of income. It would, of course, result in considerable material improvement, but more importantly, the equitable distribution of income would help to eradicate the root causes of crime and the decay of our cities, the adverse side-effects of our present system that numb our minds. Authorities estimate the nation's total losses through crime come to an incredible $25 billion a year, not to mention the hardship borne by the victims. (Blacks living in slums suffer $3 billion of those losses alone, according to Federal Reserve Board Governor Andrew Brimmer.) What if we were able to eliminate this cost through the Citizen's Wage, and make the streets of our communities safe at night, and, at the same time, reduce the amount of time and money spent in barricading our more affluent homes? For I believe that elevating everyone to a comfortable standard of living would remove much of the cause of crime which comes from hard want. We also might, over a period of time, diminish drug-related crimes also by securing and stabilizing our social environment. Maybe we could show our children that hope and fulfillment do lie in our minds and hands and not in a needle.

IT IS A FACT that some strange and sad things keep happening to the idea of work in this country today. Working conditions haven't improved all that much for most people in a century, but lately we have been treated to a new philosophy (really, a shined-up old one) by the Nixon government which sounds very much like discipline and punishment. Everybody should work—never mind at what or for what wage—because he needs the discipline, and those unable to work for some reason, as is the case with many of those receiving welfare, should nonetheless be bullied into taking any available job so as to make sure "idleness" is never rewarded.

At the same time the annual financial statistics of the nation tell us that about one-fourth of all personal income goes to people on the basis of their holding title to property and resources rather than on the basis of their actually doing productive work. You might say this just represents a reward for work that they or some relative did in the past. You might also ask just how long some particular item of enterprise or discovery deserves to be ritually rewarded. And you certainly might ask, then, why we honor the rich who get unearned income and condemn the poor who, when unable to work, also get some income for which they do not work directly, even though they may have worked like dogs for years before that.

The unjust mythologies that have grown up around the rich and the poor really make me angry. Take, for example, a multimillionaire who may never have done a lick of work in his life—perhaps because his great-grandfather made a killing rigging freight rates, selling bad meat to Indians, or selling faulty rifles to the Union Army. That fellow is honored and catered to. Presidents seek his advice—and his contributions of cash. He gets a big reputation for doing little things, giving a few crumbs to the poor and patronizing the arts like royalty of old. The truth of the matter is that in many cases this rich man is a big man through a purely random roll of the dice in the game called birth. He was born to certain parents and, bingo, he is a great person.

Now look at a poor man. Most of these folk have landed in the poverty swamp also because of an accident of birth. They didn't choose the circumstance of their birth any more than the rich man. But what awaits them? Suspicion, harassment, no honor, no dignity and a life struggle just to stay alive.

And take the average working person. Chances are he counts himself lucky to be born into the middle class, to have an education and a reasonable income. If he applies himself diligently to the job—and gets some big breaks along the way —he may make a fairly comfortable living. If the breaks are really big, he might succeed in managing or owning a business. But his chances of becoming rich are small.

By what possible stretch of the imagination, then, do we say that everybody starts out equal? Hard work is not the key factor now, if it ever was, in "getting ahead." Birth is much more important. Most economists admit that no honest man starting now, regardless of his pluck, luck, and energy, can accumulate the sort of fortune represented in the Du Pont or Rockefeller holdings, simply because those holdings include an iron grip on the very resources a man would need to re-create such empires.

If hard work was the key to success today, then the average garbage collector would live in a mansion. By the same token, there probably would be members of the House of Morgan who would live in shacks. It has become apparent that the old, simple notion of hard work has taken on a lot of new mean-ings in our time. We must not assume that work is some sort of universally shared and understood concept.

Many of our leaders have so removed themselves from the actual sweat and monotony of work that they distort its mean-ing. We find that a man in power, like the President, can con-strue work as making decisions. He enjoys his work because he enjoys making decisions. Soon he equates all work with making decisions, as if all the millions of workers on the fac-tory assembly lines and in offices spent their days making decisions. The same phenomenon overtakes the business execu-tive and the rich owners of industry. They are decision-makers, too, although overly concerned with merely figuring out how to keep the corporate coffers overflowing. The President, like the business executive, is an exploiter of lives when he sends young men off to war and demands that Americans give up bits of freedom and property to support adventures abroad. To keep the money coming in, the executive demands that workers give of their energies, ambitions, and talents under an arbitrary system of rewards which generally fail to match the workers' actual contributions to the success of the enterprise.

So long as the meaning of work in America is defined by the needs of men who presently lead society—the rich and the powerful, the businessmen and the politicians—the whole work situation is bound to be distorted. Rather than work being the means by which the people generally enrich their lives, sustain themselves, and transform their world, work becomes specifically the relationship of these people to the power and the needs of society's leaders. And that's what it is today for most Americans.

Most people understand this at some level of their experience—usually at the most basic and practical level. You ask a man why he is working and the answer is likely to be "to stay alive" and, with the next breath, "to make some other son-of-a-bitch rich." The answer is profoundly correct. Americans have permitted the economy of the nation to concentrate in the hands of the very few so that most Americans literally must depend for their lives upon the jobs controlled by that very few.

It is on this question that a people's platform must open a serious debate right now. The concentration of economic power affects every facet of our lives.

We have already examined the relationship of political power to economic power. If economic power is permitted an unchecked course of concentration, it inevitably will accumulate more and more political push and thus, more and more, deny political access to nonrich Americans.

The relationship of economic production to ecological imbalances also is well known. As long as the ownership of the country is in so few hands, changes to benefit the many will always be impeded by the power and interests of the few.

The relationship of work to mental health, the stability of family life, and the quality of life generally is well known. This country already has a high rate of divorce, unrest, and mental collapse. By removing work from any arena of democratic discussion, we are also denying people any feeling of hope or possibility and thus, in a terrible cycle, we increase the frustrations, alienation, and mental depressions which already so cloud the quality of life.

Under the current production system of this country, with its intense concentration of control, our 6 percent of the earth's population consumes somewhere between 40 and 70 percent of the entire world's annual output of minerals each year. The day when that imbalance could be rationalized because of our sheer economic superiority and military superiority has crumbled into the debris of the war in Indochina. Americans generally probably understand that they must now become part of, rather than masters of, the world community. But the demands of the great and the rich may serve to stave off that realization as long as possible. Since, under the present system, there can be no practical democratic challenge to their power, they may keep America poised on the brink of more disastrous foreign adventures, rather than accepting, as most of us would, a new relationship of fairness, rather than majesty and mastery, in the world.

BUT REDUCING ECONOMIC CONCENTRATION is not enough. In deliberating how to bring democracy into the work place, we must find new ways of making work meaningful to the person who performs it. The distance between the work a person does and the results of that work have increased steadily over the years through increasing fragmentation of tasks and more centralized corporate ownership. Fewer working people each year feel they are involved beyond performing purely mechanical acts, or that the work they do in any way enriches their life beyond providing their immediate subsistence needs.

Industrial, office, and service workers have been more and more highly compartmentalized and specialized. Orders come from increasingly remote managements. Face-to-face decision-making recedes even as a memory. Feeling a part of a whole process becomes less possible as any one person's part in the process becomes more separated, more specialized, and more repetitive.

With more people feeling this detachment there is an obvious decline in such concepts as craftsmanship. Craftsmanship is an expression of individual action and creativity. It requires that the worker care about his work and stems from his feeling of involvement, his feeling that his own values and personality are being expressed in his work. Such a feeling is impossible in a rigid, top-down, compartmentalized organization.

A man who tightens a single bolt on a car sees this as just an anonymous action in a mechanical process whose beginning he cannot see and whose end he cannot appreciate.

It has been shown in industrial experiments that the level of workmanship rises sharply whenever working people are involved in making a complete product, when they can feel they have some control over a major part of the process and are not just the anonymous servants of the machines, when they feel some participatory role and satisfaction. In short, there is ample evidence that enthusiasm and satisfaction, as well as workmanship and craftsmanship, rise sharply in what might be called a democratic or decentralized work situation, where there is participation rather than merely blind following and ordering.

There will be a temptation, in the present manner of organizing business and industry and of concentrating its control, to regard this psychic value as simply another part of the profit equation. Just pay the workers more, and let them get their kicks off the job. But, once their basic needs are met, people will seek wholeness in their lives. They will rebel against dehumanizing working conditions and against the separation of work from their personal values and interests. The mere possession of more and more things will fail to enrich their lives. Rather than being happier with their material possessions, Americans are becoming more disgruntled, more disillusioned, and, in some cases, altogether despairing—as with the young people who simply drop out of the life style based on material accumulation.

If, on the other hand, people are given a chance to express themselves in the internal organization of work tasks, they will be able to find fulfillment on the job. The satisfactions that go with the increase of participation in the organization of one's work—in apportioning work assignments, interchanging assignments to avoid boredom, etc.—are precisely the satisfactions that make people more concerned with the entirety of their lives. One reflection of such a gain in dignity will be that people will look upon the fruits of industrial production as something transcending mere bookkeeping entries and as something within the sphere of interests of all working people, rather than within the control only of owners and managers. This is especially true in a technological age since we have been relieved of most pretechnological worries of raw survival, and now must focus on how to share our abundance.

Workers must, through their local union organizations, become involved in the total functioning of the work place. I am convinced that in such a process, which stresses work place democracy and full participation of working people in organizing their own work, a generally greater and more responsible view of the place of that work in society as a whole will prevail.

I feel that the people who work in an industry or business, the people who live near the work place, and the people who use the products or services have such an obvious interest in the processes involved that they will eventually demand, and should receive a voice in the disposition of the resources, the organization of the work, and the nature of the products and services themselves.

Many models for this approach are being tried around the world by varied forms of government. The Scandinavian countries have been deeply involved in giving the workers a voice in organizing the internal affairs of business and industry. Yugoslavia has gone all the way in decentralizing and democratizing the ownership of business and industry, vesting it primarily in the people who work in a given place, but also distributing among the people in general a voice in deciding the need for products and even, in broad outline, the nature of needed products and services.

Here in America there are models for such a development that have commanded much attention. The original concept of cooperative ventures was to introduce democracy into business. Under the pressures of taxes and competition, of course, much of the social-educational nature of the cooperative movement has been submerged under traditional business imperatives, but the lesson lives on.

An attractive new approach would be to recognize this interest by giving the workers a direct place on the board of directors of the corporations for which they work. Not only those who invest in a corporation, but those who work in it and those who are affected by it should participate in the decisions at the top and in the work place, which will affect all of them. (This will be discussed further in chapter 8.) The interest of workers in the success of the corporation and in the humane functioning of the work place can, in my view, best be satisfied by giving them a direct voice in the control of the corporation and thus in the whole economy.

But even these moves are not enough, in modern America, to give meaning to work. We must also alter radically some of our presently held concepts toward work itself. One is our cherished "work ethic." Today we are still so befogged by the age-old ethic intoned by Thomas Carlyle, "All work, even cotton-spinning is noble; work is alone noble," that we condemn the mother who views caring for her children as her most important job. Politicians generally are more concerned about jobs for jobs sake than in bringing purpose to people's lives. They protect the defense industry, keep open obsolete military bases, promote unnecessary public works, and subsidize major portions of the economy just to provide jobs.

This overconcern with employment is harmful, in my opinion. It is at cross purposes with making the economy function more efficiently. As our technology advances, we need less and less manpower to turn out an ever more abundant amount of goods and services. In the years ahead, more machines and computers can be expected to eliminate more and more forms of human labor. Instead of shying away from this prospect, we should welcome it. What is the point in keeping any thinking person on a task that a mindless machine can perform?

It is time we woke up and realized that we have earned—

indeed, have paid for—the right to collect the dividends from our investment. This is what a Citizen's Wage is all about, sharing the bounty of America among all the people. Otherwise we are heading on a course where the owners will wind up with all the wealth and sentence half the people to live on some form of welfare. Don't doubt for a moment they would prefer holding people in a state of dependency. It is the way to stay rich and powerful.

If we as a nation can forge a new concept of citizen-ownership of the economy, I foresee an unparalleled growth in individual freedom and maturity in our society. The Citizen's Wage, in practice, would be a cushion, a base, for people of all income levels. How many people today find themselves in well-paying jobs but want out? How many are compelled to suffer through a middle-age "identity crisis" with no opportunity to redirect their lives into more satisfying fields simply because they can't afford to give up their jobs? With a combination of the Citizen's Wage and unemployment insurance, people would have the chance to become reeducated and change occupations. Thus we could build into our society not only security but flexibility in everyone's personal choice of career and mode of life.

7

The Prisoners of Poverty

*As a society we have not been
unmindful of the poor; we permit
them to survive.*

—Raphael Hernandez Colon
(President of the Senate,
Commonwealth of Puerto Rico)

TAKE A RIDE AROUND the neighborhoods of your city, or any
city in America, and look at the way people live. You find
there are a considerable number who are pretty well off judging by their nice homes and a great many who appear fairly
comfortable even though the lawns are smaller and the apart-
ments more utilitarian than luxurious. Then you drive into a
ghetto district and there you begin to get an idea of how the
workings of our economy affect lives—streets littered with un-
collected garbage, old buildings with the holes in the windows
covered with yellowed newspaper, older men and dudes standing around the storefronts and the bars, kids coming out of a
school that hasn't been fixed up in years, deteriorating public
housing projects, and burned-out abandoned tenements. When
you keep on driving and see how big that ghetto is, try to
estimate how many people it holds, and consider that it may
be as big or bigger than all the other better neighborhoods put
together, then you begin to realize what the "urban crisis" is
about.

You put into your head the statistics the newspapers keep printing—30 million living in poverty, 14 million on welfare, 20 percent unemployment in the cities, new housing falling a million units short of goal—and you understand who and what they are talking about. It's right here. Walk around and talk to the people and pretty soon you'll get the feeling everyone living in the dreary walk-ups with the roaches crawling over the sink and rats running in the walls is a prisoner. They hate it and they would like to escape, but they can't for one reason or another; invariably it comes down to a job or money. So they exist, hustling on the street for the numbers, for dope, waiting for the welfare check, waiting at the clinic, and waiting for the food stamps and wondering if someone's breaking into the flat to steal the TV set—waiting for something better to happen. But you can see not much is happening or likely to and that it is going to take an enormous effort to make even a little change for the better in just one ghetto.

As a nation we have tried in recent times to help the poor and we have initiated many programs to get them on their feet educationally, in work training, in financial assistance, and in care for the aged and the disabled. A lot of people have been helped and are making it today because of these programs. But not nearly enough.

It seems to me that our programs fail and we perpetuate our ghetto lockups because we do not look at the problem in its totality and we do not attempt bolder, more effective solutions. We are handicapped by a patchwork approach that is incapable of interrupting the welfare-poverty cycle. The government trains people for jobs which don't exist, puts up new housing that is inadequate, falls short in aiding schools, provides just enough money for people to subsist on. It ignores the larger issue of how to reverse the decay, the physical disintegration, of the neighborhoods that blight the lives of the poor.

Moreover, the attitude toward helping the poor is wrong; there is virtually no involvement of the poor in helping themselves. The government thrusts out assistance in a way that seems to signify the poor are too lazy or dishonest to be trusted to solve their own problems. This is counterproductive, and I think it is time we realized it.

There is only one way to eradicate poverty and that, of course, is with money, sufficient money to allow everyone basic financial security. This is a primary reason for proposing a Citizen's Wage. As I tried to convey earlier, the concept of the Citizen's Wage as a birthright share in the nation's affluence represents an important change in our attitude toward individual security. Financial security is seen as an inherent right, not a benefit or a privilege. This is the key point in freeing the prisoners of poverty. We would be making them a part of society, participants rather than outcasts. It is the key because individual financial freedom is not enough by itself to change the oppressive physical and social environment of poverty; it is going to take the exercise of will and a rejuvenation of spirit.

There must be new opportunities to build a better life for those trapped in the ghettos. A Citizen's Wage, obviously, will take time to achieve. We have to find ways now, with the means at hand, to create opportunities for self-determined improvement by the poor.

I have in mind political and economic organization, the organization of neighborhoods by the residents to gain control over their lives. I have in mind the creation of neighborhood development corporations as recognized political-economic units to bring in necessary social services and to start local economic activity. I have in mind employing these citizen-controlled corporations to rebuild the neighborhoods and regulate them to the liking of the resident, free of outside control. This is something that can be started today, and I will explain how it can be done a little later on.

I WOULD LIKE TO RETURN to our present attitude toward the poor, particularly those receiving welfare, and how it contributes to their alienation. This can be seen in Nixon's "work-fare" philosophy. His program requires welfare mothers of children over 3 years old to go to work. He has said that any kind of work for those who are able and for any amount of pay is better than none—for the poor, that is. The imposition of this discipline strikes me as highly singular, if not outright discriminatory. If work is so necessary to our national fiber, why hasn't he insisted upon a program of "wealthwork" and forced the nonworking affluent to get jobs?

I am not being facetious really, but trying to point out the dual standard which applies to the poor. We can compel the poor mothers to work because the government supports them, even if it is not in their best interest or that of their children. On the other hand, we don't seem to care about the fellow who no longer has to work because he has cleaned up on subsidies or other government largesse. Unlike the poor, he manages to stay invisible.

The whole idea of forcing welfare mothers to work is morally and philosophically repugnant. The President and the Congress have no more right to make people accept jobs they do not want than they do to conscript our young men and force them to fight a war which they oppose. This is a chain gang tactic, illustrating precisely how we do keep the poor prisoners of poverty.

I have investigated portions of WIN (Work Incentive), the predecessor to workfare and learned that by and large, it is a failure because there are not enough jobs or the ones that are available do not pay enough. In all the states which have it, except the District of Columbia, WIN has been compulsory for able-bodied welfare recipients. Under the program, people are trained for a year in a skill and usually, if a job is found, the government has to supplement the trainee's pay to bring him or her above their welfare allowance. In the District of Columbia, where the WIN program is considered superior to others because of its voluntary nature, officials have found it costs $1,900 a year to train one "client" (the welfare worker's name for a welfare recipient). In three years, 1,237 clients obtained jobs after WIN training at an average pay of $106 per week including contributions from the government. Another 738 "haven't made it at all," in the words of one program official, because they got married, had more children, became sick, or couldn't find someone to care for their children while they worked. Although the overall record was pretty good as such programs go, the program failed for more than one-third of the clients.

Officials said there was a strong desire upon the part of their clients to try WIN training because they wanted to work, which might surprise President Nixon. Indeed, more than 9,000 of the 23,000 District of Columbia welfare families with dependent children had the mother apply for the program. However, only 4,400 were accepted. Most of those rejected had no child care available or couldn't pass a physical exam. Another handicap for the applicants was the lack of a high school education. As a result, the officials said, many of the trainees had difficulty finding a job and once there found it hard to progress. As one welfare mother expressed it, "with WIN and workfare you ain't goin' up that ladder or down if you get a job. You are goin' to get the same welfare check only they call it a pay check."

Here we have the great fallacy of work for work's sake. There haven't been many jobs available in our war-depressed economy and what jobs there are are marginal in pay and importance. Those compelled to take them soon learn there is no upward mobility; the jobs are springboards to nowhere. Even worse, the mother is being taken out of a fatherless home. Many welfare workers I talked to thought this a bad mistake, because a mother coming home tired from a boring job is less able to tend her children, to check on their school work, and to keep them from running loose in the streets. In short, it will be the children who suffer from "workfare" and the satisfaction of the Nixon ethic.

If supported by a Citizen's Wage, the mothers could be

doing the job they are supposed to, rearing their youngsters. This is not to say mothers shouldn't work, if they want to. I think they should be encouraged to do so if the family situation is such that the children will not be placed in jeopardy. One essential form of encouragement is the child care center where a mother can leave her youngster while she works. Unfortunately, there are too few of these centers now to handle preschoolers and even less to look after older youngsters after school hours. There should be many more.

Beyond babysitting we must deal with the child who comes from a deprived background, and there are many such children. We should create centers to meet both the educational and health needs of this child. Mental retardation is common among poor children because of malnutrition, and they have other health-related problems which tend to make them "losers" as soon as they enter school.

In 1971 Nixon vetoed plans for a nationwide network of local, state, and regional child care and development centers, and this was unfortunate. The centers are badly needed to serve the poor, the handicapped, and the sons and daughters of all who desire special attention. I believe the program should be revived and expanded so such centers could accept children at any age from shortly after birth through kindergarten and could operate 24 hours a day, 7 days a week. Parents could then leave their youngsters overnight when necessary. The center could be an integrated hub of social, cultural, and educational learning—and perhaps for the parents as well as the young.

"A lot of people wouldn't be on welfare if they got help at the right time," a welfare mother told me in Anchorage a few months ago. She was referring to adults, but timing or assistance applies to children as well. We must reach the children before they are made captive of the hopeless, dehumanizing system the welfare "reformers" seem bent on perpetuating. That time is now and the way is through the parents.

Going into the homes and listening to the people now dependent upon welfare gives a different perspective than listening to the professed reformers preach in the halls of Congress. Remember Spiro Agnew saying, "When you've seen one ghetto you've seen them all?" The Vice-President never mentioned people, the residents of the slums. But that's what the ghettos are all about: people—all different and all human, people with intelligence, deep emotions, handicaps, and problems like you and me. There is only one thing that separates them from the rest of the community: money. Listen to the mothers:

You're never going to get rid of poverty talkin' about reform. Look at this housing development . . . there's no recreation areas. The kids are all in the streets. There's not enough schools and the ones we have aren't good. Three out of five of the pupils never finish high school. They drop out because they can't learn or because the teachers don't know how to teach them. When they put this [housing development] up all they built was a brand new ghetto.

If I get sick, I've told everybody, "Don't let them take me to the city hospital. I don't wanna die there and it's sure goin' to happen if I do." They treat the poor worse than animals. And the good hospitals don't wanna let you in. They send you away even if you're dyin' if you don't have insurance . . . and the doctors, they don' want to treat you on Medicaid 'cause they say it takes six months to a year for the government to pay 'em.

Sure there's welfare cheaters. Where the money is you always find cheating. But there's more people that's cheating on the outside than's getting rich down here.

The men leave home because they can't make a decent salary. They're ashamed to face their families. The father feels less than a man and after awhile he just doesn't care . . . the majority of black women make more than the man and they're the boss of the house. So what's to keep him there?

I think most men leave for another woman, not on account of the money. My man did. He went to live with that woman over on Minnesota Avenue.

Most of the women don't want their man to come back. Mine's bad news. He'll try to cash the welfare check and keep the money for himself. If there was enough money maybe it wouldn't be like that, maybe the man would stay and you could have a real family.

As these comments indicate, the amount of income is clearly a major factor in holding together welfare families, even though the Supreme Court has struck down the man-in-the-house rule. That rule prohibited a woman from collecting welfare benefits if she was living with an able-bodied man, even her husband, who was unemployed. Men unable to find work no longer are forced to desert their families, but they leave nonetheless. Obviously, personal compatibility cannot be overlooked as a possible reason for desertion, but it seems to me that we cannot disregard the male ego and his need to preserve "face." This is precisely why a Citizen's Wage as a birthright could be so important. It would automatically provide everyone with stature, male and female. It might be the reason for a man and woman to stick together.

IT IS OFTEN SAID THAT one should never negotiate out of fear or weakness. I am encouraged that the poor have seized this idea and are organizing into political groups to demand more consideration. The national Welfare Rights Organization and others presently are fighting for more welfare benefits and, more importantly, demonstrating that the poor do have rights. We have seen another healthy development in the provision of legal aid under the Office of Economic Opportunity.

OEO Legal Services lawyers have, in the past few years, established many important precedents bearing on the rights of the poor. In addition to striking down the man-in-the-house rule, they have reduced excessive residency requirements to qualify for welfare, abolished welfare department regulations which allowed benefits to be cut off without a hearing, and obtained decisions against the exploitive practices of small businessmen and landlords in their dealings with the poor. The lawyers also have represented the poor in millions of routine cases, usually successfully.

Indeed, Legal Services has been so successful the Nixon

administration has made repeated efforts to control its attorneys politically and administratively and, failing that, has cut back funds for the program. Nixon has also vetoed the creation of a separate nonprofit legal services corporation for the most cynical of reasons; he said he was dissatisfied with the corporation's "accountability" to the public. What he really wanted was complete political control over the management of the program. The veto demonstrates clearly the government's and particularly the President's attitude when it comes down to the nitty gritty of assisting the poor. It is the reason we, as citizens, must find the correct solutions and implement them through a people's platform.

Earlier the point was made that most of us own only a fraction of America's wealth and the poor own nothing. The poor occupy large territories in our cities, yet they do not hold the title. Because they are tenants and not owners, the poor have no political clout. They are underrepresented and misrepresented in the councils of government.

It is time the poor gained ownership of their own neighborhoods and their destinies. This is the purpose of the neighborhood development corporations I mentioned earlier. Such a corporation would be owned and operated by the residents of a neighborhood for profit. It could be private or chartered publicly by the state government as a legal political entity, but this would not be necessary as long as it is recognized by the federal government and made eligible for some type of funding.

To me the Neighborhood Development Corporation is the natural complement to a Citizen's Wage. With the latter we can build the economic base of the individual and with the NDC we can rebuild whole cities, physically and economically, by reclaiming the neighborhoods and making them places fit to live in and enjoy.

By neighborhoods I mean identifiable communities within cities or regions. They could be of any size, from New York's Harlem to the 1 square mile Woodlawn section of Chicago.

Geographical boundaries do not count, but a resident's ability to identify with his community does.

Under my proposal, the NDC would be formed by a vote of more than 50 percent of the permanent residents aged 16 years and above in a neighborhood. The corporation, once formed, would issue stock, either free or for a nominal sum, only to those qualified to vote in its formation. The stock would be nontransferable, except when a resident moves from the neighborhood. Each share would mean part ownership of the community, for the corporation would acquire the vacant, abandoned, and run-down property of the community. Private property would be retained by individuals living in the community and brought into the corporation's development plans.

Today, as most of us are aware, poor neighborhoods are treated like colonies by outside interests. Because they produce nothing, poor neighborhoods must import everything they need from outside. Money from goods and services sold to the poor flows to outside ownership. How often has it been said in the ghettos "the money leaves at 6 o'clock when the storekeepers go back to the suburbs"? It is the mission of the NDC to set forth economic policies which will reverse the money flow and generate wealth for its own people.

The neighborhood corporation, like any other corporation for profit, must have the power to raise capital. At first this will have to be done in tandem with "soft" government and commercial loans and, in some cases, grants. The creation of capital, especially in the ghettos, hinges primarily on control over land usage. The corporation will need to acquire abandoned property through eminent domain. It has to be the proprietor of neighborhood territory, enabling it to use the land as the basis for credit, to mortgage part of it for the good of the whole, and to regulate both public and private interests.

Once in command of capital the corporation can go about acquiring social services and eventually industry, bringing them into the community either by providing good operating conditions and other incentives, or by the outright purchase of productive technology. Moreover, in contracting for services and industry, the corporation can ensure that people living in the neighborhood will be employed and therefore that most of the money earned there stays there.

For major redevelopment undertakings, the corporation could go to public bonding. In recent months considerable alarm has arisen over housing, especially low-cost dwellings. Fast-buck operators have been reaping windfalls at the expense of the consumer and the government. One basic reason for this, it seems to me, is that the government is not enforcing any realistic standards and there is no one in charge, except the developer, who controls things to his own liking. Visualize how different the situation would be if a neighborhood development corporation were in charge. It could insist upon housing being built to its standards, and in its contractual arrangement with the builder the corporation could also regulate the sale and rental of the property so that residents get the best possible price advantage. As it is now, much of the low-cost housing really isn't so low, because some builders put up shoddy, cramped buildings and charge as much as they can get away with. This would not happen with firm citizen control at work.

Housing is but one example. The corporation will be a responsible part of overall planning for the community. It can provide open spaces for recreation, room for industrial parks, new schools, hospitals, disease detection centers, child care and development centers. And it can contract with the government to provide many of these social services. The NDC can develop business and shopping areas, residential areas, and retain that part of the neighborhood which defines its character and individuality.

All of this work means jobs—a lot of them and interesting ones during the redevelopment and afterward as the economy of the neighborhood picks up. In short, a neighborhood corporation can regenerate its community and imbue its citizens with a new sense of dignity and purpose.

That it is possible is already being demonstrated in poor neighborhoods in several cities including an Office of Economic Opportunity project in Columbus, Ohio. Many of these new corporations, however, lack full political control over their neighborhoods. To be truly effective they should be upgraded to the NDC concept.

Lest anyone think the idea of sprouting neighborhood corporations in the middle of cities is a radical idea, one can trace the history of town and village corporations back to the beginnings of the country. Many are still in existence today.

Moreover, the Congress has recently sanctioned the concept of regional development corporations in the Alaska Native land claims settlement. The legislation allows the Natives to establish corporations to manage the $962.5 million and 40 million acres of land they received in payment for property taken from them by the white man. These corporations will be profit-making business ventures and the Natives will hold all the shares of stock. One might consider them a rural counterpart to the urban neighborhood development corporation.

The Natives of Alaska will develop their own plans and programs for the use of their money and land. This will have unusual economic benefit for all of Alaska since the Native areas are presently deprived and contribute very little to the economy. Their ability to plan and execute their own affairs intelligently has been proven repeatedly—most recently in the Tlinget-Haida settlement plan written and implemented entirely by the Indians except in a few areas where they had to get the paternalistic propensities of government out of the way. Yes, the Alaska Native will make mistakes just as all the rest of us have done. However, that's what our system of self-determination is all about.

These are the new forces that can be put into motion in the blighted ghettos and barrios of our cities and rural areas. Similarly, an improvement in Harlem would contribute significantly to an improvement in all New York City.

Realistically, it will take time to create NDCs and get them functioning, but there is no reason why they can't start now. All it takes is three citizens to file papers of incorporation. Citizen control of the neighborhood territories is there for the taking. Certainly there will be resistance on the part of downtown business interests and some government leaders, but they are powerless in the face of a true citizens' movement, especially if that movement has as its purpose the rebuilding of cities and the eradication of poverty.

We should not underestimate what such a movement could achieve once it has take root. I can visualize neighborhood corporations springing up alongside of one another until an entire city is covered. The neighborhoods could then form a federation to join in the development of mutual services such as mass transit, public safety, solid waste disposal, control of the environment, and many of the other tasks which are so incompetently done by city governments today. The federation could be the means of coordinating neighborhood industry so the production of goods and services and trade between neighborhoods are carried on efficiently and without ruinous competition. When we have to worry about avoiding the concentration of wealth in one neighborhood through this device, we will know we have succeeded.

Imagine what it would do to relieve traffic congestion if the work was brought to the worker. Employees might be able to walk or bicycle to their jobs. The streets of a neighborhood might be turned into parks and malls and become places to meet and talk and enjoy life.

We might discover that neighborhoods, once revitalized, can assume much of the burden of services that are now bankrupting the cities. They could afford to operate police and fire departments, their own hospitals through neighborhood and regional health districts, the schools, and institutions to care for the aged and the infirm.

IF WE TRULY WANT to free our nation from the blight of poverty, we must, as I said earlier, allow the people, especially the poor, to control their own lives. Not long ago I asked a welfare worker what he thought a Citizen's Wage and neighborhood development corporations could do for his city.

"You are talking about owning something tangible, like a share in a piece of property?" he asked.

"Yes," I replied. "Everyone owning equal shares of their neighborhood."

"That grabs me."

8

An Economy of, for, and by the People

Economic wealth is only of value
as a means to an end. Every nation
has the power to decide toward what ends
their means will be directed. It
is the responsibility of government
to direct the use of its wealth
toward ends that are in the best
interest of the largest number of
its citizens.

—*Barney Gottstein*
(Anchorage Businessman)

IT IS ALL TOO EASY to forget the fundamental purpose of an economic system; it is to satisfy the material needs of the people. It is not to "play for real" an elaborate game of Monopoly where the object is to own all property, collect the highest possible rents, and impoverish all other "players." It is not some kind of competitive sport or deeply rooted primitive ritual where great aggregations of power are thrown against each other to see who prevails. Whatever the effects on individual participants, from society's point of view the object is to produce an adequate amount of things people need at an accepta-

119

ble level of quality, at prices they can afford, and with the widest possible availability and minimum environmental degradation.

Measured against these tests, the U.S. economy scores high on only one point—it produces a lot. In fact, it is now generally agreed that our victory in World War II was not due to superior generals or a more resolute national will. We didn't out-fight or out-maneuver the enemy; basically, we out-GNP'd them and had the time to do so.

On grounds other than straight production, our economy is seriously out of whack with the needs of the people. The problems have often been enumerated, but their severity and pervasiveness have not been widely appreciated. I have in mind the estrangement of the consumer from the economic system, feeling that he has no control over its functioning or its fruits. I have in mind the decline in quality of products and services despite our much-talked-about "technological superiority." I have in mind the outright deception and manipulation of the consumer by business enterprise. And I have in mind the failure of government to regulate the private sector in the interest of the public at large or to conduct its own economic activities successfully in those few instances where it is itself a supplier. Let me treat each of these briefly, as much of the ground has been gone over by others.

One would think an economy that had been so successful with the problem of production, at least in quantitative terms, would have turned toward greater improvement in the quality of its products and services. In point of fact, there has been a marked decline in some product and service areas and a failure to improve in most others, as anyone can attest from his own daily experiences. Low product quality coupled with planned obsolescence seems to be more the rule than the exception—so much so that whole advertising campaigns can successfully be built around the near-uniqueness of the contrary approach. Volkswagen and Volvo (significantly, foreign corporations) present themselves as making quality improvements while fighting design obsolescence.

The almost uninterrupted success of the National Association of Manufacturers, the Chamber of Commerce, and the business community in general in convincing the public and its elected officials of the sanctity of commercial enterprise is remarkable indeed. Historically, there were a few "setbacks," as in the public outcry of the last two decades of the nineteenth century and the first decade of the twentieth in America, which resulted in the establishment of public utility regulation and antitrust legislation. But, by and large, the business community has gotten its way with vague assertions that the full blessings of its productiveness would not be forthcoming if there was "interference" by anyone.

The governmental decision-making community, which is supposed to look out for the interests of the people, has historically been "pro business-corporation." As a result the entire system is badly skewed against the consumer in our laws, our institutions, and our culture. The long battles to get consumer protection legislation through Congress attest to this bias. The "tax reform and relief" legislation of 1970 is another example. By the time it came out of Congress the bill contained little reform or relief and the special business interests emerged unscathed. Each interest had a legitimate argument for its point of view which insulated it from change.

Still more recently, President Nixon's Revenue Act of 1971 passed Congress with new tax windfalls for American business. While corporations were awarded billions in new tax relief, the individual taxpayer got next to nothing. Efforts to try to amend the bill by deleting one of the business tax breaks and substituting an income tax credit for individual taxpayers ($25 for a single and $50 for a joint return) was voted down twice. At the same time an amendment to limit the investment tax credit provision for business to purchases of $1 million and under was defeated 53 to 13. This was final proof to me that our government is really controlled by the business-corporate element in our society and that greater value is placed on business enterprise as an operating tool than on human beings.

With few exceptions public regulation of private business has been timid at best and a mockery or nonexistent at worst. Loopholes are many, enforcement has been weak, and those appointed to regulate soon become captives of the very sectors they are supposed to be regulating. To one degree or another, this has been the sad story in the communications, power, and transport sectors; the banking and finance industries; and those commercial sectors where the Food and Drug Administration and the Federal Trade Commission have a watchdog role. Nor are the courts themselves immune from a preoccupation with property rights and the preservation of corporate value for the organized few to the real detriment of the unorganized many.

Ours has become an economy of monopolistic and near-monopolistic enterprises, organized around uncompetitive markets, operating with rigged prices having no particular relation to costs, and focused on the making of money.

Our popular misconceptions about the organization of the U.S. economy are many and serious. It is usually described as a "pluralistic economy" and a "system of mixed private capitalism," having a preponderence of profit-seeking private enterprises that are assumed to be competing to one degree or another.

We make neat distinctions between the "public" and "private" sectors, according the latter a special sanctity and inputing efficiency and usefulness to it, while we view the former as at best a "necessary evil" worthy of the most limited support. We also speak of "not-for-profit" businesses as if they were essentially philanthropic or charitable in character, when in fact many are major economic enterprises which take their profits out in salaries and emoluments instead of dividends.

The continuing concentration of large corporations is well documented. Occasional business-inspired articles appear purporting to show how risky it is at the top. But the facts are that the list of the country's 200 largest corporations remains surprisingly similar decade after decade.

Besides its anticonsumer effect on pricing through monopoly and collusive practices, the behavior of big business is hurtful to the public interest on at least two other grounds: it weakens popular support for the more desirable aspects of a private enterprise system, and it encourages the excessive growth of big unions and big government as countervailing forces in our economic system.

We must face the inescapable fact that business acts to further its own selfish ends; any relation of these ends to the interests of the people is largely coincidental. But the business-corporate constituency is the dominant force in our society. What are we going to do about it?

First, I think we must recognize that the entire business-corporate structure is a tool—a necessary and effective tool to make the goods our society needs, however imperfectly it may do the job. In producing and in developing new types of products, the tool is quite good. The fact that it may be misused is no reason to destroy it. Rather, we must find ways to make it serve the more general interests of our society.

This is, admittedly, an exceedingly difficult task, because business-corporate power exerts a dominant influence over the primary mechanism for change, the government. We can try to influence the governmental decision-making apparatus on the state and national level by electing public officials who will put the interests of the people first. This will be dependent in part on reforming the financing of election campaigns.

By the very act of bringing business onto center stage of public discussion, however, I believe we can begin to zero in on two of the most necessary reforms for our economic well being.

The first is an overhaul of the corporate structure. We must widen the present decision-making apparatus beyond the existing management of the larger companies to include equal representation for the workers and the consuming public. Secondly, we must turn our attention to our grossly unfair tax structure. We should have one tax for everyone, individuals and business, and it should be a graduated income tax with no deductions and no exemptions.

I will explain shortly the reasoning behind these proposals and what they could achieve in the future. More immediately, we must continue to sustain the pressure of citizen power. There is no question that the consumer rebellion brought into focus in recent years by Ralph Nader and other informed citizens is being felt. The attack must continue in the courts, in Congress, state legislatures, and city councils, through the executive departments of government, and through universities and other institutions. These actions, illuminated by public disclosure, are forcing the business-corporations to be more responsive to public concerns. They can be made to yield further through consumer boycotts against bad products and services.

I am optimistic that we will see some major changes made voluntarily within the corporate network. Some of our brightest and most skillful citizens occupy the executive suites. They are acutely aware of the inequities industry is imposing upon our pocketbooks and the insults it inflicts on our environment, and they have reason to correct the abuses, if only because they are members of our society and consumers, too. Actually, they have an even more basic motive—an enlightened self-interest to preserve their own positions by preserving the system. They have nothing to gain and everything to lose by provoking the citizens to rebellion.

If we do not now have an economy *of* the people in terms of an effective voice for the consumer, nor *by* the people in terms of its organization, neither do we have an economy *for* the people in terms of its performance.

We have been woefully deficient in doing any national economic planning, still viewing such an activity as faintly subversive. Accordingly, the allocation of our productive resources has been haphazard at best. The production of consumer goods, especially automobiles, frequently conflicts with the development needs of our local communities and often overtaxes their social services. Substantial investment in the private sector far outweighs the underinvestment in the public sector. While the market system is valuable for certain purposes, we now know that it is a poor mechanism for allocating needed resources to the public sector. Resource allocation in the private sector would be improved by some form of "indicative planning" by government, as in the case of France where government sets out national investment and expenditure goals in key areas as a guide to the private sector.

A start on such planning will require us to develop a more sophisticated set of social indicators than we now have. In his book *Century of Mismatch,* Dr. Simon Ramo has explored this problem and, in my opinion, has identified one of our crucial long range needs.

> All agree that today it is exceedingly difficult for the government to adjust, let alone control, the economy in accordance with any plan. The economists tell us that one basic reason is a shortage of good statistical information. Available facts are late and incomplete. Something is known of some inventories, production and sales levels, employment, spending rates, and the money supply. The rest is unknown or too little or too late to use with complete confidence for decisions on major government actions to alter the economy's pattern. Moreover, if all these statistical aspects of the economy were known accurately, completely and instantaneously, we do not have accurate models of the interrelationships, the basic theory, for processing all these data into a good prediction for the future.

To know all about ourselves—to have an instant replay on everything that is occurring in our economic system—will provide the public, the businessman, and the labor leader with the means to plan intelligently and to influence corporate and governmental policy. We should also be expanding our efforts to construct quantitative models of our national economy. As Ramo suggests, these may take decades to perfect, but it is essential if we are to formulate and then seek national goals. We have the makings of an information system in the federal government's Bureau of Labor Statistics and the Census Bureau, the chief collectors of data today. These two agencies could be placed in a completely independent unit, pooling their resources to form a national data bank, a computer-operated information processing and decision-aiding device. This could be the key to solving many of our problems.

There is ample evidence to support the old cliché, "figures never lie, but liars sure can figure." We have seen the Nixon administration, in its desperate efforts to cast a rosy hue in the depths of the recent recession, put pressure on the Bureau of Labor Statistics to produce positive indicators on the direction the economy was going. This sort of political influence cannot be tolerated in a national data bank. We need a reliable information system, one we can guarantee is meticulous in gathering, processing, and reporting data. Hence, in funding the proposed model's operation, it is imperative that we allocate the necessary money to fund an adversary group of data and statistical experts to check on its accuracy and the reliability of its projections. Properly put together, the bank could become a primary resource, the basis for achieving a soundly planned economy, voluntarily executed by informed citizens in a free enterprise system.

But, of course, mere information or quantitative calculations will be useless if they do not form the basis for effective action by citizen groups and the bureaucracies of government and business-corporations. Only if citizens organize themselves to press their demands, inform themselves on economic conditions, and then make their voices heard through the Congress and through their representatives on corporate boards, will their needs be met and the productive apparatus of the society utilized to the fullest to meet the people's needs. Left to their own devices, corporate managers will certainly plan, but they will be thinking primarily of the maximum profits for their corporation which is their first responsibility; it will be up to the citizenry to insist that social criteria enter the planning and decision process.

BUT I BELIEVE more direct steps must be taken to reform the corporate juggernaut. We now realize that its goal of maximizing profit by selling through the market place is not sufficient to meet the needs of our complex urbanized society. The general public, as consumer of both private goods and public services, as sharer of the environment, and as bearer of the economic consequences of investment decisions, must be involved in the making of those decisions.

I have come to believe that it is now necessary that corporate decision-making be broadened beyond the representatives of the investors, the stockholders, who now select the board of directors, to include the other major constituencies affected by the corporation's activities, the workers and the general public. What I envision is a new form for corporate structure in which all corporations that produce and sell in interstate commerce would be chartered by the federal government, rather than in just one of the states as at present. The main requirement of this charter would be a governing board which gave equal representation to the stockholders, the workers (to include management), and the public. The views of each constituency would be brought to bear on the major decisions of the corporation, and the interests of each would be protected, albeit in a manner that would have to take account of the possibly conflicting interests of the others.

The "status quo" corporate interests resisting this concept must realize that the new public awareness of the environment and the latent worker dissatisfaction festering in the work place can lead only to greater government control. Take your choice, bend with the wind and amalgamate these forces of change and correction or hold tough and lose the corporate system with its diffused and fractionalized base to the ownership of ever-growing government.

The concern has been expressed that the financial interest of the investors, who now control the boards of the country's corporations, would not be protected as well under the new system. But this fear could, in my view, easily be allayed. The prosperity of the corporation is as much in the interest of the workers, who depend on the corporation for their jobs, and of the public, who need the goods, economic activity, and jobs produced by the corporation, as of the investors. At the same time, these constituencies would have other interests that the investors would have to recognize and that the operating management of the corporation would have to consider in its day-to-day decisions. The workers would want not only good wages, but also healthy, stimulating working conditions. The public would want high quality products which meet real needs in society and assurance that any by-products of the company's activities would not pollute the environment or inflict hidden costs upon the surrounding community.

I believe this country will have made a major social advance when it recognizes the crucial stake which its people have in the decisions made by the business-corporate structures of our nation. Once that recognition is achieved, we will have to develop the mechanisms which can institutionalize the public's representation in those decisions. I have suggested above that the public should be represented on the boards of directors, and we should begin to consider the many advantages that such representation could bring to us all.

Selecting the public's representatives will be a difficult matter. One would not, at this juncture, want to place this responsibility in the hands of the executive branch, which historically draws its leading officials from the ranks of the business community and is most solicitous of its interests. It might be suggested that the appropriate committees of the Congress should select the public's representatives. However, I do not think this is a satisfactory solution, given the influence that the business-corporate constituency is now able to wield in the halls of Congress. If the election financing reforms suggested in chapter 3 were carried out, though, this might change, and congressional appointment could become a workable means of making this selection.

The expanded functions of the Governor's Conference could possibly provide the selection of public members in our new corporate structure. A council of mayors within each state could perform similarly if the states choose to restructure the corporations doing business only within the state.

The restructuring of corporate control to the hands of owners, workers and the public would also permit an approach to the problems posed by multinational corporations in conflict with our national interests. These organizations could be required to have federal charters stipulating the board of director membership be made up equally by the workers in each nation where the activity is performed, the owners from the parent company, and the public members qualified and selected by a commission of the United Nations.

IN EXAMINING THE IMBALANCES in our present economy, it is apparent that the single greatest deficiency is in the distribution of income and wealth. Politicians and business-corporate spokesmen are fond of saying that our economy is creating more affluence for more people than any other. However, numerous studies have shown that the distribution of income and wealth has remained virtually unchanged for the past 75 years. Since 1910, the richer half of the population has claimed three-quarters of the national personal income while the poorer half has had to get along on the remaining one-quarter. Today the richest one-fifth of our citizens command fully 42 percent of the personal income while the lower three-fifths combined receive 31 percent. And if we look at the richest 5 percent, we find that they take 17 percent of all the income while the bottom 40 percent of the population gets only 15 percent.

The pattern of the distribution of wealth—the ownership of America—is even more inequitable. Currently it is estimated that less than 2 percent of the people own 32 percent of the prime wealth of the nation. They own 100 percent of the tax-free municipal and state bonds, 80 percent of the stock in corporations, and more than 50 percent of the unincorporated business assets—all sources of revenue which increase their wealth.

Ownership for the so-called affluent middle class is largely confined to their homes (most of which are mortgaged and therefore partly owned by banks) and their personal possessions, a good number of which also have shared ownership with the bank, credit union, or finance company. Less than 2 out of 10 families own businesses, stocks and bonds, and other income-producing assets.

As for persons in the bottom half of the population, they hold only 10 percent of the wealth, and a great many own nothing.

The question of how to redistribute income and wealth so that most people are in comfortable circumstances has long begged an answer. Attempts to spread the largesse more evenly through the income tax and inheritance taxes have not succeeded. Those with wealth have exerted influence on the government to create loopholes, to the point where they pay about the same taxes in proportion to their income, as the rest of the population. Moreover, since they control the economy, they are able to compensate for loss of income through taxes by raising prices and profits of their business enterprises. They also influence government to return a good part of the tax money in subsidies and in the war machine, leaving little to redistribute to those who need it.

In my opinion the best way to redress the balance is through the total overhaul of the federal tax system, replacing the intricate latticework of taxes with a single graduated income tax applied to every individual. There must be no exemptions or deductions of any kind for anyone, and no other taxes that disguise a shift of the burden back upon the low income segment of our population. We should have one simple, easy to understand tax that is fair and removes all loopholes and incentives for evasion. Indeed, this is the only way we will ever see reform and an enforcement of what we think our tax policy should be.

We have played around with the federal tax structure too long under the illusion of reforming it. All the structure does now is encourage people with money to hire accountants, financial experts, and tax lawyers to escape what they should be paying. Besides fostering a huge tax industry it also requires huge administrative and enforcement costs.

There is only one way to assure equitable taxation and that is simplicity. Make it so everyone knows precisely what he is paying and what everyone else is paying or should be paying. Make it easy for the government to enforce and guarantee that everyone is carrying his full and fair load. The single tax will lower the cost of goods for our citizens by dropping the hidden taxes and the excise taxes which inflate their cost. The simplicity of the single tax is a guarantee to each citizen that he will have automatic enforcement and equitable treatment.

The inequities of today's tax system rob the lower and middle income citizens, while favoring the rich and supporting huge and highly profitable corporations, whose owners are taxed at only a fraction of what they should pay. People with annual earnings below $2,000 pay about 40 percent of their income in taxes of all kinds. People earning between $2,000 and $50,000 pay about 30 percent. And only for persons earning over $50,000 does the *effective* tax rate begin to rise, but even then only to 45 percent. We find the burden of taxes falling just as heavily on the poor as on the well-to-do, partly because everybody has to pay state, local, and federal taxes that tend to be highly regressive—sales, gasoline, personal property, real estate, and social security taxes—and partly because of the loopholes built into the present federal income tax system.

The largest loophole is the break given the rich who have capital gains income obtained through increases in the value of their stocks and other property. Today such income is taxed at a much lower rate than earned income. It represents yet another odd example of how our society values property above human beings. Capital gains should be treated as ordinary income and taxed accordingly. Another dodge is the tax-free status of state and municipal bonds which are owned exclusively by the rich and allow many of them to escape without paying any taxes at all. This tax-free gift costs the federal government some $3 billion annually in revenue and should be discarded.

I would also eliminate the tax on corporate profits. The corporate tax does not, in fact, reduce the income which the holders of corporate stock receive in dividends. In an era when the major corporations can administer prices to ensure any profit return they wish, they simply take the tax into account, no matter at what level it is set, and adjust their prices accordingly. As the *Wall Street Journal* observed, the tax is "treated by the corporations as merely another cost which they can pass on to their customers."

In fact, close examination of the tangled corporate tax structure shows it only serves to inflate costs of goods and services to consumers. Take, for example, the expense account living for which American business executives have become notorious around the world. They can live high because half the cost of such "expenses" is picked up by the federal government—the taxpayers—through exemptions. There are numerous other loopholes which serve to subsidize industry. The total subsidies of all kinds—tax and direct grants to business enterprises—are estimated at $60 billion or more a year —all paid out of the public treasury, directly or indirectly. While at the same time corporations are only paying *in* $26 billion a year in taxes.

Obviously, if we eliminated all corporate taxes and subsidies the ordinary taxpayer would come out far ahead. And that is exactly what the single tax approach would entail. Does this mean the corporations' owners—the stockholders—would get a windfall? Not at all. First, when the tax is removed along with all exemptions, exclusions, and deductions, every cent that corporations spend would come directly out of their pockets. This would have the disciplinary effect of making their operations much more efficient and competitive. Prices would come down to a lower, more normal level compared with today.

Dividends to stockholders would be taken care of as straight income in the single tax on individuals. For with individuals, like the corporations, all loopholes would be plugged and all exemptions, deductions, and exclusions would be eliminated. This would apply across the board to the poor and rich alike: no more preferential treatment or tax privileges. Every citizen would be obliged to pay something, if only a token amount, greatly broadening the tax base.

At the same time, *all* other federal taxes—social security, customs duties, federal excise, inheritance, and gift levies— would be eliminated. These sources of revenue along with the corporate tax must be made up by increasing the yield of the new individual income tax.

It would seem at first glance that everyone would have to pay more. But that is not the case. The net effect of greatly broadening the tax base, on the one hand, and doing away with all other federal taxes, on the other, is that now we are in a position to establish a single income tax, based on the ability to pay according to a truly progressive rate scale. This scale would be adjusted so that middle- and low-income earners would pay a lower tax than the *total* of all the federal taxes they are presently paying (see table 1). We would be able at last to shift the tax burden from the low- and middle-income brackets to the upper and highest brackets where it belongs.

Table 1 shows how the effective taxes compare for selected income brackets.

If you are filing a joint return as a married couple with two children, and your income is one of those I've chosen for illustration in column 1 you can compare how you really fare under the present batch of federal taxes with how you would do under a single tax plan. The results in columns 5 and 6 are notable indeed.

For example, if your income is $5,000, you would pay on the average of $493 less under the single tax, a drop of 48 percent. If you earn $10,000 you would save about $850 or

TABLE 1
Present Tax of Married Couple, Family of Four
Filing Joint Return Compared with Single Tax Plan

(1)	(2)	(3)	(4)	(5)	(6)	(7)	(8)
		Present Income	*In-*			*Differ-ence*	*Change as Per-centage*
Sample Income Levels	*Present Taxable Income*[1]	*Tax and Soc.*[2]	*direct Tax Total*[3]	*Total of (3) and (4)*	*Single Tax Total*[4]	*Between (5) and (6)*	*of Present Tax*
$ 2,500	$ 0	$ 270	$ 202	$ 472	$ 170	$ −302	−64%
5,000	700	638	395	1,033	540	−493	−48%
10,000	5,500	1,985	685	2,670	1,820	−850	−32%
15,000	9,750	2,867	848	3,175	3,580	−135	−4%
20,000	14,000	3,862	1,030	4,892	5,800	+908	+19%
30,000	22,500	6,282	1,530	7,812	10,940	+3,128	+40%
50,000	39,500	13,017	3,525	16,542	22,640	+6,098	+37%

SOURCE:

Underlying data furnished by Office of the Secretary of the Treasury, Office of Tax Analysis, and author's computations. March, 1972.

[1] Assumes all income is from wages and salaries (no capital gains income, for example) and that 15 percent is taken in deductions.

[2] Assumes all social security taxes shifted ultimately to employees.

[3] Derived from column 5, table 5, *supra*.

[4] Computed from column 5, table 2, *supra*.

32 percent of what you're paying now. In fact, in the examples I have chosen, everyone with salaries of $15,000 and under is better off under the single tax than presently.

At the higher salaries, on the other hand, there would be tax increases as a result of the more progressive tax rates in my plan. Persons earning $20,000 would pay $908 (or 19 percent) more than they do now; those with $30,000 incomes 40 percent more; and those with $50,000 incomes an additional $6,098 (or 37 percent) more.

The tax rate schedules used to make these comparisons (and the analysis that follows) are presented in table 2.

The nominal income tax rates applicable to taxable income under present law (for single person and joint returns) is arrayed in familiar fashion against the income brackets

TABLE 2

Individual Income Tax Nominal Rates[1] Applicable to Taxable Income Under Present Law and Under Single Tax Plan

(1)	(2)	(3)	(4)	(5)
Taxable Income Bracket ($ thousands)	*Present Law[2]*		*Single Tax Plan[3]*	
	Single returns	*Joint returns*	*Single returns*	*Joint returns*
$ 0.5 or less	14%	14%	2%	2%
0.5– 1.0	15	14	10	2
1.0– 1.5	16	15	10	10
1.5– 2	17	15	10	10
2 – 3	19	16	22	10
3 – 4	19	17	22	10
4 – 6	21	19	31	22
6 – 8	24	19	38	22
8 – 10	25	22	46	31
10 – 12	27	22	46	31
12 – 14	29	25	55	38
14 – 16	31	25	55	38
16 – 18	34	28	55	46
18 – 20	36	28	60	46
20 – 22	38	32	60	46
22 – 24	40	32	60	46
24 – 26	40	36	60	55
26 – 28	45	36	60	55
28 – 32	45	39	60	55
32 – 36	50	42	60	55
36 – 38	50	45	60	60
38 – 40	55	45	60	60
40 – 44	55	48	60	60
44 – 50	60	50	60	60
50 – 52	62	50	60	60
52 – 60	62	53	60	60
60 – 64	64	53	60	60
64 – 70	64	55	60	60
70 – 76	66	55	60	60
76 – 80	66	58	60	60
80 – 88	68	58	60	60
88 – 90	68	60	60	60
90 – 100	69	60	60	60
100 – 120	70	62	60	60
120 – 140	70	64	60	60
140 – 160	70	66	60	60
160 – 180	70	68	60	60
180 – 200	70	69	60	60
over 200	70	70	60	60

SOURCE:

Underlying data furnished by Office of the Secretary of the Treasury, Office of Tax Analysis. March, 1972.

[1] Percentage rates apply only to levels of income indicated. Income up to that level is taxed progressively at the various rates as shown. For example under the single tax $10,000 of income for persons filing a joint return is taxed at a rate of 2 percent for the first $1,000, 10 percent for the next $3,000, 22 percent for the next $4,000, and 31 percent for the final $2,000.

[2] Marginal rates of tax applicable to respective levels of taxable income as defined under present law.

[3] Marginal rates of tax applicable to respective levels of taxable income as defined under single tax plan.

TABLE 3

Elimination of Exemptions[1]	$180.0 billion
Elimination of Exclusions[2]	20.0
Elimination of Deductions[3]	120.0
Subtotal	$320.0 billion
Present Personal Income	$400.0
Grand Total	$720.0 billion

SOURCE:

   Underlying data furnished by Office of Secretary of the Treasury, Office of
   Tax Analysis. March, 1972.

   [1] e.g. $750 personal exemption, blind and student dependency exemptions.

   [2] e.g. long term capital gains, dividend exclusions.

   [3] e.g. standard or itemized, medical, real estate, mortgage.

that appear in federal tax forms. They range from 14 percent
to 70 percent on the individual income slices of column 1.
The latter are marginal rates that almost no one really pays
in the higher income brackets. Everyone pays a good deal
of course in federal taxes of other types not reflected in the
present tax rate schedule.

In columns 4 and 5 I have presented a sharply progressive
rate schedule ranging from 2 percent to 60 percent which *does*
reflect the total reliance on the single income tax in place of
all other federal taxes we now pay. The important thing to
note, as will be shown in the rest of this chapter, is that despite
these apparently "high rates" at early income levels under my
tax model, the net results are lower *total* tax payments for
a much greater number of taxpayers.

The explanation for all this can readily be seen by walking
through the following summary steps. This is how we get
there.

The present tax base from which the individual income tax
draws is about $400 billion. By doing away with all exemp-
tions, exclusions, and deductions to personal income, the tax
base is increased to $720 billion. See table 3.

The next step is to break down federal taxes by major
source. In table 4 we see the total amount of tax receipts the
single income tax is required to recoup under my plan.

TABLE 4
Federal Tax Receipts from Major Sources, 1971
(In Billions of Dollars)

Individual Income Tax	$ 82.7
Social Security Tax	50.6
Excise Taxes	15.0
Corporate Taxes	26.0
Estate and Gift Taxes	4.0
Customs Duties	2.6
Total	$180.9

SOURCE:
U.S. Treasury Department. March, 1972.

This has the obvious effect of forcing income tax rates upward to cover the receipts foregone from repeal of these tax sources, though the average rates must remain the same since the total is unchanged.

We can demonstrate that the expansion of the tax base under my plan more than offsets the necessary increased burden on the individual income tax so that a new and more highly progressive rate schedule can be fitted to collect the same total that we are now paying through a whole array of taxes.

In table 5 the new income base is expanded from $400 billion under present law to a new taxable income of $720.6 billion by doing away with the major exclusions and exemptions. This amount is arrayed by the familiar Adjusted Gross Income (AGI) classes in column 2.

In column 3 are displayed the present individual income tax yields by AGI classes. Column 4 contains the same information for social security taxes on the assumption that both the employer's contribution and the employee's contribution are ultimately paid by the latter. To these two taxes (individual income and social security) I have added in column 5 the present $47.6 billion in customs duties, inheritance, gift, federal excises, and corporate taxes we take in annually, and I have allocated them over the AGI classes in order to get the

TABLE 5

**Estimated Federal Revenues from Individual[1] and Corporate Income,
Social Security, Customs Duties, Federal Excises, Inheritance,
Gift Taxes, and the Single Tax Plan, All Distributed
to Individuals; by Adjusted Gross Income Class[2]**

(1)	(2)	(3)	(4)
Adjusted Gross Income Class	*New Taxable Income[3]*	*Present Income Tax Yield*	*Social Security (1973 Rates)[4]*
$ 0– 3,000	$ 43.3	$ 0.3	$ 2.9
3,000– 5,000	43.9	2.0	3.8
5,000– 7,000	56.4	4.0	5.0
7,000– 10,000	114.9	10.1	10.3
10,000– 15,000	185.5	19.2	15.6
15,000– 20,000	109.1	13.9	7.7
20,000– 50,000	112.8	18.4	4.6
50,000– 100,000	29.0	7.2	0.5
100,000 or more	25.7	7.7	0.1
Totals	$720.6	$82.7	$50.6

SOURCE:

Underlying data furnished by Office of the Secretary of the Treasury, Office of Tax Analysis, and author's calculations. March, 1972.

[1] Includes individual and corporate income, social security, excise (including the major federal trust funds), estate and gift taxes, customs duties. Excludes federal unemployment taxes (FUTA) and certain other miscellaneous revenue sources.

[2] The distribution of indirect taxes assumes full forward shifting to consumers. Estimates assume 1971 levels of income and present laws applicable to 1972 unless otherwise noted.

[3] A comprehensive income base consisting of present law adjusted gross income plus excluded long term capital gains plus excluded dividends. This expands the tax base from $400 billion to $720 billion.

[4] Taxes collected under social security (F.I.C.A.) at rates proposed for 1973: 5.4 percent of the first $10,200 of wages paid each by the employee and the

total dollar amounts of all federal taxes presently borne by individual taxpayers in column 6, some $181 billion.

The payoff for my single income tax approach can be seen in column 7 when compared with the results under present

(5)	(6)	(7)	(8)	(9)
Customs Duties, Inheritance, Gift, Excise, and Corporate Taxes[5]	*All Federal Taxes Now Paid by Individual Citizens*	*As Percentage of Income in (6)*	*Single Tax Plan*[6]	*As Percentage of Income in (8)*
$ 3.5	$ 6.7	15.5%	$ 3.2	7.4%
3.5	9.3	21.2%	5.7	13.0%
4.4	13.4	23.8%	9.2	16.3%
8.7	29.1	25.3%	21.7	18.9%
11.3	46.1	24.9%	41.1	22.2%
5.7	27.3	25.0%	29.5	27.0%
5.7	28.7	25.4%	41.0	36.3%
2.6	10.3	35.5%	14.6	50.3%
2.2	10.0	38.9%	14.8	57.6%
$47.6	$180.9		$180.7	

employer. It has been assumed here that the employers' share of this tax is fully shifted to wages and is born by the employee.

[5] $2.6 billion in customs duties, $15.0 billion in excise taxes, and $26.0 billion in corporate taxes were allocated to the AGI classes using the Ohio sales tax table contained in the 1971 federal income tax forms, estimating the amount of side taxes paid if taxpayers nationally followed these spending patterns, and deriving percentages of the resulting total which were then applied by AGI classes to spread $47.6 billion actually collected. It was assumed that expenditure patterns for excise, customs, and corporate taxes are the same and that all of these taxes are shifted forward to the individual consumer. Estate and gift taxes of $4.0 billion were arbitrarily distributed over the top two AGI classes, $2.0 billion and $2.0 billion.

[6] Applies the following marginal rates of tax to the comprehensive income base shown in order to yield the same total federal tax receipts of $181 billion.

law in column 6. While collecting the same amount of *total* federal tax receipts I have redistributed the burden upward to the larger income classes and sharply reduced the tax burden at the middle to lower end of the scale. Persons who make up the $3,000 to $5,000 Adjusted Gross Income class, for example, who presently are taxed $9.3 billion would pay a total of $5.7 billion instead. And those in the $7,000 to $10,000 AGI class would pay a total of $21.7 billion instead of the $29.1 billion they contributed. At the $15,000 to $20,000 income class, slightly more would be collected under my proposal ($29.5 billion as against $27.3 billion) and the top two income classes taken together would contribute almost $30 billion versus the current $20 billion.

Another way of portraying the striking results of the single income tax is to look at columns 7 and 9 in table 5 which translate the dollar amounts into percentages. Here we see the lower AGI class taxpayers would pay half as much as they do now; at the $5,000 to $7,000 income class one-third less; and at $10,000 to $15,000 of income, 10 percent less. On the other hand those in the $20,000 to $50,000 range would pay about 50 percent more than they now do (25.4 percent vs. 36.3 percent); and those in the top two income classes about 45 percent more.

In short, here is a method to institute a realistic tax reform scaled solely on ability to pay. I believe there are many tangible and intangible benefits to accrue from taking this step, and even from suggesting it.

We cannot fool ourselves. We have never had tax reform in the past and we never will in the future so long as the wealthy control our society and the government. The people cannot shuck off that control—and the propaganda in their tax return tables which shows the rich taxed at rates they never actually pay—until we have a goal and a plan to achieve it.

The inducements in a single tax are many. For one thing we could discard much of the expensive administration and enforcement of federal taxes and their attendant infrastructures in the private sector. The cost of compliance would plummet. Everyone's tax liability and computation could be handled on a postal card. The elaborate and counter-productive tax consulting industry that has fed off the complexity and inequity of the tax system would be put out of business. The important and long-neglected tests of simplicity, economy, and equity would finally be met in our federal tax system.

If this were accomplished, then the citizenry could look to their states to follow suit. There is no justification for the states to continue their regressive tax systems either. The principle of being taxed on the basis of ability to pay should hold throughout the nation.

What could be achieved in the end, if this proposal were adopted, would be the restoration of public confidence in the tax system and the foundations of the government itself.

While Congress, as presently constituted and influenced, would hardly appear disposed toward enacting a single tax, citizens could bring it about themselves through a taxpayer revolt. In a recent Harris Poll, 69 percent said they could sympathize with a "taxpayers' revolt." Eighty-two percent felt that "the big tax burden falls on the little man in this country today." Sixty-four percent agreed that taxes have reached the breaking point. The mechanism for action could be either through a constitutional amendment requiring a single tax (see Appendix G) or, alternatively, a constitutional amendment which allows citizen initiatives to pass both laws and other constitutional amendments by national referendums. (See Appendix F.)

To win a constitutional amendment for a single tax, citizens must organize and obtain passage through their state legislatures. Thirty-eight of the fifty legislatures must approve the amendment to make it law and thus institute a fundamental change without a single voice or action by the U.S. Congress.

If citizens were successful in obtaining ratification by thirty-eight legislatures for a constitutional amendment allowing citizen initiatives to pass both laws and constitutional amendments by national referendums, they could completely bypass the legislatures and Congress if need be. What a revolutionary step! Then the people would really have the power to make their own laws—directly.

One thing we should think about in striving for a single tax, regardless of its benefits or imperfections, is that it is a simple concept we can all grasp and, as such, it can become a standard by which we measure any future attempts to sell us "tax reform."

Taxes will never be pleasant, but they can be fair—if we insist. It is in the larger interest of true citizen power to use that power to tax ourselves adequately and justly.

9

The Medical-Industrial Complex

For every social wrong there
must be a remedy. But the
remedy can be nothing less
than the abolition of the
wrong.

—Henry George

A FEW YEARS AGO IN ANCHORAGF, during a political campaign, I knocked on the door of a retired plumber, a man who
had worked hard all his life and who now lived in an expensive
trailer with his wife. He had an automobile and a pickup truck
with a camper and was obviously proud of his independence.
He was now enjoying the fruits of his life-long labor. While we
talked he raised the subject of medicine and how he was against
providing free care to anyone. He said everybody should pay
for his own health needs, observing "socialized medicine is bad
stuff."

About a year later I happened to be in the neighborhood
and, hearing the plumber's wife had died recently, paid him
another call. When he opened the door, I was shocked. From a
robust Alaskan in his mid-sixties he had turned into a despond-
ent old man. And then he told me how his wife had contracted cancer and how he had used up all his financial re-

sources to ease her suffering. The bank account was empty. He had mortgaged the trailer and sold the pickup truck and camper. One illness had wiped him out.

I've never been able to forget that man's face. It made me sad and angry. Angry because it was such a senseless, mindless penalty to pay on top of his grief. And I am angrier still at how commonplace this sort of outrage is in our society and how we tolerate it. We are allowing sickness to literally wreck the lives of millions of people—the average citizen and the poor alike —by putting the cost of proper care out of reach.

No one has to be told about the painful prices. There is no escape from what the druggist charges for a handful of pills, hospital rooms costing $80 to $100 a day, inflated doctor fees. Yet we put up with them and with the fact that our entire health care delivery system is really in a shambles. Comprehensive care that provides for the early detection of disease and treatment is virtually unavailable. There are not enough facilities and manpower in the right places. There is no organized effort to assure that health problems will be checked in the whole population. The so-called "organized" medical establishment in my own state, for example, has scores of associations and groups, yet they rarely come around to figuring out what they could do to improve the health of the people at less cost. The same conditions prevail everywhere. When you get sick, you are on your own in seeing to it that you find the correct treatment. The process is time-consuming and expensive because it can be strictly hit or miss in obtaining the right diagnosis.

The disparate condition of the health care delivery mechanism of the world's most advanced technological power has been stated forcefully by the National Advisory Commission on Health Facilities in its 1968 report to the President.

> There is alarming disparity in health status among certain groups in this country. There are census tracts and neighborhoods in which the infant mortality rates are between 2 and 3 times the national average. In many areas health resources to cope with

either minor or serious illness are virtually inaccessible . . . Survey data show that as family income decreases, there are striking increases in the prevalence of heart disease, mental and nervous illnesses, arthritis and rheumatism, orthopedic impairments and dental problems. Poor people seek and receive much less medical attention than the affluent, but need more. There are critical problems—rising costs, inappropriate use of health services, population groups receiving inadequate care, and the quality of care sometimes compromised.

The report made it clear that, despite impressive medical resources and substantial progress in eliminating most infectious diseases and prolonging life, we do not have a health care delivery system. Rather it is a completely disorganized aggregation of manpower and facilities that has never been designed to serve all Americans.

It is obvious to me that this "nonsystem" came about through an absence of community control. As citizens we have abandoned the planning and delivery of services to those who do the delivering. We, the medical consumer, have no voice, no authority, in prescribing how our community health needs will be met, even though we are paying the bills. This basic fault, more than any other factor, is responsible for soaring costs and the tremendous disparity in the availability of adequate care.

A fundamental principle of a people's platform must be to establish citizen control over the public and private medical-industrial complex.

Let us examine what can be done about reining in the outrageous costs of medicine. For several years the nation's health bill has been jumping upward at an annual rate of more than 10 percent. In fiscal year 1968 the total was $53.1 billion and three years later, in fiscal year 1971, it hit $75 billion, an increase of nearly $22 billion or 41 percent.

On a per capita basis, the 1971 bill was $358 for every man, woman, and child in the country. Approximately 37 percent of the bill was paid by government sources and the remaining 63 percent either directly or indirectly by the private citizen.

Of course, as taxpayers we are paying the government share as well.

It is important to keep this government and private distinction in mind, however, because it is a key element in the breakdown of control over costs. Take Medicare, the first major government-insured health program. What the government did was agree to pay at the going rate all the medical, surgical, and hospital bills incurred by persons over 65. No cost controls were imposed. As a result, the providers of Medicare service, and later Medicaid to the poor, found these programs to be enormous financial boons. Physicians could now charge patients the full price, or higher, where before they had carried them on reduced prices. To expedite payment of the full price and wring as much money out of the program as possible, some physicians called in specialists and sent patients to hospitals whether or not they required hospitalization. This, in turn, overtaxed hospital facilities and manpower, causing shortages and expedient measures which drove costs still higher.

This is not to say the poor and the elderly don't deserve the best of care, but it does illustrate the lack of control inherent in the present nonsystem. It is obviously not proper to allow a doctor to put a patient in the hospital just so he will be sure to collect his check from the Social Security Administration, which runs Medicare, and at the same time deny that bed to someone who needs it. If the medical profession condones and abets this greedy pursuit, it says something about the whole practice of medicine and the American Medical Association, whose doctor members, ironically enough, fought the introduction of Medicare for years. The AMA fought under the banner of private medicine. But strip away the slogans and you are left with this simple fact: if you are sick, someone is making a buck on it.

A people's platform must encompass as a basic principle that the direct profit relationship between doctor and patient is absolutely inimical to the treatment of human suffering. What we now call private medicine and what we protect as a doctor-patient relationship has been used as a weapon against the trusting individual who is given the choice: your money or your life.

We have been drugged for too long by the rhetoric of the American Medical Association which sees the specter of socialism in every government move to broaden and improve health services. "Socialized medicine" is portrayed as some subversive menace that would undermine the capitalist system. Yet we never hear the same logic applied to our public school system—that we are allowing "socialized" teachers to mold the minds of the young. Is that because even doctors, as taxpayers, prefer our schools to be operated at the lowest cost, on a nonprofit basis? How inconsistent can you be over the manner in which our two most basic social services are to be delivered?

I find equally specious the argument that the patients have the right to avail themselves of all the benefits of the free enterprise system. The practice of medicine does not operate as an open market. You may have a choice of doctors, but doctors do not offer their services competitively. You can't invite bids from three surgeons to perform a hysterectomy. You can't get them to put on paper what special skills they have that another doesn't. Moreover, in any given community the doctors and dentists all tend to charge almost identical prices. They regulate the licensing of doctors and control the hospitals in a paternalistic fashion that deliberately discourages competition. There is, in short, no competitive discipline at work in what they want to call free enterprise—and the medical consumer is the loser.

Fortunately, there are good doctors. We have many dedicated men practicing medicine today who do put their patients first. There are brilliant surgeons pioneering life-sparing techniques, public health service physicians, the doctors who work the emergency wards of our hospitals, specialists and general practitioners, the researchers and disease control specialists who daily perform honest miracles. We depend upon these people and are grateful they exist, and it is with full awareness of their services that the criticisms are made here. For these

men, and many doctors I know personally, are aware of the
abuses that have crept into the health care system and would
like to see them corrected.

There is no argument that doctors and the other medical
personnel supporting a competent health care delivery system
should be amply rewarded for their services. The practice of
medicine is an art demanding expert knowledge and years of
intensive training. The responsibilities can be enormous, the
decisions agonizingly difficult. But by its very definition, im-
planted in the Hippocratic oath, medicine is a profession to
serve mankind—to heal, not to exploit.

Yet, in recent times, under the guise of "improved," "more
efficient," "specialized," "technological advances," medicine as
we know it has undergone radical changes. The family doctor
with his revered kindness and personal interest has all but vanished and no one has taken his place—except television's Marcus Welby, who will be the only doctor to enter most American
homes this year. Private practitioners have shifted their businesses to the depersonalized, profit-oriented surgical team. And
now the Nixon administration is trying to promote the profit-
oriented Health Maintenance Organization (HMO). This is a
new gimmick in making money out of what the Nixon people
think is preventive medicine. Under the concept of the HMO a
subscriber member pays a monthly fee. The operators of the
clinic say they will keep you fit through regular medical surveillance. Their discipline, or incentive to do so, is that they
will have to pay the cost of any surgery, hospitalization, or
nursing care if you become ill. The healthier you stay, the more
money the HMO makes. Sounds like a fair enough deal. But
what if you are stricken by a major illness, one requiring a
great deal of surgery and hospital treatment for six months or
a year? Where is the incentive to see you through your sickness? You are suddenly eating into the profits, a liability. As
far as an HMO would be concerned, you would be better off
dead. A true capitalist believes in cutting his losses. Or, take a
less extreme case, like an option to perform corrective surgery

on a displaced disc in your spine. Will the HMO look at it as an option when the operation will come out of the net profits for the year? Would there be a temptation to say it is inoperable and you will just have to bear the pain? I wouldn't care to trust myself or my family to such pliable medical economics.

As a group, medical practitioners are presently among the wealthiest class in the nation. Many doctors are millionaires. They are able to take the large cash flow from their practices and parlay it into still larger fortunes by investing in real estate, drug firms, and kindred enterprises where their medical work helps increase the sales and profits. When you pay a visit to some doctors today, after waiting hours to get in to see them, you have reason to wonder whether they are concentrating on you or on some big deal they are swinging across town. This is where the medical "free enterprise" system can hurt you personally.

But it hurts in bigger ways, too. Your doctor-businessman is presently in control of most of the planning of your community health services. He sits on the hospital boards which decide whether to expand facilities and manpower and where to locate new medical and dental clinics. Invariably the decision is weighted to place the facility where the people with money are —where the profits are. One has only to canvass the medical facilities in any big city ghetto to see how this thinking works. Where the need is greatest, the resources are scarcest. It took a riot to locate some clinics in the Watts section of Los Angeles. Before the people acted in their own behalf, they had to travel hours by bus across the city to the nearest medical convenience. And it was the government, not private medicine, which finally constructed the clinics in Watts.

It is axiomatic under a profit-making system that when there is a shortage of goods or services, prices will rise as demand increases. This is precisely what has happened under our health care nonsystem. Citizens under Medicare and our increasing population have vastly broadened consumer desire for more and better treatment. Whether by design or shortsightedness, your doctor-businessman has never been able to plan ahead to keep pace with this demand. Instead we are at the mercy of a perennial shortage of doctors, nurses, technicians, dentists, and hospital beds.

The day is long overdue to strip the American Medical Association, the American Hospital Association, and allied interests of their power in regulating the supply of medical professionals and facilities. This can be done under a proposal I will discuss later.

Control must also be exerted over other segments of the medical-industrial complex—the profit-making companies supplying pharmaceuticals and other goods and services and the private health insurance corporations. Since the advent of Medicare, this country has witnessed a sickening raid on the U.S. Treasury by private industry capitalizing on the nation's humane desire to alleviate the financial hardship of human suffering. Prices have been jacked up and profits have soared in the rush to mine the golden depths of misery. Established drug firms and new corporate empires specializing in nursing care, health products, and other services have become the darlings of Wall Street because they can make so much money from government care programs. Many men like billionaire H. Ross Perot have struck a bonanza. A congressional subcommittee not long ago revealed that Perot's company made $72 million over a four and a half year period by computer processing those Medicare claims I discussed earlier. Somehow, according to the subcommittee, Perot managed to garner 90 percent of the subcontracted computer work on Medicare claims. This kind of exploitation of the taxpayer can and must be stopped.

The cruelest joke of all in our health care nonsystem is private insurance. For years it has been aiding and abetting the rapacious rise in the costs of medical services without covering them. The Blue Cross and Blue Shield hospitalization and surgical insurance plans were launched by doctors theoretically to make it easier for patients to pay their bills. But history also shows that a primary motive was to ensure that the doctors could collect payment for their services. The system of "maximum benefits" for various services and procedures established in these doctor-controlled plans was, in reality, a minimum price structure. Doctors could always charge more, but they were guaranteed the amount listed in the plan. It didn't take long for them to discover the way to make more money was to raise the maximum benefit and, of course, raise the premium, that is, the cost, of insurance. The same pattern has been followed by other insurers.

In addition to providing the mechanism for raising prices, the great fallacy of private insurance is that it covers only those who can afford to pay. Further, it is based strictly on the treatment of illness, not its prevention, and it does not pay for minor sickness. A family of four today may be charged $500 a year for a major medical plan and still have to pay $500–$1,000 in out-of-pocket expenses that are not covered because of the tricky way one has to qualify for insurance "benefits." So, unless one is unfortunate enough to be stricken by a major illness, private health insurance is more a liability than an asset.

A Social Security report shows how insufficient insurance benefits are in covering total medical costs. In fiscal year 1971, insurance benefits amounted to only $15 billion of the $57 billion paid by the private sector, mostly by individuals. Add to that another $1.6 billion—the insurance companies' costs and profits. This meant $42 billion was uncovered; more than 70 percent came directly out of our pockets. What kind of "insurance" is that?

LET US TURN NOW to how we can redesign this monstrosity; what we as citizens can do to make it responsive to our needs and infuse it with human values.

A people's platform must hold that every American has the right to comprehensive medical-dental-mental health care. Henceforth, the entire health care complex must be placed under public control and run on a nonprofit basis like our educational institutions.

I propose that we carry out this policy through a national health program which will cover everyone's needs from the time they are born until they die. National health would be financed like social security insurance, but graduated according to the ability to pay.

Public control over the delivery of services would be exerted through the creation of community and regional health districts. Members of the boards operating the districts would be elected as school boards are now. In this way, when a citizen has a complaint about a doctor or a hospital, like being made to wait because of insufficient staff, he will have someone to complain to, an elected official who can act on a problem to solve it.

Health boards must have the authority and the financial resources to take over all existing public hospitals and clinics and the power to create new facilities where they are needed. Private clinics and practices would not be affected, except that doctors availing themselves of health district hospitals would abide by the district's standards. These standards would apply to the quality of medicine practiced and prices for services. The boards also would be able to control the supply of medical manpower to assure adequate delivery of services and assure the prompt introduction of new equipment and techniques.

The boards would promulgate and enforce community standards for occupational safety and environmental health according to national standards.

A key facet in redesigning community health services must be the establishment of neighborhood disease detection centers equipped with the best diagnostic methods available, so that preventive medicine can be provided for everyone. The centers can concentrate on the early detection of such major killers as heart disease and cancer. They can be sensitive to particular problems in segments of the population, such as sickle cell anemia among blacks, mental illness and conditions prevalent among the aged and the poor, venereal disease among the young. By recent estimates, there are two million cases of VD in the country and the infections are spreading because there is no organized system for mass screening of carriers. This public health problem could be overcome through the ability of the disease detection centers to give every citizen a yearly checkup and to screen a whole segment of the local population, such as 16- to 24-year-olds, in a short period of time.

The centers should have mobile units to reach out to the schools and people unable to leave their homes. All the centers should be connected to hospitals for speedy referral and treatment of patients.

An effort must be made to humanize medicine. It could be done by assigning a physician at a hospital or disease detection center to act as a "family doctor" for a neighborhood. He could be the advance scout for the center and be responsible for seeing patients through an illness, from diagnosis through convalescence.

Hospitals should be made into friendlier places by encouraging more individual attention of patients. We need more volunteers, more paramedical personnel to spend the time in nursing the sick back to health. We should be making much wiser use of the thousands of medics and other technicians who have been in military service. There should be in-hospital work-training programs where these men can apply the skills they have now while studying to improve them. They could advance professionally at the same time they are providing badly needed patient services.

On the national level, a national health administration must be the agency to take responsibility for the recruitment and education of medical personnel. It must assume the role of planner to meet long-range needs and oversee the operation of medical, dental, nursing, and other technical schools. These schools already are largely tax-supported.

A particular effort must be made to bring minorities into the system. Today there are only 5,000 blacks among the nation's 300,000 physicians and surgeons. This means there is only 1 black doctor for every 5,000 blacks, against 1 white doctor for every 600 persons in the rest of the population. The present shortage of black physicians and surgeons results mainly from a lack of financial resources to gain the necessary training. They can't afford it. It is also true that doctor-businessmen governing admission standards at some medical schools have practiced racism in excluding blacks. Only recently have they grudgingly granted some concessions in the way of fellowships and tutorial assistance for the disadvantaged to allow a few more blacks to gain entrance to the profession. It is no great wonder that black medical needs have long gone unmet.

National health policies must be developed to ensure the deployment of medical manpower and resources to rural areas as well as inner cities. All personnel in the system must be salaried. Pay incentives may be applied to locate personnel in less desirable areas, as well as to channel them into a specialty, research, or teaching. Health districts, like school districts, can compete for the best manpower. But there must be a form of equalization so that poorer districts are not deprived of equal services. This can be done in the form of grants and agreements on pay scales. Pay scales should be attractive, but obviously we don't want to set up a system where they will keep escalating and drive up costs.

It is on the national level that the other half of the medical-industrial complex should be controlled. The national health administration must have the power to convert the industry to a nonprofit basis. Where it is impossible to achieve this policy voluntarily, companies should be nationalized. We have to produce drugs and other hospital and medical supplies at the lowest possible cost and in quantities that meet the demand. Costs of drugs alone can be greatly reduced simply by abolishing all the expensive advertising and promotion presently being done by the industry and paid for by the consumer.

The national health administration should establish a national clearinghouse for all information on drugs. This should be the primary source for fully reliable and objective data on the safety and efficacy of drugs. Doctors should not rely, as they do now, largely on the propaganda generated by profiteering drug companies.

If drug advertising were halted, the American Medical Association would be deprived of a main source of revenue which it uses to lobby against what it considers "socialized medicine," for most of this advertising is done in the AMA's journals. Why should we consumers have to bear the cost of this advertising in higher drug prices just to allow the AMA to use the proceeds against our best interests? Let the doctors use their own money.

To achieve its goals, the national health administration must coordinate all its efforts closely with the local health districts. As a further safeguard, the agency must function under the surveillance of an adversary unit, a group of experts and investigators who will monitor the agency's programs and policies and report their findings to the public. I have discussed the adversary principle at length in chapter 3 and I think it is particularly applicable in this critical area of bringing the health system's costs and services under control. The adversary technique can help make the system manageable, efficient, and effective just by alerting the public and Congress how the stated goals are being met.

The concept of a national health service, while alien to this country, is not new. It has worked successfully for years in England and other nations. The difficulties and dislocations will be great in implementing it here, but the step must be taken. A truly citizen-run health system is the only hope for bringing sanity out of today's chaos and ensuring the health of America.

As citizens we do not have to wait for Congress to pass enabling legislation to organize local and regional health districts. We can start now. We can begin by making models of how we want a health district to be designed; by holding public meetings and discussing our needs and how they can be met; by drawing up charters and presenting them to state legislatures to define health districts; by going ahead with the political work to establish our districts and health boards through elections.

Indeed, we should seize this initiative now. I feel certain once citizens make it their right to oversee the health care systems in their own communities, dramatic improvements will be forthcoming. I have in mind first the accumulation of facts. How many of us have any accurate picture of how health care is delivered in our cities and towns? How many hospitals are there, who do they serve, and how well are they run? How many doctors and other personnel are we supporting, how much do they charge, and why do costs of all services keep going up? How many sick people must be cared for and how many are being ignored or receiving shabby treatment?

These are pertinent questions that are generally impossible to answer today because the surveys haven't been made. Or if they have, the information hasn't necessarily been collected with the entire community in mind to determine how improvements can be effected. A community health "profile" made through an independent survey should be the first goal of a health district; it is here that the flaws will become apparent and a plan can be developed to correct them.

If our experience on the national level is any guide, we know that many government-run health services tend to become bureaucratized. We spend a great deal of money on paper shuffling, on maintaining some marginal facilities and over-staffing others. Every community has the same problems to a greater or lesser degree. The great need is to bring them out in the open and to discover where the hidden costs and the waste lie.

When we go about taking over the management of our health services, we cannot overlook one factor which is fundamental to their successful operation—the medical education of the individual citizen. Several young doctors I have talked to recently believe that probably our greatest failing in health care is a lack of public knowledge about medicine. Our schools offer little outside of rudimentary hygiene in teaching a person how to stay healthy; the ways of the body and how to care for it are left as dark mysteries to be plumbed only by licensed practitioners. And nothing is taught about the delivery and quality of health care. This is a defect which concerned citizens can begin to correct now by insisting that comprehensive medical instruction be included in school curricula. If we can teach youngsters the secrets of making a gasoline engine run, we certainly can instruct them in the mechanics of their own bodies. Indeed, it is in this form of instruction that preventive medicine begins and it is here we could start to lower the enormous costs of health care.

10

Closing the Education Gap

Next in importance to
freedom and justice is
popular education, with-
out which neither freedom
nor justice can be per-
manently maintained.

—*James A. Garfield*

AMERICANS HAVE ALWAYS had a love affair with education. Ask any American father and mother what they want most for their children and "a good education" invariably will be near the top of their list. It is part of our national dream of equality; the means by which the disadvantaged can achieve for themselves economic well-being and social acceptance; the stimulus for individual enrichment and achievement; and the prerequisite for national advancement. It can provide the major and enduring solution for problems of crime, prejudice, and poverty.

Despite its obvious virtues, however, education today is the victim of growing criticism, some justified and some not. There is a crisis of confidence among the people in the ability of education to fulfill its role as, what Horace Mann termed, "the great equalizer of the conditions of men." They rightly complain that education today too often is unequally dis-

158

pensed, ineffectively administered, and lacking in relevancy and creative innovation. In order to strengthen education, therefore, a people's platform must demand that it be developed as a humanizing institution and that it progress by economic and political means toward this end.

Education has become one of this nation's biggest businesses. Although some Americans derive satisfaction from the fact that during the current school year more than 60 million people are engaged in our education enterprise as students, teachers, or administrators and that some $74 billion—over 7 percent of the gross national product—is spent on education, I do not. We need to open the doors of education to even more Americans, of all ages; we should expand the ranks of qualified teachers and administrators; we must provide additional funds for increased salaries, improved facilities, and more modern equipment; and we need to see to it that those monies are raised by a formula based on ability to pay and redistributed according to need.

I find little solace in the fact that some education is available to most young Americans. It does not disguise the imperfections of a system that often favors the haves over the have-nots and produces an ever-increasing number of teenage drop-outs, while adults who want to drop-in find a scarcity of educational opportunities available to them. In short, we must reevaluate the merits, and perhaps even redesign the structure, of an educational program that elicits campus strikes and boycotts by dissatisfied students and fails to meet the expectations of parents or the demands of society.

Unless the existing educational system is improved sufficiently to meet the needs and demands of today's changing society, we shall have to consider the implementation of entirely new methods for dispensing education. One such possibility is the so-called voucher system soon to be tried on a very limited experimental basis. Under this proposal, parents would be given educational vouchers which could be used to send their children to any school of their choice, public or private, or, if they prefer, to engage in specialized education activities such as apprenticeships, study projects, or even travel. The cash value of each voucher would approximate the amount spent on the education of one child each year by the local school district. The system does offer the flexibility and the element of individual choice so often lacking in our educational institutions today and this is important. However, many contend it would undermine the public school system and could be used as a device to perpetuate segregation. Nonetheless, it is an innovative, imaginative concept, something found all too seldom in education today, and for that reason it merits further study and serious consideration.

At the same time, we must not be too quick to blame our present educational system for all our educational problems. The malaise of a society racked by continuing racial strife, unwanted war, unemployment, poverty, and a myriad of other social and economic ills, plants the seeds, long before the student arrives in school, which produce such deplorable conditions as riots in the classroom, policemen in the corridors, and dope in the gym lockers. The times have created new challenges and placed new demands on education. Education now must rise to the occasion.

While recognizing that education is perhaps our best long-term solution to problems, it is first necessary to understand that, paradoxically, education is also the source of many of our problems. The uneducated knew only what they experienced. They were unaware that they could make life better for themselves. They could not read and they did not socialize with people outside their socioeconomic class who knew how. It was not until schools were opened to them that they began to learn that they did not have to remain in their present position. They became dissatisfied and they rebelled. An awareness developed and a new impatience extended to everything that men had previously accepted. The more men knew, the more they expected. And they did not want to wait. "The evil which was suffered patiently as inevitable seems unendurable as soon as the idea of escaping from it crosses men's minds," de Tocqueville observed. "All the abuses then removed call attention to those that remain, and they now appear more than galling. The evil, it is true, has become less, but sensibility to it has become more acute." The result is our age of confrontation and, in its extreme form, anarchistic violence.

But educated men did not only complain. They also were busy doing other things. Some built industries that polluted the waters, automobiles that polluted the air, buildings that blocked the sky and replaced trees and grass, dangerous freeways that carried us to our man-made monstrosities. Some did look to the less fortunate and juggled their school boundaries to separate black children from white. It was, after all, educated men who concocted questionable aptitude tests that minorities could not pass to justify policies of perpetuating social classes.

Some of the best minds from the best schools created the greatest injustices. Somewhere, somehow, morality was lost, and although we now know how to do thousands of things, we have not distinguished which ones are worth doing and which are better forgotten. The purpose of machinery, we all know, is to serve man. We all must know how to make a living, but we must also learn how to live. If the schools are to teach us this, they must be made into humane institutions. "There is a horrible example in history of what the Educated Society might easily become," Peter F. Drucker of *Careers Today* magazine has written, "unless [society] commits itself to the education of the whole man." His example is China during the T'ang and Sung periods when "commitment to the purely intellectual in man destroyed what had been the world's leader in art as well as in science, in technology as well as in philosophy." The development of the complete person, his total human potential, has to be learned. Therefore, creating and maintaining a humane environment within the school system is most important.

I see a humanistic school as one that accepts, even cele-brates, personal differences and yet emphasizes the common qualities men share. It is one that aids the student in under-standing his predecessors and in growing from them without being restricted by them. Its goal for the student is superior scholarship so that he can contribute to his society while further developing his own personality. It supplies the means for the student to mature by examining his own life. "Men are men before they are lawyers, or physicians, or merchants, or manufacturers, and if you make them capable and sensible men, they will make themselves capable and sensible lawyers or physicians," John Stuart Mill observed in his Inaugural Address at the University of St. Andrew.

EVEN THE MOST HUMAN INSTITUTIONS require proper funding to be effective, however, and the financial inadequacies block-ing full development of our educational system are appalling. The greatest offender in this regard is the federal government. While piously extolling the virtues of quality education for all Americans, the government consistently fails to put its money where its mouth is or to give the issue the priority it deserves.

The task of providing every American with the best possi-ble education, for example, is too important and too complex to be treated any longer as the stepchild of a divided-interest federal establishment such as the Department of Health, Education, and Welfare. The current downgraded status of the Office of Education should be elevated to the position of a full and independent department and its commissioner should be made a member of the President's cabinet. (For that matter, the same should be done with the Bureau of Public Health; Welfare, eventually, should probably be inte-grated with the Social Security Administration.)

The federal government's share of the $40 billion spent for elementary and secondary education by the federal, state, and local governments in the 1970–1971 school year, was only 7 percent or $2.8 billion. Compare this with the more than $80 billion spent on defense. The cost of the obsolete anti-ballistic missile system alone would enable Washington to increase the federal education expenditure fivefold! What a terrible price we are paying for the poor judgment of a leadership which cannot recognize that in deciding to increase our overkill capacity, it was deciding on much more than the mere expansion of a missile system; it was deciding on a lesser quality of education for our children.

What damning evidence this presents to prove that the public does not have the weight needed to protect its interests. Oh, the public-interest rhetoric is there, in the White House and on the floors of Congress, but when the chips are down the decision-makers will respond most quickly and most favorably to the special monied interests which helped to place them in office. This is why a people's platform must insist, as detailed in chapter 3, that the election process be based on public finances rather than private contributions. Too many preelection "contributions" are paid off with postelection "favors." If it makes sense for our hard-headed corporate types to invest in someone's election to public office in anticipation of rewards, certainly it should make equal good sense for the public to do the same thing by appropriating the money to pay for the cost of electing officials in anticipation of some rewards for itself.

This is the reason the executive (where the money is in government) responds so generously to the pressures of the powerful military-industrial complex, while state and local governments have to come up with a whopping 93 percent of the education price tag. Small wonder citizens at the local level find themselves economically smothered under ever-increasing property taxes.

Property taxes, it should be noted, are not only economically burdensome, they also are an unfair and unequal basis for financing education at the local level. Now it appears they may be illegal as well. The Supreme Court of California ruled on

August 30, 1971, that the financing of schools in California through local property taxes violates the equal protection clause of the Constitution's Fourteenth Amendment. "We have determined," the court declared, "that this funding scheme invidiously discriminates against the poor because it makes the quality of a child's education a function of the wealth of his parents and neighbors." As the decision points out, "Affluent districts can have their cake and eat it too; they can provide a high-quality education for their children while paying lower taxes. Poor districts, by contrast, have no cake at all."

Former U.S. Commissioner of Education Harold Howe II, writing in the November 20, 1971, issue of *Saturday Review,* suggests that the easiest thing to do might be to remove the taxing authority of local school districts. "Under such a system the state could presumably abandon the property tax and seek other forms of taxation, or devise a system of property evaluation that is comprehensive and fair throughout the state."

A program along these lines has been underway in the Canadian province of New Brunswick since January, 1967. With the goal of providing a single standard of education to all communities, the province assumed the full cost of financing education. It restructured its tax system by eliminating property and nuisance-type taxes and enacted a uniform real estate tax of 1.5 percent of market value as determined by provincial, rather than local, assessors. Sales taxes were increased from 6 to 8 percent and a 10 percent surtax was levied on income tax. The state take-over of school costs has resulted in a more equal provision of services and, of additional benefit, it has fixed political responsibility for school support.

As we take steps to correct the inequities of financing education at the local level, we also must begin to escalate our national commitment to education beyond the present 7 percent of our gross national product to 8, 10, 12 percent or more

—whatever is needed. And, at least one-half of that dollar amount should be put up by the federal government.

At the same time the federal government must make up whatever dollar differences are required to meet the special needs of impacted areas and those localities which have deficiencies in their fiscal abilities.

There are other steps needed to achieve equal opportunity in education. State aid must be adjusted to take into account the higher costs of education in certain areas and funds must be allocated on the basis of whatever is needed to provide full educational opportunities for children with special problems or special skills, such as the retarded, the handicapped, and the exceptionally gifted. I take exception, however, to the matching-fund formula or the use of special subsidies for rewarding districts which spend more money on children requiring extra attention than is usually spent on "normal" children. Such financial arrangements again favor those affluent school districts which are better able to raise the necessary funds for such purposes. If a school district needs more money to meet the requirements of all its students, it should receive it without any ifs, ands, or buts. Providing matching funds or special subsidies to upper socioeconomic school districts serves only to siphon off the available funds that should be going to all or to the more needy school districts.

Simply raising more money, of course, is not enough. The funds must then be distributed in a manner that will do the most good. This means allocating finances on a basis of need rather than according to the wealth of the school districts. We must spend more money in our poverty areas than we do in our affluent areas. It is unacceptable for the ghettos or the impoverished rural communities to receive less assistance than the more fortunate neighborhoods surrounding them, or for the retarded and the exceptional to get something less than the best. The time has come to redefine equal educational opportunity in financial terms. Every student learns at a different rate; an equal number of dollars, therefore, will not bring equality of educational opportunity. We must change the thinking that resulted in the 1968–1969 per pupil expenditure for the city of Los Angeles, where the lower socio-economic school districts are located, to be set at $636, while neighboring affluent Beverly Hills received $1,131 per pupil. The same pattern was found to exist throughout the nation: Cleveland, Ohio, $630 per pupil, Shaker Heights, $968; Boston, Massachusetts, $655, Newton, $842; New York City, $1,031, Scarsdale, $1,626; Detroit, Michigan, $575, Grosse Pointe, $875. Financially speaking, the conclusion is obvious. Children who need education the most are receiving the least.

Take your choice. You can pay the cost differential of $300–$400 per year for bringing these individuals into productive society during their school years or you can wait for a larger percentage of our deprived population to run afoul of the law. At that time you will have to pay more than $1,200 annually to lock them up in prisons, while you pay the cost of barricading yourself in your own home because you couldn't get them all locked up.

THE NEEDY CHILDREN of our society are getting the short end of the stick when it comes to the quality of instruction as well. It is understandable that the most experienced, best qualified teachers would usually choose to pursue their profession in the more wealthy neighborhoods. After all, that is where one finds the finest schools, the best prepared students, and the nicest and safest surroundings. Yet, it is the not-so-safe neighborhoods, the not-so-fine schools, and the not-so-advantaged students which most desperately need the specialized expertise of skilled teachers. The long-range solution, of course, is obvious: eradicate urban slums and rural blight, transform them into safe and comfortable places in which to live and work, and build better educational plants. In the meantime, however, I propose a federally supported supplementary salary program to reward those men and women who elect to risk the dangers, endure the discomforts, and accept the added challenges of teaching in our educationally deprived areas. Surely if we can pay government workers and military personnel as much as a 25 percent bonus for serving in so-called "hardship" areas around the world, we can do as much for our teachers here at home. Such a program would enable the financially struggling lower socioeconomic school districts to compete more favorably with their wealthier counterparts in recruiting the talent to provide the quality of instruction needed by our disadvantaged youngsters.

We must also make more efficient use of our expensive educational facilities. It is ridiculous for these costly institutions to remain idle and unused for three months out of every year. The summer vacation is an archaic custom instituted by an agrarian society that needed to have its children on the farms to help with the summer and early fall harvesting. Schools should be operated on a four-quarter schedule, and parents should be able to withdraw their children for one quarter for vacation or travel, if desired. What a boon this would be for those families in which parents have jobs that make it difficult or impossible to take time off during the summer. And think of all the people who might prefer to take a late fall, winter, or early spring vacation, but must now wait until school lets out. Imagine the healthy economic side effects. Travel agencies, airlines, resorts, vacation-related industries of all kinds would enjoy business activity on a year-round basis instead of being inundated seasonally during a brief three-month interval and around holidays. And the vacationers would benefit, too. Conditions would be less crowded, rooms would be easier to obtain, and rates would tend to be equalized instead of being jackedup to capitalize on the seasonal influx. The whole seasonal cycle in the recreational part of the economy could be leveled out.

Not only must we utilize our public educational facilities more fully, we must recognize the value of using private schools to help meet our educational problems. I see no compelling reason why private schools should not receive federal funds as long as they are primarily education-oriented, instead of religion-oriented, with the understanding, of course, that they cannot bar enrollment of any youngster because of religion, race, or economic background. The existence of parochial schools, for example, has eased the burden for many underfinanced and overpopulated school districts. This has been dramatically proven in those districts where parochial schools have been forced to shut down because of a lack of funds and their students have suddenly been thrust into the public school system. The only criteria which should matter in qualifying for federal financial assistance is whether a school provides quality education indiscriminately and effectively.

AFTER YEARS AND YEARS of children failing in tremendous proportions, some parents who had accepted "disadvantaged" as the explanation began to wonder where the fault really lay, on their children or on the "system." A new notion has developed called "accountability." It is time that schools and their professional staffs now share the responsibility that was assigned only to the children. Parents who were worried about their children's failure were not the only ones interested. Federal and state governments insisted on meaningful reports which were required to show where the money was going in the schools. And a job market that could no longer simply absorb drop-outs, but required high school diplomas and junior college degrees, added to the development of the idea of accountability.

Accountability is not something to be limited to issues of money and curriculum, however. The system of individual accountability currently is abrogated once a teacher gains tenure. This is not to say that most teachers will not continue to provide their best efforts, but if it is important to have checks and balances outside the educational system, certainly it is as important to have them within the system. The debilitating effects of seniority ascribed to our legislative halls are no less so when found in education or anywhere else for that matter. A teacher who is no longer effective in the classroom, whether it is because of age or ability or for any other reason, should not be able to escape accountability because of tenure alone. A method must be devised, through administrative procedures and hearings and with the end decision being taken by elected school board members (subject to the wishes of the people affected) to strike down the immunity of tenure when poor performance warrants it.

STARTING FROM PRESCHOOL, it is generally assumed that schools are fixed and immutable. Therefore, changing the child to fit the school is the solution. I think often changing the schools would be more appropriate. Research does indicate that underprivileged children do not learn well because they enter school without many of the attitudes and the linguistic, cognitive, and affective skills that are absolutely necessary for them to succeed in school. It is easy to say, then, teach them that before they come to school.

To improve the "system," teachers' attitudes have to continue to change. They have been oriented to expect a certain performance from their students. They must stop now and reorient. Teachers who think their students are incapable of learning very often find this to be true. Yet, a different teacher with the same class and a different assumption sees them become interested in learning.

I was not a very good student when I was a youngster growing up in Springfield, Massachusetts. I was a poor reader and had considerable difficulty in expressing myself clearly. As a consequence, I became disinterested and unresponsive. School was something to be endured, not enjoyed; learning was a chore to be avoided.

In my senior year of high school, however, something happened that changed my attitude and my life. A remarkable and dedicated teacher, Brother Edgar Bourque, recognized my reticence as but a problem to be overcome. Because of his interest, his willingness to tutor me in speech and reading beyond the classroom demands, I discovered the joys of learning and was imbued with the desire to maximize my talents.

I have never forgotten that experience or failed to benefit from it. I was one of the fortunate ones, and I often wonder how many boys and girls will never realize their full potential because there are not enough Edgar Bourques in the teaching profession or because, for some other reason, they will receive something less than the kind of education they need to develop fully and to compete well in our society.

A primary goal in education should be as John Comenius stated, "To seek and to find a method of instruction by which teachers may teach less, but learners learn more; by which schools may be the scene of less noise, aversion, and useless labour, but of more leisure, enjoyment, and solid progress." Educators must be made aware that how they teach and how they act may be as important as what they teach. Doing is more effective than simply talking in terms of shaping values. For education to solve all our problems, the "system" itself has to be improved. Placing a dedicated genius in every classroom would be the perfect solution, but as John Dewey asserted some seventy-five years ago, "Education is, and forever will be, in the hands of ordinary men and women."

But these men and women, ordinary or not, must and can meet the challenge and learn why students who had been lively and eagerly interested upon first entering school are quite bored by the time they reach fifth grade. This is especially true in lower-income schools, although it is hardly absent in higher-income ones. It is time to make education more exciting, more interesting, and purposeful. Curricula which fail to satisfy and enthuse the students must be studied and revised or replaced with imagination and daring. Details are only steppingstones to understanding concepts which are of fundamental importance. Alfred North Whitehead advised teachers, "Do not teach too many subjects" and "what you teach, teach thoroughly." Teachers must know their subjects well enough to reach their students in a creative way and be able to relate them to both their own and their students' educational goals. As Plato's *Dialogues* illustrate, a teacher cannot simply start his students where they are; he must also take them elsewhere.

A people's platform will demand more than just equal educational opportunities for every American; it will demand the right education for each individual. To achieve this, we must first look to the students and the parents themselves for guidance and provide them with an effective means for participating in the formation and implementation of educational programs.

The phenomenon of college boycotts and student and teacher strikes must be viewed for what it is: a demonstration of dissatisfaction not with education itself, but with the quality and relevancy of the education. Indeed, activism is a healthy sign because it indicates an acute awareness of the fact that knowledge and the future of society are at stake. In their idealism, our youthful activists are rebelling against the traditional and authoritative, condemning them as thwarters of academic and personal freedom. They are justified in complaining about a system that often concentrates too much on unnatural order, discipline, neatness, and silence. A humane institution wastes less time on such peripheral issues.

Of course, the schools must retain some authority. There are all kinds of authority. Some that are necessary. Sociologist Robert A. Nisbet remarked, "There is the authority of learning and taste; of syntax and grammar in language; of scholarship, of science, and of the arts." But authority has to be distinguished from power. Thus, while the schools must try to retain authority, they must also try to understand that they exist as a democratic institution that should open its ears to legitimate complaints from students about irrelevant-to-learning rules and inadequacies in curriculum and quality of instruction.

College students should be represented and have a voting

voice on all university boards and committees. This is already happening to some extent with the advent of the 18-year-old vote. Students are running for state boards of regents and are being elected, and this, I believe, will have a salutary effect. The new power now enjoyed by this heretofore disenfranchised constituency will serve to break down the alienation so often found between the receivers and the dispensers of education.

The remoteness of the public school boards from their constituents, especially in the big cities, must also be overcome. Jack Witkowsky, a former Chicago school board member, suggests in the November 20, 1971, issue of *Saturday Review*:

> If large urban school systems are to become viable institutions again, it seems clear that they must be decentralized . . . much of the power now held by the general superintendent must be broken down into smaller units, and each of the local districts within the school system must be given considerable autonomy in running its own schools.
>
> Residents of each district should be free to form a district school board to oversee their schools. Residents in activist communities would probably want to do so; in other communities where the schools were functioning reasonably well, the residents might prefer to establish a more informal means of supervising their schools. In any event, the community should have a direct line to the central board of education.
>
> The central board itself should remain and a small central staff should be available to the general superintendent of schools; but the decision-making powers should fall on the community and the district superintendent.

This is the best ideal for a citizen's democracy with regard to education and it is a primary demand for a citizen's platform.

ELEMENTARY AND SECONDARY SCHOOLS are not the only segments of the educational system that need help. Vocational, adult, and higher education face numerous problems that must be solved soon. The need for vocational education in our technological society is self-evident. Vocational competence as well as personal and social traits for relating to people are necessary at work and at home. With thousands of different jobs that this modern society can supply, programs are needed to teach students how to measure their aptitudes, interests, and abilities, and too few schools offer these programs.

Adult education has to be expanded for people of low income who want to boost their earning power, people with high incomes returning to school simply for the pleasure of learning, and people who need further education for various licenses and apprenticeships.

The recent growth in higher education has been spectacular, rising in the past ten years from 3 million to 8 million students. The share of the gross national product devoted to this expanding enterprise has increased from 1 percent to over 2 percent and is expected to be over 3 percent by 1976. As the colleges and universities grew, however, problems multiplied. Programs became too big to coordinate, priorities were hard to determine and establish, state and private support needed to be integrated, and universities became heavily dependent on federal aid. Here, too, there is a great need for equality of opportunity in the form of funds and places in the institutions for the less affluent students. Costs are rising faster than inflation. The cost per student has risen about 5 percent per year since World War II. In leading universities, the increase rate is 7.5 percent. The problem of adapting to new technological devices for learning, such as language laboratories and computer-assisted instruction, also exists. And the universities in the cities that have opened their doors to more students find that many are less prepared and not as motivated as the typical middle-class students.

Specific kinds of institutions must cope with specific kinds of difficulties as well. Negro colleges have to deal with the fact that public and private universities are recruiting the best black students and teachers, who would have gone to these institutions before integration began. Now they are often fortresses of black power. Private liberal arts colleges now compete with the universities, state colleges, and community colleges. They do not get state or much federal support, and often their curriculum is too general for the many students who want specialized courses. State colleges have identity problems; they are caught between community colleges and universities. Community colleges are spreading across the country as the answer to the American dream of higher education for all. Their open-door policy promotes the equality of opportunity through minimal entrance requirements and minimal fees. However, created as vocational as well as two-year liberal arts schools, they must develop counseling services that fit each student into his proper program. All of these institutions are in need of policies and funds for construction, student aid, and special programs. Much of the solution to their problems lies in the purse strings of the federal government. They must be supported now.

The dramatic rise in the number of adults seeking additional education and in the number of community colleges and other adult-education oriented institutions which attempt to satisfy their demands bring us to a central premise of any people's platform. Education is a continuing process. It is not something to be offered for a set number of years and then set aside. Like health services, education should be made available to every American from birth until death. It should begin with federally supported child care and development centers, as I propose in Chapter 7, and it should never be withdrawn.

One of the most glaring inequities in our present approach toward education is the exclusion from the continuing education process of millions of working Americans who do not have the financial resources or the available time. Trapped in a work-a-day environment, the adult's education virtually comes to a halt while elsewhere new discoveries are made, new information is acquired, and new educational techniques are perfected. He is continually frustrated to discover that his children at home and the recently graduated employee at work have received knowledge inaccessible to him.

I suggest this is unfair to the individual and wasteful for society. Better educated people make better citizens and better workers. Therefore, I propose that every American worker be afforded the opportunity to avail himself of a year's educational sabbatical leave once every ten years. Financed by a combination of his Citizen's Wage, set forth in chapter 6, and the amount of unemployment compensation required to provide him with a total income equal to his current annual salary, the individual could then elect either to enhance his formal education or job skills through classroom study and specialized training programs, broaden his knowledge and cultural awareness through travel, devote his time to help correct a social ill by working with the poor, the sick, and the disadvantaged, or, if he prefers, rejuvenate his mental and physical capabilities through rest and relaxation. The totally educated man, after all, is not the product of the classroom alone, he is the sum of his experiences and activities at all levels of society.

The concept of educational sabbaticals is not new. Teachers periodically are granted time off to travel and otherwise acquire fresh understanding and information which can be translated into more effective and meaningful classes in the schoolroom. Industry and government, too, recognize the value of continually upgrading the performance and the worth of selected employees by sending them to colleges and universities so they can keep abreast of improved management procedures and technological developments. A few industries, in fact, have established educational programs of their own, not merely to improve skills related to the performance of a particular job, but to raise the overall educational level of the employee. More of this needs to be done at all levels of the economic spectrum. How much better it would be, however, if each individual had the opportunity to select for himself the educational programs he desires.

Eligibility for the sabbatical would be automatic for any person who has worked a total of ten years and would renew itself every ten years thereafter. A person's qualifying time would not be limited to the number of years spent in any one job, but would be accumulated and transferred with the worker if and when he changed positions. A potential employer, in this way, would know when the employee's sabbatical would take effect and could plan for a temporary replacement or a rejuggling of responsibilities and duties needed to fill the gap caused by the worker's absence. Instead of asking whether any individual's military service obligation has been met, the employer would want to know when his sabbatical is due.

Imagine the benefits to be accrued to the economy alone. Thousands of sabbatical workers each year would travel, enroll in schools, and engage in new activities. They would stimulate increased services, buy new products, spend money in different places. It could not help but mean more jobs and a more viable economy. Most important, however, it would keep faith with a people's platform that demands we provide continuing educational opportunities for all ages and at all levels.

11

Shaping Our Future Energy Policies

*We travel together, passengers on
a little spaceship . . . preserved
from annihilation only by the care
and, I will say, the love we give
our fragile craft.*

—*Adlai Stevenson*

IT MAY STRIKE SOME PEOPLE as odd that anyone from Alaska
with its rich deposits of oil and coal (yes, there's a vast amount
of coal there, too) would be concerned about the production
of energy in the year 2000. But I am concerned, very concerned, about the environmental impact of civilization's in-
satiable demand for heat and light and power-driven machinery. We are burning up oil and gas at an alarming rate. In 30
to 50 years most of those billions of gallons of oil under the
North Slope and elsewhere will have been pretty well pumped
up and burned. Coal supplies may last 400 to 1,000 years
more, but the environmental problems of strip-mining and of
carbon-dioxide pollution are serious, and they remain even if
we convert the coal into clean gas and oil before we burn it. So
we had better develop other sources of energy or face the
prospect of lights which may go out, wheels which may stop,

177

or pollution which may threaten the fragile web of life itself.

The question that alarms me is what source of energy will we employ as an alternative. Our government and the energy production sector of our economy are pursuing the development of nuclear power almost to the exclusion of other far less dangerous sources of energy. I consider this to be an extremely unwise policy. It seems to me we are not thinking clearly about the long-range environmental hazards as we plunge ahead investing billions of dollars in the construction of nuclear reactors. We are rapidly becoming wedded to a course where we, as citizens, are given no right to choose the bride.

We appear to be captive of a guilt psychosis. Our leaders are burdened with the idea we have to prove atomic energy is good. It was the United States that wiped out Hiroshima and Nagasaki with atomic weapons, and we are driven to prove there are really benefits for mankind to be derived from the research which resulted in that terrible weapon of war, which only we have used. That is why we have an Atomic Energy Commission and an Atoms for Peace program, why the government has spent $3 billion in the past 17 years on nuclear energy development. And it is the main reason we haven't explored the broader spectrum of energy-producing sources. The most promising alternatives—fusion energy and solar energy —are potentially limitless in supply and, by any ecological yardstick, a million times cleaner and safer than atomic energy. (Fusion is a nonexplosive nuclear process which generates energy by combining rather than splitting atoms in a semigaseous state called a plasma.)

It is folly to allow a guilt psychosis to force us down a road that holds grave potential for contaminating our entire planet. What possible benefit can it be to mankind if we elect to pursue a form of energy whose by-products are the most deadly substance man can create—and just to boil water? For that's all a reactor is, a furnace which makes heat by the fission (splitting) of uranium atoms to boil water to turn a steam turbine. The by-product of this process is not a "little" harmful radioactivity from "burning" atomic fuel as the AEC would have us believe. The amount of radioactive waste, which is small only if measured by the space it fills, is already enormous if measured by the billions of people it could kill. If the plans of the AEC and other nuclear nations are realized, construction of 1,000 or more immense nuclear fission plants will be completed in the next 30 years. Every year these 1,000 plants operate, they will produce radioactive fission products equal to the debris of a million Hiroshima bombs.

All of this material must be contained in a Pandora's box— the reactors and many other boxes—to handle the constant deluge of wastes for thousands of years before the radioactivity will decay to the point where it is no longer lethal. Obviously, we are setting for ourselves a future environmental problem of impossible proportions.

Indeed, the AEC has discovered it already has a fantastic headache in the disposal of atomic "garbage." Presently the AEC is holding over 80 million gallons of high-level wastes, that is, extremely intense radioactive material, in leak-prone storage tanks. The tanks from government reactors and weapon-production are on AEC property. Tanks for commercial wastes are privately operated. The AEC wants to have the wastes solidified and buried somewhere—but no one will have them. The agency would like to squirrel them away in underground beds of salt in Kansas. The people of Kansas, however, are protesting because the AEC cannot prove it will be safe. There is a possibility the heat released by the casks of decaying radioactivity, or geological forces, could crack the salt. If the waste reaches water, radioactivity could then find its way into subterranean streams and poison drinking water. No one knows whether this would actually happen, just as no one knows what will result from all the radioactive waste that has been dumped in the oceans and is still being dumped by other nuclear powers. And that is precisely the point: we won't find out until it is too late—after the radioactivity has escaped.

I am convinced that our nuclear guilt complex also led to

the dropping of checks and balances which allowed the promoters of atomic energy to push us as far down this perilous road as they have. As citizens we have wanted to make amends for the awesome destruction our technology had wrought. Imbedded in our national conscience is a hope our nuclear scientists may yet right a wrong. This explains why we were willing, even eager, to give them plenty of latitude and why we have not imposed more careful scrutiny on the AEC's secrecy-shrouded activities.

Our attitude has been a mistake. It is imperative that a people's platform bring atomic energy—and the entire problem of developing ample amounts of safe energy—under firm citizen control. We must institute a system of checks and balances through scientific adversaries which will expose the true nature of the dangers of making the atom a part of our future, a next-door neighbor in our cities. And we must direct far more research funds into the nonnuclear technologies.

Energy is so fundamental to our existence, it is foolhardy to rely solely on the atom. A people's platform must insist on the restructuring of our research under an Energy Commission— an agency which will be charged with intelligent development of all feasible sources of power. The work of the Atomic Energy Commission should continue, but that work should represent only one of many areas of research under the unified direction of an energy commission. I do not advocate the abandonment of nuclear power research; there may be places on this earth where it is the only efficient method of generating electricity, provided the hazards of radioactivity can be safely managed. Our objective should be to develop concurrently every energy source, be it fusion, solar, geothermal, magneto-hydrodynamic, the winds, or the wave power of the oceans, and meld them all into a system. After all, when we developed our natural fossil fuel resources, we didn't single out just one and ignore the others. We have separate technologies embracing coal, oil, and gas, and even subtechnologies like the gasification of coal. We are never going to have the benefit of all the potential alternate energy sources, if we remain locked solely on our present nuclear fission course.

I hope we can learn by our past mistakes, and the biggest mistake is public ignorance. There is no room for ignorance when it comes to something as basic to society as energy, because we not only live by electricity, we must live with the generating plants. We have the right to know the danger any type of plant poses to our health and general welfare. Financial liability, when fully known and assumed, is an important check in itself.

In the field of nuclear energy it is a fact that the people who know the most about the danger—the government and the developers and operators of atomic plants—have the least financial liability. The people who know the least about it, because they haven't been told all the facts—the general public —have almost all the liability. This ridiculous situation has arisen through government insurance (and a limited amount of private insurance) of the nuclear industry under the Price-Anderson Act. This law is not widely known and the key provision sets the maximum liability for a nuclear accident at $560 million. However, numerous independent studies have shown the release of radioactive material from the core of a large power reactor near a population center could cause substantial loss of life and damages exceeding $8 billion. An entire city could be contaminated and rendered uninhabitable by one accident. Because of the limitation on liability, many victims of such an accident would be denied compensation. Obviously, such injustice is intolerable and wouldn't be tolerated if the public were fully informed.

The Atomic Energy Commission and the atomic energy industry contend the risk of an $8 billion accident, or any major release of radioactivity from a reactor, is exceedingly small. They claim to have mastered the problem of containment so that even if a reactor lost its cooling system and went out of control, there would be little or no danger to the surrounding population. In an interview, which appeared in the October

18, 1971, issue of *U.S. News and World Report,* Dr. Edward
E. David, Jr., President Nixon's science advisor, supported
this contention: "There could be a conflagration inside these
atomic reactors, but they are designed so that the risk of that
breaching the wall of the compartment is extremely small."

I say we should put this to the test. I have introduced legislation which would repeal the basic provisions of the Price-
Anderson Act. Let the nuclear industry assume its own financial liability and with no limitations. But, of course, the
industry doesn't like that idea. It doesn't want to lose its comfortable shelter.

Actually, the industry feels it cannot do without a shelter.
Not long ago I met in New York City with a group of bankers
who were heavily invested in nuclear utilities. They said they
regarded me as a responsible person and they couldn't understand why I would sponsor such "radical" legislation as repeal
of the Price-Anderson Act. One of the bankers, who considered
himself an expert in the field, said to me, "Don't you realize
your bill could bring the whole atomic power program to its
knees?" I replied, "If that is the case, it is better that we
brought the industry to its knees now before it is too late. If
atomic energy is dangerous, better that we face it now."

Then I asked the banker, "If you can't get private insurance
on a reactor, then why are you putting up your own money?"
It was a question he couldn't answer. It was a question which
seemed to strike him and everyone else in the ego. But when
I thought about it, who could expect a group of bankers to
suddenly admit they may have made a mistake and should
change their policy? Private bureaucracies are just as suscep-
tible as the government is to hide or fudge unpleasant facts.
It is always more convenient to look at what you may have
done right than what you may have done wrong.

In a way, the bankers have been taken in like everyone else.
I honestly believe they don't have a full appreciation for the
dangers inherent in nuclear energy because, like the rest of us,
they haven't been told all the facts. The cocoon of obfuscation

woven by the AEC is difficult to penetrate. And when you combine the withholding of unsavory evidence with a concerted propaganda campaign extolling the wonders of "clean" atomic electricity, it is easy to be misled.

Congress must bear its share of the responsibility for the deceptive selling of atomic energy. The Joint Atomic Energy Committee, created because of the unique aspects of atomic weaponry and its peaceful applications, is supposed to be the primary check on AEC activities through legislation. However, the Joint Committee has come to act like a board of directors of the AEC and, like a private corporate board of directors, it is prone to manipulation by the management. Rather than being an adversary, the Joint Committee became an advocate of almost everything the AEC wanted. In Congress, therefore, we have what you might term a built-in structural cop-out. I might add that the Joint Committee is not alone in this fault. The same cop-outs occur through the Armed Services and other committees with a proprietary interest in particular segments of government and industry.

Over the years the Joint Committee, composed of members from both the House and Senate, has fostered a policy of creating a private nuclear power industry with the ultimate aim of making it self-sufficient and free from government subsidy. Outwardly this would appear to be a sound policy. But in practice it is as defective as it is shortsighted.

In the first place, the Joint Committee should never have permitted the AEC to assume its present all-powerful role. The AEC is charged with developing and fostering the peaceful uses of the atom and at the same time it holds sole authority to license nuclear plants and regulate their safety. It is judge, jury, witness, defendant, and plantiff, all at once.

Secondly, it is an error to allow the AEC to make both peace and war. The weapons program and the peaceful atomic energy program should have been separated and placed in independent agencies, the latter, as I have suggested, in an energy commission.

It must be granted that those pushing atomic power are men of good will. But I was very disturbed to learn not too long ago that a certain degree of cynicism surrounded the start of the Atoms for Peace program. It was actually the Pentagon which gave the program its impetus. Leaders of the defense department were concerned how Americans would react to the fact that nuclear bombs were rolling off the assembly line and being shipped around the country and around the world. It was feared there would be an outcry and it was decided a ploy was needed to overcome the citizens' natural abhorrence of these weapons. The result was a public relations hard sell of the peaceful uses of the atom to build up the public's tolerance and acceptance of the proliferation and possible use of atomic weapons. As we can see today the strategy was highly successful.

The Joint Committee apparently never perceived what was happening, just as Congress as a whole never realized that it was making a mistake in focusing all our energy research on the atom. It is unfortunate but true; Congress allowed itself to be mesmerized by the AEC's flatulent claims that given the money its scientists could tame the atom to do any kind of trick. Only in recent years has the thinness of these claims shown through.

In the meantime, however, the $3 billion "seed" money sown by the government in nuclear power research has spawned a substantial and growing industry. Private sources, like my banker friends, have invested $17 billion and are prepared to put up more. Perhaps another $100 billion by the year 2000. We have in this industry a number of growing interests having high stakes in the economic success of the atomic reactor program—the people who mine and process uranium into reactor fuel rods, the contractors and equipment manufacturers who build the power plants, and the utilities who operate them. There are more and more jobs involved as the capital investment grows and feeds upon itself.

We cannot allow this investment to grow any larger until

we take stock of where we are heading. I am very suspicious of the AEC's ambiguity regarding radiation hazards. If they are correct in their safety claims, they should welcome a public dialogue. But just declaring they are doing the right thing by the world isn't enough. They are human beings and they are capable of human error. It has the familiar ring of our early days in the Indochina war, the statement "we're doing the right thing—just trust us."

The same sort of rhetoric is being employed by President Nixon and his advisors to justify the spending of more billions to develop a "second generation" reactor, the so-called plutonium breeder. In July, 1971, the President announced he had selected the breeder reactor as "our best hope today" for meeting the electricity demands of tomorrow. Several months later, to a small audience of atomic workers at Hanford, Washington, Nixon conceded, however, "this business about breeder reactors and nuclear energy is over my head." He went on to express confidence in science, observing "in terms of nuclear power we must not be afraid. We must explore it."

Regrettably, Nixon has not expressed the same confidence in, nor requested substantial money for, expanded research to master the technologies of fusion and solar energy which have little or no vested interests. The administration's position, as enunciated by science advisor Dr. David, is to give the alternate energy sources lip service and token funding. David contends "it will be another 30 years before we see the fusion reaction producing power on a commercial scale. Hopefully, we will solve the basic problems within three to five years. Then there will be another 20 to 25 years of work to solve the many engineering problems." David avoided the fact that fusion research is receiving minimal federal funding, a total of $450 million over the past 17 years, compared to $3 billion for the fission program. (Solar research has received only $1 million of tax dollar support in the same time period.)

Nor did David say what a concerted effort comparable to the nuclear fission program would do for his projected fusion timetable. But even assuming it would take 30 years to become commercially viable, why must we rush off now on the breeder reactor route? What can be wrong about spending a few more years to do the research into fusion and solar power to gather the information on which to decide the wisest course? The decision could determine the future of the planet.

This view is supported by Dr. Hannes Olof Alfvén, the winner of the 1970 Nobel Prize for Physics. In April, 1971, he wrote me as follows:

> In the long run fossil fuels cannot satisfy the rising energy demand in the world. There are only three sources of energy known which are sufficiently powerful.
>
> (a) Solar energy
> (b) Fusion energy
> (c) Fission energy
>
> The first one is completely pollution-free, the second one almost pollution-free. The third one is necessarily combined with production of large quantities of radioactive poisonous elements.
>
> In my opinion, the dangers associated with the fission energy have not received necessary attention. Whether the pollution caused by fission reactors in normal operation is below a safe level or not is a controversial matter. If a reactor goes out of control, the consequences may be terrible. Even if extreme safety precautions are taken, the large quantities of radioactive material in them, constitute a permanent danger. For example, in periods of political or social unrest, sabotage against reactors may cause catastrophes. Furthermore, in a full scale fission programme, the radioactive waste will soon become so enormous that a total poisoning of our planet is possible. Under such conditions safety margins which are acceptable in other fields, are inadequate. It is not evident whether the waste problem can be solved in a satisfactory way.
>
> If solar energy or fusion energy were available now at comparable cost, no one would use fission energy (for peaceful purposes). Unfortunately this is not the case. Solar energy is available but at prohibitive cost. However, there are new interesting solar energy projects which should be examined carefully.
>
> Concerning the fusion energy, there is a general agreement that

no fundamental obstacle is likely to prevent the construction of a fusion reactor but there are a number of difficult scientific and technical problems which must be solved. There is much speculation about how much time is needed to solve these problems, but it is just as much a question of how much effort has to be spent.

In my opinion a solution of the fusion problem is less distant today than the Moon was when the Apollo project was started. This means that if a national effort of the same kind as the Apollo programme were now made, the fusion energy would be available in a comparable time. If this is achieved, the fission reactor, especially the breeder, will be of interest only as a danger which must be eliminated as soon as possible.

The views expressed here are shared by many competent physicists. They are basically different from those on which the present policy is based. An important decision about the future energy policy of the USA—and the whole world—should not be made until a thorough discussion has taken place involving advocates for all the three different alternatives for solving the energy problem.

It is significant to me that our government has never entertained public debate on this fateful issue. The AEC harps on the coming energy "crisis" as if it were just around the corner, indeed, as if there were no time for rational discussion. We must lunge ahead immediately with the breeder reactor and erection of nuclear plants or all is lost, we are told, because our consumption of electricity is doubling every ten years. Utilities are employing the same tactic: don't get in our way, we haven't a moment to lose. Electrical demand is king and must be served.

Strangely, there is virtually no mention of energy conservation or what could be done to stretch out our fossil fuel reserves. Why is it that the utilities continue to adhere to a regressive rate structure which encourages consumption by lowering the per kilowatt hour cost to the customer as he uses more power? Why are the utilities continuing advertising campaigns to switch to "all-electric homes"? Why aren't consumers being encouraged to use less power by turning the rate structure and the propaganda in the opposite direction? Obviously the "crisis" has not reached the point where the utilities can possibly think in terms of reducing their revenues. But citizens can.

The question of generating national debate in the absence of governmental encouragement must be resolved. In 1971, as one possible recourse, I proposed legislation to provide funds for major debates on nuclear safety and hazards among scientists of opposing views. The debates, to be held publicly, would be conducted before a jury of scientists who would clear up the reasons for the disagreements and report their findings to the public. In this way vital information would be brought into the open on which to base an intelligent policy, but whether such a series of debates will come about is another matter. However, as citizens we can't afford to wait for such a device to halt the nuclear juggernaut. Many citizens have already perceived this.

Citizen power presently is being exerted effectively to hold up construction of numerous nuclear plants around the country. People are learning to organize, to bring suits, to use the legal provisions in the AEC's licensing procedures and Environmental Protection Act statements to voice their objections. The efforts of individuals and groups have had a remarkable impact in policing the industry where Congress has failed. The AEC, for example, has been compelled to tighten up on its standards regulating the amount of radiation that is permitted to leak into the air and water from reactors. It was citizen scientists in universities who first raised the problem of thermal pollution—the ecological changes caused by heating of lakes, rivers, and streams by water used to cool power plants. In Chicago the Citizen's Action Program organized residents to withhold payment of their electrical bills and to put the money in escrow until Commonwealth Edison did something about its pollution practices.

In June, 1972, Californians, who represent one out of every ten Americans, are to vote yes or no on an initiative which includes a five-year moratorium on nuclear power plants and many other measures to restore a healthy environment in the state. If California's citizen initiative wins, the legislature cannot water it down or repeal it.

Nineteen other states have constitutions permitting similar citizen initiatives. They are: Alaska, Arizona, Arkansas, Colorado, Idaho, Maine, Massachusetts, Michigan, Missouri, Montana, Nebraska, Nevada, North Dakota, Ohio, Oklahoma, Oregon, South Dakota, Utah, and Washington.

Clearly, paths have been opened to combat the nuclear incursion on the local, regional, and federal levels. A logical next step is to form a coalition of concerned citizens to shape our overall energy policies on the national level. We must widen the debate, through Congress and across the land, on the issue of whether we want to gamble our lives and the planet's future on a radio-active source of energy or develop safer nonpolluting sources of electrical power.

Early in 1972 a coalition of 60 citizen environmental groups formed the National Intervenors to challenge the AEC's criteria for reactor safety systems. The systems are intended to stop a reactor from melting down and bursting a radio-active steam cloud over the surrounding population in the event the reactor loses its primary coolant system. In AEC hearings, still under way at this writing, the Intervenors had succeeded in gaining admissions from the AEC's own top experts that they did not think the present emergency systems were technically "defensible." In other words the AEC now has been shown to doubt severely the safety of its own product.

12

Of Crimes and Punishments

As long as we permit unfair laws to exist, deny speedy trials or equal justice to all, and operate prisons to punish rather than to rehabilitate, our society will be guilty of a far greater crime than any committed by those it prosecutes.

—*Walter Karabian*
(California Assemblyman)

ALL NATIONS and their governments must choose one of two fundamental risks. One is to seek total control of the lives of their citizens, so as to ensure "order" and "security," but at the risk of a bloody and destructive revolution when the collective human spirit can no longer abide such repression. The other is to risk the broadest possible freedom for all citizens, in the belief that people in a democratic society will so flourish in such freedom that their national common sense will ultimately repulse the periodic tides of demagoguery or anarchy which flow in and out of the lives of all nations.

The founding fathers of the United States emphatically chose to take the risk that comes with freedom, and they embodied it in that remarkable document known as the Bill of Rights.

Unfortunately, a repressive climate has developed in this country in the past few years, which is distinctly threatening to the fundamental protections which the Bill of Rights seeks to provide for every American. Equally disturbing is a recent poll (CBS News Poll, March 20, 1970) showing that, when the provisions of the Bill of Rights were read to a cross-section of Americans, they either did not recognize them, opposed certain provisions (76 percent would restrict the right to peaceful protest), or, according to a wire service poll taken in California, thought they sounded "communist."

Many thoughtful people today contend that America is currently living in an atmosphere of repression. I agree. Dramatic reforms must be made if we are to reverse the trend toward repression and return to the ideals this country supposedly represents.

Many factors have contributed to the current climate of repression. Most of them are rather obvious: our huge and rapidly growing population, our crowded cities, our complicated technology, our economic interdependence, our gigantic governmental structure, our huge, hungry and ever-growing inanimate economic units known as corporations, our racial divisions, and the divisions created by the breathtakingly rapid changes in our life style stemming from technology, such as widespread displacement and the increasing awareness by the have-nots in our society of the many goods and pleasures readily available to the middle and wealthy classes.

It is perhaps this increased awareness by the have-nots— an awareness sharpened by the arrival of television and the general explosion of information through media—that is most responsible for today's climate of repression, for it has evoked strong reactions from those who are better off. The poor, the black, the Puerto Rican, Spanish-American, and Indian minorities are ever more mindful that it is they who are afflicted by our system of unequal justice, it is they who fill our prisons, it is they who languish in our death rows, and it is they to whom the doors of equal employment opportunity, equal housing, and equal education are kept shut.

As this arising awareness results in increasing demands, America's great uninvolved mass of middle- and upper-class citizens are forced to confront new ideas which are often alien, even hostile, to them. Integration? School busing? Open housing? Welfare? As protests from racial minorities and the poor are multiplied by groups of women, students, migrant farm workers, the old, the counterculture, and the antiwar, those with the traditional keys to power often become confused and feel threatened. They have already been conditioned to put the blame on phantoms by living through a generation in which anything and anyone "different" was "communist" and could therefore be put down with clear conscience. If control of the threatening ideas meant making exceptions to protections supposedly guaranteed all citizens, so be it. Necessity dictated it and, besides, it wouldn't really affect the good people.

As pressures increased despite efforts to suppress demands for justice, those seeking to halt change—the comfortable, settled, generally contented, and traditional middle—sought more controls. Not control over the conditions creating the pressures, of course, but over the people who protested against those conditions. Most of what the people in power saw as menacing could most conveniently be lumped under the broad stereotype "crime" and its twin "permissiveness."

One of the traditional acts in any effort to control people who would upset the status quo with new demands has been to repress the avenues of communication through which these persons sharpen their awareness and make known their demands. America today is no exception. Freedom of speech, freedom of assembly and freedom of the press—all guaranteed by the First Amendment—have never been under heavier attack.

As Franklin Haiman, Professor of Urban Affairs at Northwestern University, noted in a recent pamphlet:

Holders of power, when seriously challenged, tend to respond repressively. Hence, the most intense controversies over freedom of expression in America have swirled around those groups which have been on the cutting edge of the social change process, those most profoundly discontented with the status quo and most aggressive in urging its reform.

Haiman also observes that the more the holders of power

feel that freedom of expression threatens to be effective, that it represents significant and growing power, the greater their intolerance becomes. Shortsightedly, they imagine that by suppressing expression they can hold onto the status quo. Free speech, in their view, may be allowable when it is relatively harmless, but when speakers mean business, it becomes a luxury they feel they cannot afford.

I seriously doubt if the United States has ever had a national administration whose personnel, from top to bottom, have been so uniformly lacking in an understanding of the indispensable role a free press plays in a democratic society and so unremittingly hostile to that role.

The high (or, in this case, low) water mark was reached in June, 1971, when for the first and only time in our entire history, newspapers were officially prevented by the federal government from publishing something they deemed newsworthy. The event, of course, was the suppression of the Pentagon Papers. It marked an attempt, successful for 15 days, by the government to suppress disclosure of material revealing the moral bankruptcy and intellectual ineptness of the men primarily responsible for conducting an illegal war which has killed hundreds of thousands of innocent people and has torn at the very fibers of our nation. The material was kept classified for the obvious motive of covering up official ineptitude and protecting those responsible. It had nothing to do with "national security." Its disclosure was in the highest tradition of the responsibility of a free press to provide citizens the fullest possible information about the performance of their paid public servants. The government's action was a clear violation of First Amendment free press guarantees. Even more unsettling, the Supreme Court's too close 6-3 decision seemed to leave the door open to further such actions by deciding the case on the narrowest of grounds, all but ignoring the fundamental principle—the First Amendment— which should have guided the decision and made it an easy one to reach.

But if the Pentagon Papers marked the low point in the administration's acknowledgment that we are bound by a Constitution and a Bill of Rights, there were plenty of other instances along the way. Among them:

Explosive attacks on the broadcast media by the Vice-President, with thinly veiled warnings that official pressure could be brought to bear through federal licensing powers if the news was not presented in ways more pleasing to those holding that power.

Subpoenas of reporters, their notes, even unused TV film, for the purpose of forcing disclosure of confidential sources—a step which would clearly restrict reporters' ability to ferret out news.

Efforts by the attorney general to establish his "right" to wiretap or bug, without a warrant, any citizen whom he deems a security risk (this in the face of the fact that the same man is the chief political operative for the President); arguments by then-Assistant Attorney General William Rehnquist that no court orders were needed for this practice because citizens could rely on the "restraint" of the executive.

Intelligence officials and informers posing as reporters.

Efforts by the House of Representatives to issue a contempt citation against CBS for its refusal to submit to the government all film used in preparing the documentary "Selling of the Pentagon" (the House finally rejected this move by the disturbingly close vote of 226 to 181).

Use of ridiculously vague "conspiracy" laws to defuse the legal efforts of peaceful antiwar groups, and the use of equally vague laws against persons who cross state lines with the alleged intent of causing a riot. How anyone determines what thoughts were in the mind of a person so accused or just what thoughts are "illegal" is left vague enough to support the impression that illegal thoughts consist basically of ideas displeasing to the administration in power at the time of the arrest.

Excessively heated attacks by the Vice-President against the 500,000 Americans who exercised their right to peaceful dissent by attending the 1969 Vietnam Moratorium, in which he implied that citizens opposed to the war are anarchists or communists, whom the country can "afford to separate . . . from our society." This same administration could contend that the speech of others, holding far less powerful positions, was an incitement to riot, but apparently saw no connection between the vitriolic language of the Vice-President and the subsequent series of savage attacks by hardhats on completely peaceful war protestors in New York and other cities.

The actions of the Department of Justice in sending agents to make inquiries of transportation companies under contract to transport citizens to the November 15, 1969, Vietnam Moratorium.

Massive surveillance by the Army of the perfectly legal political activities of thousands of Americans, and the cancer-like growth of the use of police informers inside political organizations.

The virtual absence of TV coverage of the 1969 Moratorium—surely the largest mass protest in American history—apparently due to the chilling effect of the administration's battering ram attacks on the broadcast media concurrently with its equally strong diatribes against citizens seeking an end to the Vietnam war.

A presidential executive order of July 27, 1971, authorizing snoopers of the House Internal Security Committee to inspect more than 20 years of tax records of any person or organization in this country; a presidential executive order of July 2, 1971, expanding the power of the Subversive Activities Control Board to condemn and blacklist organizations for activities they regard as "subversive" and to bar their members from federal employment. This is an effort at thought control in its purest form.

Mass arrests in the May Day demonstrations in Washington in 1971, in which dragnet tactics were used, thousands of innocent persons were arrested without any evidence whatsoever, arrest forms were falsified, and citizens were detained illegally in unsanitary, unhealthy facilities.

WHILE ALL THESE CONDITIONS were developing, the phenomenon popularly called "crime in the streets" was also growing. The increase in violent crime was, and is, very real and very serious. The trouble is that those resisting necessary social change have tried to cloak their opposition to it by labeling all the protest movements—most of which have been over-whelmingly peaceful—as crime in the streets. This served the double purpose of justifying social denials while refusing to correct them.

But it did not do anything toward solving the real crime problem. The policy, at best, could only fight a holding action. In the words of Albert Seedman, Chief of Detectives of the New York City Police Department, "Robbery grows out of social unrest, out of poverty and out of a society that is in flux. We can't do much about these root causes of robbery, but we can arrest more of the robbers." That may have been an answer. It is not a solution.

"Solution," indeed, took the form of a "law and order" campaign for the presidency by Richard Nixon in 1968, with its strong racial overtones and the implication that more cops, more guns, more toughness, no more coddling, and—presto!—no crime.

It didn't work out that way. During each of the three years of the Nixon-Mitchell crackdown approach, violent street crime went up and up. Meanwhile, in 1970, the nation had 13 percent of its total population living below the poverty level. These 25.5 million persons had increased by 5.1 percent over the previous year, the first time since compilation of this data had been begun in 1959 by the Bureau of the Census that the number had not decreased. Until 1970, there had been an average 4.9 percent decline each year.

The number of Americans receiving welfare assistance had grown from 9,274,000 in 1968 to 14,399,000 in 1971. The number of unemployed had risen from 2,817,000 in 1968 to 4,600,000 in 1971. If such staggering figures cannot demonstrate the real problem, nothing can.

Russell G. Oswald, Commissioner of Corrections of New York State, pinpointed the real problem succinctly: "Society has done damn little in ending poverty and illiteracy that provide the seeds of unrest and problems that lead people to prisons."

The nation also had a serious new problem: while our highest officials were busy condemning college students for protesting a war which these officials themselves soon stopped defending, a genuine threat was building within the ranks of another mass of young people—the children of ghetto whites, blacks, and Puerto Ricans.

Author Shane Stevens, who spent years living in their neighborhoods and writing about them, explained in his November 28, 1971 article in *The New York Times Magazine:*

> By the start of the seventies, the country's racial rupture and economic inequalities had filtered through to consciousness in the minds of the youthful poor. Black power—and the White Power backlash, especially among the frightened poor whites in the cities—set color as the determinant of one's enemies. The depressed economy meant even less money in the slums, and the young, as always, were the first to feel the crunch. Spending money had to be got from the outside, and so the whole city became the arena. Rip offs were to be done anywhere, to anybody— preferably to a member of another race, religion, nationality or culture, but basically anyone with money. Violence became an accident of time and place.
>
> The phenomenon is now seemingly endemic to large cities. In New York, as might be expected, it involves predominately those youths who have the least opportunity and the most grievances— largely, but far from exclusively, black and Spanish-speaking residents. While the gangs and groups of the past fed on their own, today's rat packs, formed along racial lines—all white or Puerto Rican or black—feed on everybody else.

The lesson is clear. More police, more jails, more tough talk will not help. None of these traditionally instinctive reactions to crime can stem the rising tide. So long as injustice and inequity in the larger society exist on the gross scale that they do today, all the reasoning and rhetoric and police clubs in the world will not stop the have-nots from going after the goods they seek through the only avenue they feel is open to them—crime. So long as we delay the basic reforms, that long will our cities continue to half-exist, in fear, behind locked doors.

Over ten years ago, Dr. James B. Conant, the educator, warned that we are seeding "social dynamite" in our cities by the enforced idleness due to failures of schools, jobs, housing, and recreation of hundreds of thousands of young people. "When hope dies, its heirs are desperation and despair," said Conant. Today that prophecy has come true. Hope has indeed died, and desperation is embodied in the social dynamite we call street crime. During the second quarter of 1971, for example, the teen-age ghetto black unemployment rate was a staggering 39.4 percent, compared with 4.6 percent for adult whites. For black adults between ages 20 and 24, unemployment was 19 percent. We are paying a price for those figures. The price is the random, desperate, unpredictable nature of today's bold, hit-and-run street crimes, and the universal fear that results from it.

As long as we maintain policies that confine the poor and the colored to ghettos, deprive them of equal education, and keep them in the lowest job categories, they will be the victims of their desperation, but we will be the victims of our fear. So no one wins. The only way out is for America— white America, with its access to all the levers of power that make our society go—to face this truth, put aside its selfishness and prejudice (even if that requires doing it through legislation and the courts), and open up the avenues of escape from and improvement of what are now ghettos. A people's platform must present the ideas which can be the tools to bring about the necessary social and economic reforms. Some of them are not new. Indeed, some are decades old. But they have either never been tried or never been given the chance to work.

A BROAD RANGE OF CHANGES must be made in the way we operate our system of law. When we see hundreds of laws prohibiting people from doing what they would otherwise do (or *do* do anyway) in large numbers, then public "order" is artificial, coerced, and unstable, because respect for law is shallow.

The people will accept order when it is based on equitable representation, fair taxation, humane utilization of people and resources, and opportunity for free and open discussion, dissent, protest, and access to information.

The people will accept order when the laws make sense and when they are equally enforced. One of the largest areas of abuse today, one that affects millions of citizens because it touches on their daily activities and personal preferences, is in the category of crimes known as "victimless crimes," i.e., activities relating to drinking, gambling, sex, and drugs, which will be discussed later in this chapter.

This is an area in which everyone can see that the law is grossly misused, because it is enforced in an obviously unequal way, because it is hypocritical, because it relates to activities which most people do not regard as a crime, and because often these laws are used only as a means for punishing selected individuals while ignoring the rest. For example, it was common, not very long ago, to see so-called drug raids being made on places where antiwar activists were known to gather. Obviously, no great social good was accomplished if the police happened to discover a marijuana cigarette in someone's shoebox; the real goal was to harass, intimidate, and neutralize people who made the government's war policies look as bad as they actually were.

The police power of the state is so pervasive and overpowering when juxtaposed against an individual or small groups that we must continually overcompensate with our checks and balances in favor of individual freedom. Without this effort and the relentless vigilance by citizens, the state can undertake new repression and warp old safeguards, as is being done by the Nixon administration. One of the most important legal protections Americans possess, for example, is the grand jury, which is intended as a device to hear whether sufficient evidence exists to warrant arrest and prosecution of a suspected offender. The Department of Justice has radically shifted this role by activating a nationwide pattern of using grand juries as "fishing expeditions" to seek evidence which approved law enforcement methods have failed to unearth (most of the time because the evidence does not exist).

During 1970–1971, some 13 federal grand juries were used in this manner as part of the government's attempt to suppress three politically active groups: young new left radicals, antiwar intellectuals, and the Catholic left. Author-lawyer Frank Donner, who made a study of the practice, observed that the grand jury subpoena was becoming the government's substitute for the badly discredited congressional witch hunt committees of the 1950s. The present administration sought to revive in 1971 the same witch hunt approach, through a broad, but probably unconstitutional, expansion of the powers of the moribund Subversive Activities Control Board, thus further shifting initiative in the security areas from Congress to the executive.

Attempts to unearth the means through which the Pentagon Papers were given to their rightful owners, the American people, were made through grand jury fishing expeditions in Boston and Los Angeles. What an irony that the grand jury system, which was a tool designed to protect citizens from the police power of the state, should be used to thwart acquisition of a study paid for by the citizens and to be used as the knowledge base upon which to exercise collective judgments concerning their own affairs.

Attempts to stymie the Catholic left were channeled through the even more remarkable grand jury proceedings in Harrisburg, which sought to justify the wild charges made before Congress by J. Edgar Hoover in which he accused the Berrigan brothers and others of plotting to blow up heating tunnels under Washington and kidnap presidential advisor Henry Kissinger. Unable to back up the charges, but unwilling to discredit Hoover publicly, the Justice Department employed its new policy of indicting first and then seeking supporting evidence by interrogating witnesses in the grand jury room, a rather shocking distortion of law and order by a regime professing dedication to law and order.

Indeed, so flimsy was the Harrisburg case that the government eventually replaced its original indictment with what is called a superseding indictment. The superseding indictment was worded so that the government could obtain a conviction without ever proving a bombing-kidnapping plot at all! Relegating the alleged bomb plot to a minor role, the government inserted new charges, accusing the defendants (from whose ranks they had already dropped the name of Daniel Berrigan) of plotting to destroy draft files in several cities. Of course, the defendants had already publicly admitted the latter actions as a matter of principle, but by convicting them of acts they had already confessed, the Justice Department apparently hoped to confuse the public by giving the impression that the defendants had been convicted of the initial, hugely publicized charges and that Hoover had saved the nation once again from another fiendishly diabolical plot by dangerous subversives.

That any democratic government would go this far to repress opponents of its own discredited war policy is unnerving enough. That it would so distort vital judicial safeguards in the process is even worse. Since rules currently defining the role of the grand jury are apparently vulnerable to abuse by officials who do not respect the law, a people's platform must include strict new limitations to protect against further such distortions. Citizens selected for jury duty who see its perversion in this manner should reject it.

Our personal freedom must be protected from another insidiously expanding practice, one which stands in sharp juxtaposition to the highly sophisticated invasions I have just mentioned. That is the practice of so-called "no-knock" entries by police into private residences. We must restore strict observance of the principle that no searches may be conducted without a warrant. No-knock laws must be repealed, along with that odd set of laws which springs from the same mentality, preventive detention laws. I describe them as being odd because it is odd, to say the least, that some public servants apparently feel that they are omniscient enough to know which arrested persons will commit crimes, if released on bail, and which persons won't.

Even more repugnant are the so-called conspiracy laws, which again require that police be mind readers in order to enforce them. The conspiracy laws, like the no-knock laws, have proved nothing more than another tool for arresting political activists. They have done nothing to deter actual crime, and they should be repealed.

Certainly one of the most basic planks of a people's platform is the reassertion of one of the most fundamental intentions of our Constitution: the right to dissent. We must encourage, not discourage, those among us who are moved to dissent and to nonviolent civil disobedience. Dissent has played a consistently vital part in our nation's finest achievements going all the way back to her very founding.

In the face of the disappointing determination of the Nixon administration to stifle dissent, through the abuse of administrative authority, citizens must call out for the strongest possible support for reestablishing a climate in which full appreciation of freedom's most profound meanings can flourish Since every citizen is ultimately responsible for what his country does (or at least so the United States said in prosecuting men for "crimes against humanity" at Nuremburg), the platform must stress that the final power of every citizen is the power to say "No"—the right to dissent. The people must never forget that without them, their rulers are helpless.

To foster the climate of free and open dissent, we must modify all laws which lend themselves to thwarting legitimate protest. Laws ranging from trespass to disorderly conduct, public nuisance, and unlawful assembly must be modified to protect responsible protest and resistence. Civil disobedience should be protected by jury nullification in the favor of defendants when the public conscience is at stake.

The right to dissent must be recognized as extending through that most extreme situation in which the state may place its citizens, the right to refuse to kill or support killing by the state. This means, as I proposed in an earlier chapter, a prompt return to our long tradition of no obligatory military service except in times of extreme and declared national emergency (the peacetime draft is a relatively new phenomenon, having established itself only since World War II).

IN ADDITION to reasserting the protections that are vital to our basic political and social freedom, drastic reform must be made in another major area: our entire philosophy of criminal law and our dual system of justice. We can no longer tolerate one system of justice for persons with money and another for those without it.

Americans have acknowledged the truth of dual justice for a long time, but have done nothing about it. Why is this? Some observers believe that along with our system of laws, which has always reflected our desire to impose white middle-class values on everyone else—whether through the slaughter of American Indians and the forcing of their children into training schools or the repeated oppression of each new immigrant group—guilt about the gulf which separates our material comfort and security from poverty and oppression accounts for some of the irrational fear and even hatred exhibited toward the poor and the oppressed.

Our system of crime and punishment is so grossly weighted against the moneyless that it seems impossible it could exist in any society that is even remotely fair-minded. Pay the bail or go to jail. That is the fact of it, and being poor is too often the real crime. Abhorrent as I find the advocacy of preventive detention by the Nixon administration, the truth is that we have actually practiced preventive detention for years on a wide scale. Over half the prisoners in our county jails, just for one example, have not been convicted of anything; they are simply locked up awaiting trial.

If we accept the idea that much of what we traditionally call crime is the result of the deprivations of life in the slums, we must face the fact that in locking up someone to prevent crimes that could be avoided by social reforms, we are making the prisoner a scapegoat rather than protecting ourselves from a public enemy. Former Governor Michael DiSalle, in his observations on prisoners in death row, put it this way: "During my experience as Governor of Ohio, I found men in death row had one thing in common: they were penniless."

In "Struggle for Justice," a recent study prepared for the American Friends Service Committee by a large team of experts, it is noted that this distortion of justice has historic roots. Fraud, bribery, commercial deception, embezzlement, and exploitation of the poor and helpless impose costs to their victims' lives, health, and property hundreds of times greater than those of conventional theft and robbery. But, noted the report, "In the nineteenth century, just as in our own, this systematic white-collar conduct was not what was meant by the crime crisis."

Our failure to prosecute all crimes equally and to redirect crime control efforts to the root causes of crime is perhaps best dramatized by the fact that police never even manage to arrest those who commit most muggings, robberies, and similar violent crimes. It is the height of hypocrisy and deception, then, to blame our serious crime problem on "permissive" court decisions, as was done in the 1968 presidential campaign. Most crimes never result in anyone's being brought into court in the first place. The crime problem will never approach solution until we face the real problem: inequality of opportunity, denial of basic rights, and unequal application of the law.

Reform of our system of criminal law is too large a topic to be covered in this limited space, but a few basic and immediate changes to be included in a people's platform would be these: police review boards composed of civilians from a true cross-section of each community; policemen assigned to patrol their own neighborhoods wherever possible; reversal of the present trend toward paramilitary police forces; effective redress for victims of police misconduct and the victims of the offender (which I will discuss later); reduction of the tactic of using arrests rather than summonses; almost total prohibition of pretrial detention; reaffirmation of every citizen's right to counsel; stronger protections against abuses of the interrogation-confession process; major reduction of the presently excessive discretionary power of prosecutors; restrictions on the overly broad sentencing discretion given to judges, discretion which results in shocking examples of unequal punishment for similar crime; renewed stress on appellate review of sentences; strict requirements for speedy trials; better salaries and broader social education for police, as well as opportunities for sabbatical leaves; expansion of the concept of a citizen's right to a jury of his peers, to include at least some jurors, not more than half, chosen by the defendant on the basis of his economic, religious, and ethnic definition of his peers; a truly full-scale attack on organized crime and total exposure and prosecution of all politicians and business figures implicated in it; and financial compensation paid by the state to victims of violent crimes.

This last idea—financial compensation by the state to victims of violent crimes—has already been established in at least seven states and has been proposed in the U.S. Senate for crimes involving federal law. The program has already met with success where it has been tried. In Maryland, for example, officials found that none of the apprehensions they felt upon passage of the program in 1968 proved to be justified. Patterned after the workman's compensation law, the program provides a top payment of $45,000. Victims can be compensated only if they cooperate with the police and only if they report the crime within 48 hours after its commission.

A federal program was introduced late in 1971 by Senator Mike Mansfield, calling for payments of up to $25,000. The bill would establish a grant program to the states so that individual compensation boards could be set up. As Senator Mansfield observed when he introduced the legislation, society has an obligation to compensate crime victims when it fails in its duty to protect them. Additional legislation on this issue was introduced in early 1972 by Senator John McClellan of Arkansas.

IF WE are to bring about these and many more reforms in the field of criminal justice, an intensive educational program is imperative to reduce today's widespread reactionary resistance to progressive change. A vital first step, of course, is an end to the simplistic, inflammatory, self-seeking rhetoric of politicians pursuing cheap votes through so-called law and order programs which provide neither law nor order nor justice.

Equally as important as a shift to calm, reasonable, and humane rhetoric, however, is a program setting the stage for reform by helping Americans take an educated look at the fallacies in a number of basic assumptions about crime.

First of all, why do we punish (and sometimes try to rehabilitate) offenders on the assumption that crime is a matter of individual pathology, when we have no scientific evidence that there is such an identifiable pathology or that it is treatable? And why, while we base our system of "treatment" on that assumption, do we continue it in the face of more convincing indications that criminal behavior, if we can generalize about it at all, is more likely to be the result of conditions of life in the slum and the ghetto? Furthermore, the assumptions we make about individual pathology are based on studies of that small percentage of offenders who are caught and defined; virtually no research exists which uses a control group consisting of persons who did not turn to crime. The sample we do study is further narrowed by the fact that virtually everyone in prison is from a poor or minority background; the percentage of white middle-class persons we actually jail is infinitesimal. So what we are actually operating today is a massive system of crime and punishment in which we really have no idea what we are doing or why we do it.

Another assumption we must question critically and painstakingly is why, in our system of individualized treatment, we give to prosecutors, judges, and correctional administrators a range of discretionary powers that we grant to no other authorities in our society, a range that is aptly described as "awesome in scope and by its nature uncontrollable." As the authors of "Struggle for Justice" point out, standards for making the countless individual decisions that determine the fate of anyone caught in the criminal process are "nonexistent or so vague as to be meaningless." Yet it is evidently accepted without question that absolute power does not corrupt when exercised by government agents upon criminals.

Those who fill the air with praise for this system, however, "would not for one moment surrender to the discretion of those same judges and agencies the assessment of their income and property taxes" in accordance with these same officials' individualized judgments on the person's value as a citizen. Indeed, say the authors,

> the best antidote to being swept off one's feet by the claims made for the necessity and importance of the discretion that permeates criminal justice administration is to [compare] criminal law with the laws governing taxation, corporations and commercial transactions. When it comes to matters concerning their vested interests, the men who have the power to write the law in this country give short shift to discretion. Criminal justice is the last surviving bastion of absolute legal discretion.

And so it is. Nowhere else in our system of law do individual administrators have so much discretion with the very life

and death powers they exercise over other human beings, beginning with the policeman's decision whether to bring in a
vagrant because of his skin color, through the hundreds of
vagaries of the trial process, to the staggering range of choices
open to judges (there is a black man named Lee Otis Johnson,
former head of Houston's Student Nonviolent Coordinating
Committee (SNCC), now serving 30 years in Texas for the
sale of a single marijuana cigarette), to the literally unlimited
discretion of wardens and prison guards who operate outside
the range of public scrutiny, and on to the equally excessive
discretion available to parole boards and parole officers, who
have the power to make self-fulfilling prophecies of any label
they choose to affix to persons in their power, from "good risk"
to "poor risk."

It is easy, if painful, to see that we must make an exhaustive
study of all the assumptions on which our system of criminal
justice is based and put its findings into action, even though
they will surely upset every myth we now accept without question. It is imperative, both in the name of humanity and for
the future internal peace of our nation, that we promptly en-
act the reforms which such a study will call for.

WE GENERALLY ACCEPT THE IDEA, for example, that our prisons are the last step in the course of a criminal proceeding.
We will have to readjust to the likely discovery that, more
often than not, prison is the first, not the last, step on the road
to a pattern of criminal behavior. Dostoevsky wrote: "The
degree of civilization in a society can be judged by entering
its prisons." Perhaps that is why we place our prisons in isolated areas and erect every possible barrier to their access by
the public. Perhaps, subconsciously we are ashamed and de-
graded by what we do in the name of "rehabilitating" criminals and "protecting" society. We know that our prisons do
neither. We know that they are schools for crime and that
most people who come out of them are less equipped to live
in peace with their society than when they went in. We know

they are a burden and a moral disgrace to our society, not a protection for society or a solution to the problem of crime.

Dr. J. Ray Langdon, President of the Alaska State Medical Association, sums it up this way:

> So long as any group of society can be looked on and treated as non-people or animals—in this case prisoners, convicted or not, in the past all hospitalized mentally ill—so long can the whole society be regarded as inhuman or depersonalized.

It will take a certain period of time to complete a thorough reappraisal and reform of our system of crime and punishment. Meanwhile, thousands of prisoners languish behind bars. Waiting for reform to come is no consolation or help to them. The needed reforms are encompassed in a document known as the Prisoners' Bill of Rights. It is based on three premises.

The first is that prisoners are entitled to every constitutional right exercised by the outside population except for those inherently inconsistent with the oppression of the institution. The burden must be on the institution to show why it is necessary to deprive inmates of certain rights, rather than on the inmates to show why they should not be deprived of them.

Secondly, since prisons are governmental institutions, the public has a right to information about the operation of prisons and access to the prisons. Prisoners have the right to public scrutiny of prisons for the same reason that the accused have a right to public trial. Any student taking a sociology course in college should be required to visit a prison for at least a day and a night.

And, thirdly, prisoners are dependent for their survival and well-being on the same essentials as their fellow citizens outside the walls. As an example, they should be able to organize themselves, with each prison being a unit, in a national prisoners' union. Their dues could go, among other things, toward the study of their own psychological and physical conditions. These studies could then be made public.

The Prisoners' Bill of Rights includes the following 12 provisions.

1. Unrestricted access to the courts and to confidential legal counsel from an attorney of the individual's choosing or from a public defender. Adequate opportunity to prepare legal writs.

2. Freedom from the actuality or threat of physical abuse whether by custodial personnel or other prisoners.

3. Adequate diet and sanitation, fresh air, exercise, prompt medical and dental treatment, and prescription drugs.

4. Maintenance of relationships by frequent meetings and uncensored correspondence with members of the immediate family, personal friends, public officials, and representatives of the community. Regular opportunity for conjugal visitation by the granting of home furloughs.

5. Reasonable access to the press, through both interviews and written articles.

6. Freedom of voluntary religious worship and freedom to change religious affiliation.

7. Established rules of conduct available to prisoners in written form. Prohibition of excessive or disproportionate punishments. Procedural due process in any disciplinary hearing that might result in loss of good time, punitive (involuntary) transfer, or an adverse affect on parole decisions. Due process includes the right to independent counsel, the right to cross-examination, the right to subpoena witnesses, and the right to avoid self-incrimination.

8. Opportunity for the prisoner voluntarily to avail himself or herself of uncensored reading material and facilities especially provided for vocational training, counseling, and continuing education.

9. Opportunity in prison through work-release for work at prevailing wages. Eligibility for social security, unemployment compensation, and public assistance benefits upon release. Exclusive title to and control over all products of literary, artistic, or personal craftsmanship produced on the prisoner's own time. Freedom from compulsion to work.

10. A judicial proceeding for the determination of parole that incorporates full due process in the determination of sentence and parole data, including established rules of parole-board conduct. Parole may be revoked only upon conviction of a crime and only after a judicial hearing.

11. Full restoration of all civil rights and privileges upon release from prison. The right to vote in any election in which a prisoner would be entitled to vote if he had not been confined.

12. Unrestricted ability to petition for a redress of grievances.

A separate authority with the power to correct instances of mal-administration, abuse, or discrimination. Freedom from reprisals for making complaints.

It takes no more than a reading of this list to cause one to stop and think: if these are what is needed to make it possible for prisoners to live in a semblance of the "normal" life society will demand of them when they get out, and if these are the things we now compel prisoners to do without, how miraculous it is that even 1 percent of those released back into society from such deprivation ever manage to remain out of prison. It would seem that our present "corrections" system is all but deliberately designed to insure that no one, once caught in its web, will ever be able to remain free again. How does anyone come out of such a nether world without feeling such frustration and hostility toward the society that put him there that he can operate from then on only through an attitude of total rage?

While there are many specific conditions included in the Prisoners' Bill of Rights, there are many other particular reforms that a people's platform could also enunciate. It is not necessary to enumerate all of them here, because the list is potentially endless and would vary depending upon the particular needs springing from the particular conditions of each situation. All of them, in one degree or another, would be variations of the overall theme that emerges upon a full reading of the Prisoners' Bill of Rights, that is, the reforms recognize the humanity of prisoners and the needs they share in common with all other human beings. Such needs, when denied, make people a danger to themselves and their community, but when recognized, enable people to live constructive lives.

Nevertheless, a brief listing of other reforms is in order, being worthwhile for the seeds it may plant. It includes: freedom for convicts to wear beards, mustaches, and the clothing and hair styles of their choice; convict athletic teams, musical groups, drama groups, etc.; home furloughs for all prisoners regardless of marital status; letting of binding contracts for convicts to operate such businesses as are reasonably possible; letting of contracts between prisoners and the judiciary to establish programs with clear-cut goals for prisoners which, if and when they achieve them, guarantee release for the prisoner; minimum legal requirement of 12 weeks for guard training and six-month probationary periods for guards; higher salaries for guards; publicly sponsored job recruiting programs for exconvicts; more community programs for exconvicts; a restitution house where property violators will live while they fulfill a contract to repay the victim his financial loss, thus enabling the violator to live outside prison and keep his job; working with law schools to set up a model ombudsman program for prisoners.

I suspect some readers will think these ideas are "far out," pie in the sky, too theoretical ever to work in real life. Such persons will be pleased to know that every program I just listed was already in some stage of operation in 1971 in the state of Minnesota, under the direction of Corrections Commissioner David Fogel. Moreover, certain of these programs are also underway in other states. It is interesting to note that almost all of them, along with many provisions in the Prisoners' Bill of Rights, can be made operative without even waiting for the sometimes tortuously slow process of passing legislation. They can be started merely through administrative directions, which, of course, can be prodded by citizen committees.

I subscribe fully to Fogel's concise evaluation of our correctional systems. "Prisons are a failure. They don't work," says Fogel. "I don't think we need prisons. I do think there are people who are so violent they have to be helped, and held somewhere while getting that help. We must bring in the psychiatric and medical professions, which have ignored prisons." Focusing on the economic roots of so much of our crime, Fogel asserts, "If prisoners were paid the going rates for their labor, prisons would disappear." Fogel has put that theory into practice not only by initiating various work and business programs, but by arranging for prisoners' earnings to be deposited in interest-bearing accounts.

Until now, prison reform has received only lip service. It made headlines after every riot, but promised reform always faded with the headlines. Today, thanks to more education and more understanding of the harm done to all of us by the total failure of our prisons, the climate is right for genuine reform, and I have no doubt that it is imminent. I am likewise aware that the imminent will come even faster as a result of the government's mixing in one final ingredient, a new class of prisoners—the intellectual elite of the peace movement, along with the young men who refused to kill for their country as a matter of principle. The latter went to prison because of the vagaries of the draft law which did not take their act of imprisonment as proof of conscientious objection. These new elements could add a dimenson to prison reform never before experienced in our history.

Almost nothing has been written about women in prison, despite the fact that in 1971 there were 15,000 women in confinement. Very few women are incarcerated for crimes of violence. Sexist discrimination against women begins when young girls are sent to reformatories for sexual behavior which, on the part of boys, is smiled upon as a sign of "young manhood." One of the most vicious practices is the arrest of women whose children are elsewhere at the moment of arrest. Such women have often had to wait days and even weeks before learning if their children are all right.

The most frequent "crimes" of women in prison are disorderly conduct, vagrancy, and prostitution. There is no excuse for jailing women for any of these situations. Most women in prison have children and are strongly urged by the authorities to give them up for adoption. "It's very hard to get your children back from welfare," says author Kitsi Burkhart, an expert on women's prisons. "You must prove you're a fit mother, and the assumption is that since you were in jail, you're not a fit mother."

Women's jails—nearly all county or city lockups—are no better than those for men. There have been revelations, within the past year, of jails in America where women are sometimes kept in tiny stone closets, naked, on cement floors, for many days. There are women's jails with restraining straps, women's jails where gassings and beatings occur, where food and health care are unfit for human beings, and where every vestige of human dignity is stripped away. Many is the female parolee who has been returned to prison for the crime of getting pregnant. She is incarcerated "for her own good."

As with men's prisons, broad basic reforms could be made overnight. They merely require an acknowledgment of the humanity of prisoners, and the changes could be made administratively. "They talk about money," says one female exconvict. "I don't see where humane treatment costs money."

Every reform cited in discussing the rights of prisoners applies to women's prisons as well as men's.

BECAUSE SO MUCH CRIME is the product of people who were trained for crime through confinement in prisons, an obvious means of reducing crime is to drastically reduce our prison population. That can be done, at no danger to society, almost overnight. How? By eliminating a whole host of common social activities from the law's list of "crimes."

Common activities for which we now punish people—so-called "victimless crimes" because they affect no one but the participant—include drinking, prostitution, gambling, homosexuality, and use of certain narcotics and drugs. What is the point of jailing people for these practices? What more towering hypocrisy, what more potent breeder of total disrespect for the law, can there be than these "crimes," which are practiced by millions of citizens, but for which only a few are singled out for punishment?

Not only do these laws spawn crime, not only do they fail to decrease the behavior they condemn, not only are they irrelevant, they are also vicious, for they are too often used as devices to punish people whose life style is displeasing to police, prosecutors, or judges, whose wide latitude of discretion enables them to pick and choose those they decide to select for punishment. We all know of cases of judges offering to drop marijuana charges if young defendants would get a haircut. We all know of cases of police harassment of "longhairs." Hair styling is subject to no laws, and in persecuting people for such a harmless practice, police and judges are themselves offending the spirit of the law. They are practicing de facto legislation.

No valid purpose is served by retaining victimless crimes among our criminal laws. All of them should be abolished, and necessary sanctions channeled through noncriminal processes. Liquor laws, except for those against drunken driving, are utterly useless and should be dropped entirely. They are only a source of corruption. Prostitution laws, the most grossly unfair of all since they punish only the women (a vivid reminder that virtually all our laws have been written by men), should likewise be removed from the criminal code; such regulation as may be necessary belongs to civil law. Laws against private sexual preferences are nothing more than a device for persecution and there is no justification whatsoever for such laws. Pornography laws, too, concern private behavior and are essentially unenforceable. The recommendations of the President's Commission on Pornography, calling for an end to nearly all criminal sanctions, should be adopted.

Victimless crimes are a peril to our social health only in so far as they are classified as crimes. Some 51 percent of criminal arrests in 1970 were for victimless crimes. We could very nearly empty our jails by abolishing them, and thereby free our correctional system to deal properly with those who commit real crimes.

IN ADDITION TO THOSE who find themselves confined in cages, whom we call prisoners, there are two more large classes of people whose rights are in a severe state of deprivation. I am talking about juveniles and mental patients, groups whose tragedy is largely ignored by society in the manner of the old adage, "Out of sight, out of mind."

Some 500,000 juveniles are picked up every year. They do not receive due process. Once caught in the system of juvenile justice, they are stripped of almost every procedural safeguard afforded to adults. They are caught in a system that creates delinquency rather than cures it. Not only delinquent children, but dependent children, are shoveled into the system because, as the jargon has it, "suitable location could not be found." Others are put away in state mental hospitals for being part of the subculture. In some states, such as Pennsylvania, children are literally forced into involuntary servitude as peons laboring on farms, sometimes from sunrise to dark, with no pay, no school, and frequently no medical care. "A kid can be sent away because the probation officer doesn't like the way he's wearing his hair," says Lisa Richette, professor of law at Villanova University.

The history of juvenile treatment is built on the myth of rescuing children from a debauching environment. Youths have been placed on the treadmill for such "crimes" as "growing up in idleness," "living with a disreputable person," "incorrigibility," "vicious or immoral behavior." A whole range of youthful behavior that can best be handled informally can lead to the reformatory—drinking, smoking, staying out late at night, sexual promiscuity, truancy, running away, disobedience to parents and teachers.

Supreme Court decisions have recently begun to provide some of the procedural rights already available to adults, but many others are needed to block such abuses as confusion of child neglect cases with delinquency, arbitrary sentencing, and the use of unsubstantiated rumor as evidence. Furthermore, as Daniel A. Rezneck points out, "the Court has thus far dealt only with one of the three stages of juvenile proceeding—the adjudicative, or trial phase. It has not determined the rights applicable in the pre-trial and dispositional phases."

I do not think we can wait for the awful failings of the juvenile system to be corrected by the courts. The problem should be solved quickly, through legislation. A citizen's platform should call for the National Commission on Children and Youth to investigate and make recommendations for prompt implementation on the treatment of delinquents, their rights, and the problem of child-abuse.

I would expect such legislation to include, among other things, the requirement that counsel be appointed automatically for any juvenile involved in any administrative or judicial process; use of rules of evidence similar to those in adult courts; safeguards against use of hearsay from investigative reports compiled for juvenile proceedings; jury trial for alleged violations of criminal law; strict separation of fact-finding from investigative and accusatory functions; transcripts of hearings, for use on appeal; strict application of Fourth Amendment guarantees against unreasonable search and seizure; strict limitations on prehearing detention; prohibition of confinement in any adult facility; strict protection against involuntary confession, including presence of counsel during any interrogation and/or a requirement that all information from any interrogation be used only for purposes of rehabilitation, and barred from use as evidence in any hearing or trial; thorough and humane treatment and rehabilitation programs including comprehensive educational and vocational programs. (Most of these protections are drawn from the writings of Daniel Rezneck.)

No less shameful, in fact in many ways more shameful, than our treatment of prisoners and juveniles, is our treatment—I should say nontreatment—of mental patients. Not only do we confine thousands of persons in prisons who actually belong in mental hospitals, but too many of our mental hospitals are nothing more than prisons. Once again, the solution has been "out of sight, out of mind."

Bruce J. Ennis, Director of the Mental Illness Litigating Project of the New York Civil Liberties Union, offers this perspective: "If you substitute 'crime' for 'mental illness' and 'defendant' for 'patient' you will find that virtually every important right guaranteed to the criminal is denied to the patient."

Although there are three times as many mental patients as prisoners, Ennis points out that the Supreme Court "seems to be unaware of their existence. Not once in the past twenty-five years has the Court considered the procedural or substantive rights of a civil mental patient."

The pot-pourri of horrors that constitute our nonsystem of treatment for mental illness is a catalogue far too long to recite here, but a few brief notes will help to point out what must be done to rectify this wrong. Because of the countless provisions where criminal, civil, and medical sanctions are intermingled in our laws, innocent persons accused of crime have been denied trial on the "merciful" ground that they were mental cases and, therefore, were never given counsel and were confined for the rest of their lives as patients. Both competent and incompetent defendants must have the same rights to counsel and a speedy trial.

There are approximately 750,000 persons hospitalized as mental patients, more than 3 million persons receiving outpatient service, and only 23,000 psychiatrists in the United States. Most patients confined to state institutions receive minimal care. Their chances of release have little to do with their mental health. Once confined, especially if a person does not have concerned friends or family, as many patients do not, the lack of outside help can mean he is all but abandoned, a nonperson, for the rest of his days.

Despite the staggering absence of treatment facilities, there is no record of even one patient's being released from one state hospital on the grounds of inadequate care. Judges, says Ennis "are understandably reluctant to enforce the right to treatment. If they did, state hospitals would be emptied."

Thousands of persons are committed "for their own welfare" because they are considered "dangerous." They were thus categorized not because of expert diagnosis; studies show psychiatric predictions are wrong much more often than right, and psychiatrists tend to overpredict dangerous behavior for the very good reason that if one incorrectly predicts nondanger he will be castigated by an outraged community. Most of us know nothing about mental illness. We fear what we do not understand. "We don't know what to expect next," says Ennis, "so we play it safe and expect the worst. We are almost always wrong." There is absolutely no evidence that mental patients are more dangerous than average citizens, and plenty of evidence that they are less dangerous. Some mentally ill are dangerous, of course, but the important point, says Ennis, "is that a diagnosis of mental illness tells us nothing about whether the person . . . is or is not dangerous. Psychiatrists know this, but judges don't." Result: thousands of persons are committed without any proof that they are dangerous.

Practically the only state with a law even approaching an answer to this injustice is California, where a new law limits preventive detention by requiring proof of the type of danger (physical harm), the degree of danger (substantial), and the imminence of such behavior. Strict limits are set on how long a patient so classified may be held if he does not exhibit dangerous behavior. This law is a good step forward and should be a basis for similar national legislation.

Persons diagnosed as mentally ill must also have a right to clearly defined procedures such as court hearings or a trial, as the case may require. They must be given a speedy trial, lest any pretrial confinement only exacerbate their problem.

Hundreds of other problems must be worked out via a major study by experts, and money must be provided to implement every recommendation. (Money is always a problem, isn't it? Yet one can't say it too often, the money wasted on the Vietnam war could have financed solutions to virtually every social ill in our nation, from hunger to housing to health, education, and a system of enlightened justice.)

But one final problem of the mentally ill can be rectified

practically before any overall study: discrimination against former patients. "Mental illness is reversible," notes Ennis, "but its social consequences are not. If two physicians say a man is crazy, they will be believed. But if they later say he has recovered and is as well as any of us, they will not."

Result: job application forms, college admission forms, driver's license forms, and every other piece of paper standing between the former patient and a better life are filled with questions such as "Have you ever been hospitalized for a nervous or mental condition?" "Have you ever received psychiatric treatment?" These questions raise serious problems regarding equal rights. If we do not bar cured pneumonia patients, by what right do we bar cured mental patients? The use of such clearly discriminatory questions, which unfairly block access to a normal life, must be totally banned.

THERE IS ONE MORE important right which a people's platform must fully endorse—the right to life. The most obvious way in which we deny this right is through use of the death penalty. It should be abolished forthwith.

It is possible for the death penalty to be abolished through the Supreme Court, which may declare it cruel and unusual punishment, and it is possible to abolish it through the legislatures of the separate states (as of early 1972, 35 states still retained the death penalty for first degree murder).

Scientific studies of the past few years have overwhelmingly proved the case for abolition. The death penalty does not deter homicides; statistics show no lower homicide rates in states with capital punishment than in those without. Murders of policemen, a shockingly high number, are no higher in cities whose states have abolished the death penalty than in those retaining it. In short, there is no evidence that the death penalty deters murder.

One reason why the death penalty does not deter murder is that most murders take place between members of family or friends, committed in the emotional heat of an argument, enabled by the easy availability of a weapon.

There is a second reason to abolish capital punishment. It is immoral. Nothing is more demeaning and debasing for society than to legalize murder, giving official sanction to an act because we abhor it in others. If we are honest with ourselves, the real reason we have allowed retention of the death penalty for so long is not deterrence, not protection of society, but simply revenge. Yet we like to think we are more enlightened than to stoop to such a motive.

Capital punishment is not only barbarous, it is totally unfair. Only a rare few are executed while hundreds of others who committed the same crime are not. The death penalty is reserved for the poor, the black, and the ugly. Warden Duffy of San Quentin, who has seen many an execution and who deplores the practice, calls capital punishment "the privilege of the poor."

Virtually every single modern western nation has abolished the death penalty, as well as more than a dozen countries in Latin America. Several have had abolition for more than a hundred years. Just since 1930, on the other hand, there have been 3,859 men and women executed in the United States, including several later discovered to be innocent of the crime for which they had been convicted.

THERE IS ONE FINAL, major change in our legal structure that can be made at once to the great good of our society. It is a national tragedy that more than 100,000 of our young men are either living in exile, confined in prison, or branded for life as exconvicts, because of their refusal to take part in the atrocity called our war in Vietnam.

While I realize that many other young men went unwillingly to that war, where some of them died, were wounded, or became addicted to drugs, so many of the terrible agonies that rend our nation today stem from that war that we, the people, are desperately in need of some gesture of hope, some reassurance of our humanity, some positive sign of the fundamental decency that has characterized so much of American life. That gesture—Christ called it forgiveness—is available to us now. It is time for a national declaration of amnesty to erase the taint on the names of all the young men who ran afoul of any military law, whether as resisters or in other ways, connected with a war which many contend is illegal.

Why should the terrible burden of their elders' blunders be dumped on these young shoulders? Why do we sustain a huge class of permanently alienated Americans? Why do we perpetuate the poison in our national bloodstream that flows directly from this war? Amnesty has been a part of our history before, even for soldiers who opposed their own country in the Civil War, but never has there been this urgent a need for some healing gesture of national reconciliation. A complete overhaul of our system of military justice, initiated by a blanket declaration of amnesty, is a first order of business for a people's platform.

IN SUM, if we are ever to free our entire system of justice from the burden of individual repression and relieve the nation of paying the immense human and financial costs of crime, we must assume a radically different social perspective. That perspective must insist the shopworn phrase "equality and fairness under the law" means exactly that; it must insist upon protecting the rights of the victim as well as the accused, and be dedicated to understanding that most crime is a symptom and not the cause of a deeper disorder in our society.

13

An End to Secrecy

Through the devices of secrecy,
the government attains the power
to "manage" the news and use it
to manipulate public opinion.
Such governmental power is not
consonant with a nation of free
men . . .

—*Senator Sam J. Ervin, Jr.*
(Chairman, Senate Subcommittee
on Constitutional Rights)

THE PREREQUISITE for everything in a people's platform is a responsible, enlightened citizenry. If the American people are ever to become meaningful participants in the operation of their government, there must be an end to national decision-making in secret and policy implementation by executive fiat. This requires easy access to virtually all information by the public and, with rare and precisely defined exceptions, the removal of all limits on the information available to its elected representatives. The government's shrill claims of a "need" for secrecy must give way to the higher priority of the citizen's need to know, his right to know.

At present the scales are tipped heavily in favor of the government. Information is systematically classified and withheld from the public for vaguely determined reasons of "national security" and denied to Congress by the imperious assertion of "executive privilege." These two ridiculously flexible tools of secrecy, when placed in knowing and manipulative hands, demonstrate a rubbery quality that can be stretched and shaped far beyond the mere encompassment of what might be construed as legitimately sensitive defense and diplomatic data to provide self-appointed decision-makers with a protective shield against public accountability. The use of such conveniently available safeguards is difficult, if not impossible, for even the most well-intentioned administrations to resist when the stakes involve executive prestige, personal vanity, or political expediency.

As a result, the American citizen knows little more than what the state and its co-guardians of information in the mass media either want him to know or are permitted to let him know. He is plagued by doubt over the accuracy of what he is told, rightly suspects he is not being told everything, and resents the obvious lack of trust by the government in his ability to understand the issues and to make proper judgments even if provided with all the facts. He is inundated by propaganda communicated to him as gospel from far and wide in an endless stream of confusing and often conflicting images splashed across his television screen or jumbled in the headlines of his newspapers. There is, however, little he can know firsthand or with the certainty that he is not being lied to, conned by the complex and sophisticated language of the "experts" who always seem to know best, or manipulated by the carefully arranged "leaks" or semiofficial backgrounders by bureaucrats seeking to influence public opinion in support of predetermined decisions.

This is an intolerable situation for a government founded on the premise that in order to succeed it must have the active and full participation of an enlightened electorate. That is what our forefathers attempted to ensure when they created a government of laws rather than of men and enshrined that distinction in a written Constitution. That, too, is why they insisted upon attaching a Bill of Rights to the Constitution, guaranteeing maximum competition in the market place of ideas. Today, however, we find ourselves victims of a system where adopted policies often have neither the understanding nor the approval of the people.

CAN ANYONE, for example, doubt that our present system of document classification is a farce, and an expensive one at that? The practice of stamping public papers with some sort of secrecy designation has become so widespread as to be virtually meaningless. It is conservatively estimated that upwards of $50 million annually is wasted merely in attempting to protect material bearing classification markings which are either overclassified or don't qualify for classification. In testimony before a June, 1971, hearing of the House of Representatives' Foreign Operations and Government Information Subcommittee, William G. Florence, a retired civilian security classification policy expert on Department of Defense procedures for classification, claimed that "less than one-half of 1 percent" of the millions of documents bearing classification markings actually contain information qualifying for even the lowest authorized classification. "In other words," Florence contended, "the disclosure of information in at least 99½ percent of these classified documents could not be prejudicial to the defense interest of the nation." He later increased his estimate of the number of documents that need to be protected to from 1 to 5 percent, but the point of his testimony remains the same.

Following what seems to be a philosophy of "when in doubt, classify," tens of thousands of government employees routinely exercise their delegated authority to deny the public access to information through the simple use of a rubber stamp and ink pad, tempered only by the classifier's own imperfect subjective interpretation of vague classification guide lines.

The classification practices of the departments of Defense

and State and the Atomic Energy Commission, alone, re-
portedly involve some 38,000 persons and have resulted in
the secreting away of more than 22 million documents. Most
other government agencies also have authority to either use
or originate classified information. Indeed, the authority to
classify has become a liberally dispensed privilege rather than
a limited and controlled responsibility as intended. Items such
as interoffice memos, backgrounders, and public policy documents are classified more frequently for the dubious purpose
of bolstering a sagging sense of self-importance or of "playing it safe" by providing a degree of protection for the classifier's possible poor judgment or the author's unsubstantiated
criticisms or questionable recommendations, than as the result of a studied determination indicating that release of the
material would be harmful to the nation's security.

But if the excesses of government classification are outland-
ish, the abuses of executive privilege are outrageous. Information required by Congress, if it is to perform its duties
intelligently, is regularly and somewhat self-righteously withheld, enabling the administration to make momentous and
often irreversible decisions without the discipline of congressional review, the benefit of congressional advice, or the need
for legislative endorsement.

The right of Congress to demand and receive information
from executive officials must supersede the prerogative of those
men and women to keep their secrets secret. I consider the
ease and frequency with which members of the administration
hide behind the protective cloak of executive privilege to be
an affront to the people who elected the members of Congress
to represent their interests, an insulting expression of either
disdain or mistrust of individual congressmen or for congressional operations as a whole, as an indication of the low
regard held by the executive for the legislative branch's status
as an equal and independent arm of government.

The entire concept of executive privilege carries with it
the undemocratic connotation of some sort of kingly divine

right. However, it is more of a tradition than a right and should either be discontinued or defined and legitimatized by statute. Certainly the practice of permitting anyone other than the President himself to initiate such a practice must be stopped. Senator William Fulbright, who as chairman of the Foreign Relations Committee frequently has found his efforts to obtain information from various federal officials frustrated by their use of executive privilege, has rightly proposed that any member of the executive branch called upon to testify before a congressional body be required to do so unless the President personally intervenes. To put teeth into such a requirement, it has been suggested that Congress make the stipulation that it will withhold approval of appropriations for the involved agency or department until either the reluctant witness agrees to testify as requested or the President exercises his option.

Actually there is no constitutional or legislative authority for either the government's classification procedures or the doctrine of executive privilege. They have evolved out of executive order or assumption and have been more or less accepted as custom, although they are a clear contradiction to an open government and the freedom of information concept.

The dispute between government and citizen and the executive and Congress over what information can and will be made available has been going on in varying degrees of intensity ever since President Washington opened the controversy by turning down a congressional request for information on an expedition into the Northwest Territories. As might be expected, most practices of government secrecy and censorship evolved out of what has been considered the necessity of maintaining military security during wartime. The Civil War prompted direct military censorship for the first time in the nation's history and led to a major confrontation with the principle of a free press when Union zealots used it as a device to seize or suppress opposition newspapers and even to jail editors who dared differ with the war's conduct or its goals.

Perhaps because this sounded a warning bell in the minds of many believers of the sanctity of a free press, an uneasy partnership was achieved between the news media and government during the two world wars. President Wilson created a Committee on Public Information in 1917, and President Roosevelt established the Office of Censorship in 1941, each affording the press an opportunity to have some voice, albeit severely limited, in the censorship of those eras.

Even in wartime, however, no attempt to pass a law abridging the constitutionally guaranteed freedom of the press has ever succeeded in passing Congress. The problem has been that, although wartime conditions admittedly make it necessary to be cautious about the possible disclosure of information that might compromise national security, the practices of suppression once planted and rationalized, for whatever reason, usually persist long after the purported need is gone.

The reason so many of today's secrecy practices have gone largely unchallenged, for example, can easily be traced back to World War II, when the people were conditioned to believe "the enemy has ears everywhere" and that "a slip of the lip can sink a ship." There was little, if any, public news media resistance to the government's contention that strict censorship was required to maintain our security and protect "our men in uniform." Never mind the fact that the suppression of information was often carried to absurd extremes; it would have been considered unpatriotic to argue the point, especially during wartime. Although the war ended, unfortunately the malaise of secrecy did not. The indoctrination of the American people was so successful, in fact, that it was easy for the government to carry it forward from hot war to cold war and to expand it from purely military information to matters of public policy.

Because Congress has consistently balked at assuming responsibility for enacting legislation defining and limiting what government materials can be classified, establishment of classification guide lines has become, by default, the prerogative of the executive. This has been exercised in a series of executive orders, some less vague and suppressive than others, but none of which has proved to be acceptable.

President Truman's Executive Order 10290 of September 24, 1951, prescribing minimum standards for the classification and handling of publications "which require safeguarding in the interest of the security of the United States," was widely criticized for being too favorable to government and for its lack of adequate review or appeals procedures.

On November 5, 1953, President Eisenhower replaced the Truman directive with Executive Order 10501 intended to bring about "a proper balance between the need to protect information important to the defense of the United States and the need for citizens of this country to know what this country is doing." Initially praised by proponents of greater access to government information for its imposition of review and appeal procedures and its reduction of classification categories, the Eisenhower administration was later the object of severe public and news media criticism for failing to live up to its promise. Acting outside our system of checks and balances, as both judge and jury of its own executive order, the administration, then as now, liberally and self-servingly interpreted the doctrine to withhold information that to many did not seem to fall into the three categories set forth.

1. Top secret. "information or material the defense aspect of which is paramount, and the unauthorized disclosure of which could result in exceptionally grave damage to the nation, such as leading to a definite break in diplomatic relations affecting the defense of the United States, an armed attack against the United States or its allies, a war, or the compromise of military or defense plans or intelligence operations, or scientific or technological developments vital to national defense."

2. Secret. "defense information or material the unauthorized disclosure of which could result in serious damage to the nation, such as jeopardizing the international relations of the United States, endangering the effectiveness of a program of policy of vital importance to the national defense, or compromising impor-

tant military or defense plans, scientific or technological developments important to national defense, or information revealing
important intelligence operations."
   3. Confidential. "defense information or material the unauthorized disclosure of which could be prejudicial to the defense
interests of the nation."

These guide lines may seem reasonable and even justifiable
upon first examination, but the tests of time and experience
have shown that the impreciseness of language and the absence of specific declassification provisions open the way for
the inclusion of practically any materials the classifier desires
and for as long as it serves the government's rather than the
public's interests.

President Kennedy attempted to correct some of the failings of the government's classification system when he issued
Executive Order 10964 in 1961, providing that, "When classified information or material no longer requires its present
level of protection in the defense interest, it shall be downgraded in order to preserve the effectiveness and integrity of
the classification system and to eliminate classifications of information or material which no longer require classification
protection." It was a step in the right direction, but to my
mind, fails to solve the declassification dilemma because it
places the cart before the horse. The automatic release of materials should be provided for at the time of classification, not
years later, and should be strictly adhered to unless an appropriate, independent review body can be convinced by the
arguments of the affected agency that there are compelling
reasons for extending the period of classification protection
beyond the normally stipulated disclosure date.

It must also be recognized that government not only has
erected barriers to protect its own self-construed secrets from
the public, but also has adopted the role of receptacle, guardian, and perpetuator of corporate secrecy. Information that, if
made public, would provide consumers with the knowledge
needed to detect and respond to the injustices and illegalities

inflicted upon them by business-corporate interests is collected by government officials and placed under cover while the citizen continues to be victimized in the market place.

In 1966 President Johnson signed into law the highly touted Freedom of Information Act (revised in 1967), designed to force federal agencies to make more of their carefully hoarded information available to the public. Over the opposition of the affected agencies and like-minded business interests, the measure largely rewrote Section 3 of the 1946 Administrative Procedure Act to require the release of all agency data, unless specifically exempted. But therein lies the rub. The scope of the nine exempted categories, included to overcome the objections of the act's opponents, is so broad as to enable the government to withhold almost as much material from the public as before. In fact, V. M. Newton, Jr., a founder of the Freedom of Information movement, called the nine following exemptions "nothing more than an open invitation to the federal bureaucrat to withhold legitimate information from the American people."

1. Material "specifically required by executive order to be kept secret in the interest of the national defense or foreign policy."

2. Material related "solely" to agencies' internal personnel rules and practices.

3. Material specifically exempted from disclosure by statute.

4. Privileged or confidential trade secrets or financial information.

5. Inter- or intra-agency memoranda or letters which would be unavailable by law to a person in litigation with the agency.

6. Personnel and medical files "the disclosure of which would constitute a clearly unwarranted invasion of personal privacy."

7. Investigatory files compiled for law enforcement except to the extent available by law to private parties.

8. Material contained in or related to examination or condition reports of agencies regulating financial institutions.

9. Geological and geophysical information and data, including maps concerning wells.

As Robert O. Blanchard, head of the communication department at American University, commented, "Several of the phrases seem bound to encourage continued, perhaps more sophisticated, federal agency discretion in release of information."

He was right. One of the original sponsors of the legislation, Representative Donald Rumsfeld (now a trusted advisor to President Nixon) reported shortly after the measure was enacted that some agencies were attempting to avoid the law's provision by contemplating doing much of their business verbally so there would be no records, while another agency was trying "to categorize everything under one or more of the law's nine exemptions so that virtually none of the information under its control will be available."

Although some of the more enterprising newsmen and tenacious investigators, such as Ralph Nader, have been able to utilize the measure to surprisingly good advantage, I believe it to be an unnecessary hinderance to the dissemination of information.

One of the most deplorable aspects of the measure is the protection it provides for information garnered from the business community. At a minimum, the people's platform embraces the Nader proposal that no federal agency shall be permitted to treat information it receives from any business as confidential "in the absence of a showing that the business interest in secrecy outweighs the public's right to know," and that government officials who withhold corporate information without such justification be subject to dismissal or other punishment.

Ideally, however, I believe the entire FOI law should be revoked and only information covered by executive order or specifically exempted from disclosure by statute should be granted the right of secrecy. Even this should be done sparingly and under close supervision.

As PERHAPS no other single event in modern history, the controversy surrounding the publication of the so-called Pentagon Papers last year has served to dramatize how slight has been the progress made by the nation toward achieving its espoused goal of an open government and how contemptuously the citizen's right to know has been regarded. The calculated practices of deceit, distortion, and denial of information, exposed by the contents of this remarkable study, made possible the commission of a monstrous crime upon the American people: the waging of an unnecessary, undeclared war in a foreign land and the reprehensible usurping of congressional powers.

Without the carefully orchestrated public and political moods fashioned by a succession of purposefully isolated administrations utilizing the twin tools of propaganda and secrecy, I do not believe the people of this nation would have condoned the decisions made and the policies implemented. Surely, had the ordinary citizen been privy to the information and, yes, the thinking so jealously restricted to the uppermost echelons of government, our ill-conceived involvement in Southeast Asia, with its resultant and irrecoupable costs in lives, social progress, and world credibility, would never have been permitted to run its tragic course.

The abrogation of the people's right to know—one of our system's most important checks and balances—caused this nation to make this colossal mistake of waging a war that has nothing to do with our security, individually or as a nation. The crime, therefore, surrounding the public disclosure of the Pentagon Papers is not, as the Nixon administration would have us believe, that Dr. Daniel Ellsberg released these materials to the press or that *The New York Times, Boston Globe, Washington Post,* and other newspapers proceeded to publish them. The real travesty of justice is that the study was classified at all, that it became necessary to circumvent the executive's self-imposed shroud of secrecy in order to convey to the public information which was rightfully theirs all along.

What better proof is needed to refute the Nixon administration's claim that the release of the Pentagon Papers constituted some sort of shocking moral and legal crime, endangering national security, than the Defense Department's own response in hastily reproducing the material for public sale when it later learned that a copy of the study I had acquired was to be published, in its entirety, by Beacon Press.

How specious then became the administration's charges of immorality and illegality which had been hurled so vehemently against Ellsberg and the newspapers. Surely, if the Defense Department truly believed it was wrong and dangerous to disclose the contents of this study, did it somehow become less wrong or dangerous for the department to do it merely because someone else was planning to do it first. *No.* The Defense Department's act only confirmed what those of us who had read the study knew and the public was soon to learn: the Pentagon Papers contain no military secrets; there is nothing in them that jeopardizes the security of our nation or endangers the well being of "our boys" anywhere in the world; what they contain are political secrets sustained only by an appalling litany of faulty premises and questionable objectives.

Yet because of our ridiculous classification system, it took someone like Dr. Ellsberg, willing to risk personal abuse and punishment, to do what the government itself should have done—serve the public by honoring its right to know. To my mind, Dr. Ellsberg performed a citizen's act of unusual courage and should be praised, not prosecuted. Likewise, the newspaper publishers are to be commended for fulfilling their roles of uncensored conveyors of information as guaranteed under the Constitution. Public relief over defeat of the administration's surly attempt to thwart publication by the unconstitutional use of prior restraint must be tempered by the discomforting willingness of the Supreme Court to consider the matter at all and the closeness of its narrow decision in the public's favor.

Prior to the Court's decision and shortly before the government secured an indictment against Dr. Ellsberg, a major portion of the Pentagon Papers came into my possession. As I read the original documents and the memoranda written by officials in charge of the war's conduct and American policy, my worst fears were confirmed. Page after page spelled out in chilling detail how badly the people had been misled. I became convinced that this additional information had to be made public.

Many people have asked me how I arrived at the decision to place the study in the public record of Congress and how it was actually done. I must confess it was a very trying personal ordeal. I learned to appreciate fully what Ellsberg must have suffered. Where he was alone and open to legal prosecution as a private citizen, I was cloaked with some protection in my capacity as a senator. But there was no legal precedent for what I intended to do. The right of a member of Congress to divulge information the executive branch of the government had stamped top secret had never been tested in court. I thought, at the time, I might be liable to arrest or, perhaps, censure or expulsion from the Senate in view of the sentiment which seemed to be building in favor of the administration's steamroller campaign to suppress the study. I also had my staff to consider, for these loyal and principled assistants might be liable to prosecution for what I was doing. I gave everyone on my staff an opportunity to disassociate herself or himself from any part of my activities relating to the documents, because I didn't know of any other protection. The thought crossed my mind more than once, "We all may wind up in jail."

It was on the 24th of June that I obtained the papers. I planned to use them to filibuster the extension of the draft which was to expire on June 30. My strategy was to read the more than 4,000 pages of material from Tuesday evening, June 29, until Wednesday at midnight to enshrine the end of the draft and bring public attention to the simple fact that the nation would not fall apart or be invaded on July 1 without a draft. The study would be printed in the Congressional Record for all to see. The study said more explicitly than anything else that had been written why we should end the draft, and thereby take away the President's chief war-making power, the ability to raise armies.

I had another purpose in reading the Pentagon Papers on the floor of the Senate, aside from whatever personal immunity the proceedings of that body might offer. That was to represent Congress on the firing line in this momentous issue. The administrative/bureaucratic element was represented by Dr. Ellsberg. The fourth estate was amply represented by a number of newspapers. I felt it would be a tragedy for the Congress not to be represented on the firing line, too—on the right side.

During the Korean conflict, I attended infantry school at Fort Benning, Georgia. The shoulder patch we wore said "Follow me." The joke and fear of any combat infantry platoon leader was to order a battle charge and find himself running up the hill all alone. Ellsberg had said, "Follow me." It didn't seem fair to let him charge up the hill alone for all of us. I also felt that my action might then make foolish the claim that his actions were illegal.

On the day before my filibuster was to start, at President Nixon's direction, the White House and the Pentagon delivered an official copy of the entire study to the leaders of Congress. Special conditions limited access to the material to members of Congress. No staff members were allowed in the special reading room, and the nation's legislators, in the presence of a guard, were prohibited from taking notes. It infuriated me to see Congress, which is supposed to make policy for this country, submit to such schoolboy rules.

For too long Congress has played along in keeping secrets from the people and to do it again, in the midst of this crucial test of the people's right to know, was too much. It was an abdication of its own power, a condoning of Nixon's act of suppression. The President was arguing privately that release of the study might make the people lose respect for the government. I felt the contrary to be true. The issue was whether the government had lost faith in the people. The government was afraid to admit its mistakes, afraid to admit publicly that the people had been deceived.

As it turned out, my filibuster died aborning on the evening of June 29. Through a parliamentary maneuver by Senator Robert Griffin, the Republican Whip, I was denied the floor of the Senate. I must point out that, at that moment, no one but my staff knew I had the Pentagon Papers and how I planned to release them, although some rumors were spreading among the press. I decided not to wait, but to find another forum to enter the documents into Congress' public record.

At nine o'clock I convened a special public hearing of the Senate Subcommittee on Public Buildings and Grounds, of which I am still chairman.

Representative John Dowd, a principled and dedicated Democrat from New York whom I had never before met, agreed without question to appear as a witness for the hearing, and he was there when I walked into the room carrying a brief-case full of documents. I opened the hearing by saying we need more federal buildings, but we can't afford to build them. The reason we can't afford them is that we are wasting our money. And then I asked Congresman Dowd if I could impose upon his patience to read some documents which would show how we have been wasting that money in the war in Southeast Asia.

I read from the Pentagon Papers for the next four hours, placing in the subcommittee's record the futility and duplicity of our enormous expenditures. I read as much as I felt was necessary and placed the balance in the record. At that point the Pentagon Papers became part of the public domain. I then decided to read the statement I had been prevented from making on the floor of the Senate, the one with which I had intended to introduce the Pentagon Papers in my filibuster. By this time, one o'clock in the morning, I was feeling the effects of the days and nights of tension and preparation and the emotions this whole affair had stirred within me. Those emotions began to spill forth as I read from the statement a sentence about the horrors of the war, a sentence describing how we

Americans were the ones responsible for metal crashing through human bodies, for arms being severed, and women and children being killed to no purpose. It suddenly overwhelmed me that, as I sat there describing them, these terrible things were actually happening at that very moment to the people of Indochina. I found myself crying, crying over my nation's guilt. I also recall how temporarily embarrassed I was while I cried; after all, I was a man and a U.S. Senator and I was in full public view. The embarrassment, however, was washed away with tears.

People have asked me if I had it to do over would I go through the ordeal again. I have told them I am convinced the lessons to be learned from the Pentagon Papers outweighed by far any possible risk. I hoped by that action I would help shorten by even one day, the senseless killing and destruction in which we persist in Southeast Asia. And I hoped that it would penetrate the shroud of secrecy enveloping and protecting our highest echelons of government. Given the same set of circumstances, I would do it again and again. Secrecy is democracy's worst enemy.

THE PUBLIC CLAMOR following the release of the Pentagon Papers elicited the rather belated news from President Nixon that he had ordered a review of procedures and policy on the classification of documents back in January of 1971. Ironically, the presidential order setting up the study had been withheld from the public for more than five months, until after the Pentagon Papers controversy erupted, on the grounds that it was an "internal paper." Even this study of secrecy, it seems, was launched in secret.

Indeed, the administration's announced plans to declassify World War II documents at a cost of $6 million merely accentuates the ludicrousness of a system that keeps documents classified 25 to 30 years or more, when the enemies and events of a bygone era are mere shadows of history.

If it is painful for the average citizen to accept the fact that he is not being provided with all the information he needs to judge properly his government's actions, imagine how frustrating it is for a United States Senator to discover he or she, too, is unable to secure the material necessary for the proper discharge of his legislative responsibilities or, even worse, that he is deliberately lied to or misled.

In 1969, for example, I received a letter from a distinguished professor of political science at the University of Alaska in Fairbanks, Dr. Richard Feinberg, claiming he had discovered that the Army was conducting nerve gas tests on a nearby military installation. "I thought you should be made aware of this," he wrote.

Dr. Feinberg knew of my intense opposition to the continuing development and stockpiling of lethal gases by this country and of my persistent efforts to convince the administration to seek Senate ratification of the long-pending Geneva Protocol, already signed by practically every other major power in the world, banning the use of all deadly chemicals as weapons of war. He rightly assumed I would not be too pleased to learn that nerve gas tests were being conducted in my own state.

I immediately contacted a high-ranking Department of the Army official and asked point blank, "Is there any poisonous gas testing being conducted anywhere in Alaska?" The answer was as clear as the question, "Absolutely not."

In my naïveté (I had been a U.S. Senator for only a few months), I accepted this official declaration in good faith and informed Dr. Feinberg that I was sure he would be as delighted as I to learn that he had been mistaken.

Less than a month later, Dr. Feinberg succeeded in documenting his charges sufficiently for the Army to finally concede "some" nerve gas experiments had indeed taken place in Alaska. In short, I had been lied to.

The Pentagon Papers episode obviously represents one of the most spectacular and flagrant misuses of secrecy by government. But it is far from the only one, or even the most recent. Specific foreign aid planning documents, CIA expenditures, overseas military commitments, our clandestine activities in Laos, the worldwide deployment of nuclear weapons, environmental studies on the SST and atomic power plants, and many other "government papers" have been systematically treated as "sacred cows" by the executive, not to be defiled by the inquiring eyes of even a congressional committee, much less the people. Yet the Congress must pass upon, and the public is expected to accept, legislation founded almost solely upon the unsubstantiated requirements of an uncommunicative military establishment that claims "national security" and a tight-lipped administration that asserts its "executive privilege."

The government's handling of the five-megaton underground nuclear explosion on Alaska's Amchitka Island on November 6, 1971, for example, was steeped in secrecy and distinguished by an apparent disregard for the legitimate concerns of millions of Americans as well as the populations of friendly nations such as Canada and Japan. Secrecy surrounded not only the need for the test, but the very basis on which the government decided the question of safety. Internal reports containing environmental arguments against the test were deliberately denied the advantage of public examination and congressional debate. Court action finally succeeded in prying loose some of these adverse comments, but it never brought them all into the open and what was achieved was too late for the public to consider them adequately.

Not only has vital public information surrounding the Amchitka tests been kept secret since the program originated, but the Atomic Energy Commission has gone so far as to conduct a deliberate and expensive campaign to discredit anyone daring to question or oppose its series of underground nuclear explosions.

In 1969, prior to the detonation of the one-megaton Milrow blast which I also opposed, the AEC, through its prime contractor, actually opened up a publicity and public relations office in Anchorage and sent out a procession of press hand-outs and public speakers throughout Alaska which, in Mc-Carthyite style, impugned the motivations and questioned the loyalty of myself and anyone else in opposition to the AEC position. One of the actual statements made, and published in a newspaper of wide circulation in Alaska, was that those opposing the planned atomic test (Milrow) were "part of an international conspiracy to impede the defense posture of our country."

So here we have a case where not only was public information kept secret, but an elected public official was attacked with public funds for assuming the role of adversary on a vital public issue.

Even today, it is premature for anyone to claim that the 1971 Amchitka Cannikin blast was an unqualified success. Only the test of time can accurately make that determination. Although there fortunately was no immediate catastrophe as many feared, the possibility exists that the risky detonation deep under the surface of that Aleutian island might well have planted nuclear seeds of destruction yet to be reaped. The cavity created by the blast caused a distortion of the earth's crust which, like a nuclear time bomb, could still act as a trigger for larger-than-natural earthquakes. And the probable leakage of radioactivity into the surrounding ocean for decades to come presents a continuing danger to vulnerable marine life.

The concern I have over whether the right decision was made is aggravated by the secret manner in which it was made. An act of great potential danger, involving both life and environment, was undertaken and the people were precluded from participating in that decision. When the executive suppresses the internal debate surrounding a public issue, the citizen is left with little by which he can judge the government's decision. As long as a substantial portion of the pertinent technology is restricted to the government and the opinions formed on the basis of that information are treated as the exclusive property of those in high office, the government possibly may operate for the people but never by or of the people.

Two BASIC STEPS must be taken in order to supply a free flow of manageable information. First, we must uncomplicate things. Then we must declassify them.

Bureaucratic abbreviations and fantastic government and social science jargon have long been joked about. But these obstacles to public understanding should not be taken lightly. It is a matter of extreme urgency that something be done about them. Without condescension or loss of meaning, it must be possible to say important things simply and cogently. A concerted effort is required to decode bureaucratic and specialized language, so that information is correctly translated into the common tongue and categorized in manageable units connected to policy and interest. It is inexcusable to permit whatever information is made available to the public to be couched in the mystifying and stilted terminology developed by the snobbishly closed ranks of the technicians or to be rendered meaningless by the often unintelligible gobbledygook of bureaucratic officialdom.

Most important, the standards for protective classification of information must be revised immediately. The public's right to have access to available information and thinking on matters relating to its security and survival is too critical to be sacrificed to a decision-making process shrouded in secrecy and immune from the light of public examination.

An independent board, including representatives from the legislative and judicial branches of government with a majority of the members representing the public sector, should be established to study the present practices of classification, to establish new and more liberal procedures, and to recommend needed legislation. The executive branch should not be represented on this board; rather it should be required to plead its case for secrecy before the appointed board.

Any future standards for classification should be weighed heavily in favor of the public's right to know. Indeed, the public should not have to prove its need for information; the government should be made to justify any request it makes for the withholding of information. Better we err on the side of freedom of information than on the side of suppression. If this entails some risk, so be it. Freedom is impossible without risk and certainly the risks of free discussion are less to be feared than the risks of repression.

Automatic time limits should be an integral part of any items which are classified. All classified documents should be declassified as a matter of course after two years, unless the classifications board approves a government request for an extension of secrecy. The board would be empowered to send relevant papers to the appropriate committees of Congress at any time and to serve as an appellate on declassification disputes.

One of the board's most urgent tasks would be to press for revision or repeal of Executive Order 10510. At a minimum, specific language is required to insure that the classification system is applied only to information that, if disclosed, would definitely compromise our national defense posture. At the same time, it is essential to make certain no other item can be haphazardly lumped into the system unless it meets this criteria. The difficulty in obtaining release for the environmental impact study relating to the Amchitka Cannikin test, for example, was that it was considered a part of a larger classified report concerning the test's purpose of developing a more powerful anti-ballistic missile warhead. The practice of taking a public report, unrelated to national defense by any stretch of the imagination, and incorporating it as part of a national defense document so the entire work can then be classified must be stopped.

ONE OF THE GREATEST IRONIES, and dangers, of the secrecy syndrome is that people sometimes fail to distinguish between the desirability of having all of government's activities made public and the necessity for protecting the individual's right to privacy.

"All of us have our secrets," they reason, "so why shouldn't the government be entitled to its secrets as well." This feeling is largely a product of the conditioning imposed upon them by our competitive enterprise system which relies heavily on confidentiality and trade secrets. The public has been told so often and so convincingly that government and business have the right not only to keep certain matters secret, but to acquire information by secret means as well, that it has come to accept such practices as an integral part of the system.

Nonsense! The individual has a constitutional right to privacy while the government has a constitutional obligation to inform. The proposed board on secrecy, therefore, should have control over not only the classification of information, but the shameful manner in which such material is often gathered.

In 1971, for instance, it was revealed that thousands of members of the armed forces intelligence branches had been engaged, and hundreds of millions of dollars spent over several years so that the military could spy on civilians, federal agencies could keep tabs on one another, the privacy of the citizen could be invaded, and the rights of the First Amendment could be compromised. Yet even Congress seems unable to secure information on such subjects as Army surveillance of civilians or mushrooming data bank programs. Indeed, the gigantic nature of our state and corporate society, with all its demand for record keeping, makes it literally impossible for anyone, even if he wished it, to live the life of a recluse. "In the general atmosphere of apprehension and suspicion thus engendered, possibly half the population of a modern civilized country are 'security risks,'" notes C. H. Rolph, the respected British journalist, meaning the temptation to invade privacy, in the name of "security," is powerful indeed.

I believe it is this kind of atmosphere, which has developed slowly, almost invisibly, and to some extent unintentionally, that has increasingly made it easier and easier for those who argue for more and more irrelevant snooping into our private lives. The degree to which government and big business pry into matters which are purely our private affairs, and which have no possible bearing on national security, is staggering.

Stopping this reckless, and recklessly growing, practice may be the single most vital need of all those requiring immediate attention, for if we lose control of our privacy, which is in effect to lose control of ourselves, we are prisoners. And there is very little that prisoners can do to bring about change.

The growing use of wiretapping is especially disquieting. Under the broad cover of "national interest," the Justice Department admits that it has frequently used wiretaps to gather evidence. For example, it revealed the use of wiretaps to gather evidence against 20-year-old Leslie Ann Bacon in connection with her 1971 indictment for conspiring to bomb a First National City Bank branch in New York. In an affidavit to the U.S. District Court in New York, Attorney General John Mitchell contended the wiretaps were legal but said disclosure of the details of the government's wiretap would "prejudice the national interest." Would they? How? The attorney general should at least be required to explain exactly what "national interest" would be jeopardized. Perhaps the release of such details would give technical information to criminal elements that would somehow aid in the commission of future crimes against the state. If so, this should and could be explained without divulging technological specifics.

The seemingly irrepressible growth of this gross invasion of ourselves becomes even more dramatic, and more frightening, when one realizes that, since the legal concept of the "inviolate personality" was introduced in 1890 by Samuel D. Warren and Louis D. Brandeis, the right to privacy was recognized and supposedly protected by more than 35 state legislative enactments and over 400 Supreme Court decisions.

How then do we account for such phenomena as the conclusion of Aryeh Neier, Executive Director of the American

Civil Liberties Union, in his study of the dissemination of derogatory data by the FBI, that "At the very least, millions of
people have been injured by data dissemination functions that
the FBI has taken on which go beyond the Bureau's legislative
authority."

Using data drawn from federal court records in the 1971
case of *Menard v. Mitchell and Hoover,* Neier reported that
in 1970 the FBI received an average of 29,000 sets of fingerprints per working day, of which 16,000 came from non-law
enforcement agencies such as banks, insurance companies, and
government agencies engaged in employing or licensing people. Upon receipt of these fingerprints, standard procedure
"was to report to the submitting agency the material in the FBI
files on the person fingerprinted."

The trouble is a great deal of this data is raw and unverified.
For example, although nearly half of all arrests for actions
other than traffic violations do not result in convictions, there
is no indication on arrest records whether the arrested person
was ever convicted.

Yet because the FBI has almost no control over what hap-
pens to this information once it sends it out, these records are
inevitably acquired by the multi-tentacled credit industry. In
a report undertaken for the ACLU, Ralph Nader stated that
the Association of Credit Bureaus of America (ACBA) keeps
105 million files. "These economic interests have almost total
control over the information they collect and sell," reports
Nader. "They are not accountable to anyone except those who
seek to purchase the information. Further, for reasons of profit,
these companies place a premium on the derogatory information they assemble."

An arrest record, as noted in the *Menard* case by the U.S.
Circuit Court of Appeals for the District of Columbia, "may
subject an individual to serious difficulties. Opportunities for
schooling, employment, or professional licenses may be restricted or non-existent as a consequence of the mere fact of
an arrest, even if followed by acquittal or complete exonera-

tion." The court cited a survey showing that 75 percent of New
York area employment agencies would not accept for referral
an applicant with an arrest record. Another survey of 75 employers showed that 66 of them would not consider hiring a
man who had been acquitted of an arrest for assault.

Dogged by an arrest record for victim and victimless crimes,
a record that follows him even if charges were dropped or he
was acquitted or never prosecuted, a citizen in today's tightly
intertwined society finds the doors closed to credit, bank loans,
mortgages, apartment rentals, licenses, and admission to
schools. Moreover, because the FBI does not differentiate between juvenile and adult records, a minor youthful misstep
can have the same crushing consequences. They can, indeed,
twist the entire future of a young life.

With all these doors shut to an arrest victim, doors which
control access to nearly all the necessities and amenities of life
in twentieth-century America, it is no wonder some people slip
into a life of crime and thoughtful people cry out against the
"dossier dictatorship." It is logical to ask, as Neier does in
concluding his study,

> Is crime being controlled or reduced by the dissemination of
> this data? It would be more reasonable to say that the FBI's data
> dissemination policies have served to increase crime. Once people
> have been denied jobs, licenses, homes, admissions to schools and
> credit, the likelihood that they will commit crimes would seem
> to rise rather than fall.

Clearly the time is long overdue for severe controls to be
clamped on the dossier industry, both inside and outside of
government. Strict requirements must be placed on the information that can be placed in them in the first place. Why
should the FBI collect data on anyone other than persons
convicted of a crime or fugitives from some law enforcement
agency? Juvenile records must be clearly marked as such. The
dossiers should be available only to law enforcement agencies
and those needing the material for judging sentencing, probation, or parole. (Fortunately, some of these limitations were

imposed by Judge Gerhard Gessell in his *Menard* ruling in June, 1971, when he ordered the FBI to stop disclosing arrest records to private or non-law enforcement agencies. Legislative efforts to neutralize the ruling, however, were soon introduced in the Senate, one at the behest of then Attorney General Mitchell, so this battle for the right to privacy and, indeed, the right to a normal life, is only beginning.) Finally, since it was the cloak of secrecy which enabled the FBI to follow such promiscuous practices of data dissemination in the first place, legislation must be enacted to provide for thorough public scrutiny of the Bureau's practices.

The FBI is by no means the only agency whose practices constitute a threat to our vital right to privacy; some 20 federal agencies are engaged in intelligence activities. Among them are the Internal Revenue Service, the Post Office, the Secret Service, the Customs Bureau, the Civil Service Commission (which lists 15 million—repeat, 15 million—names of "subversive activity" suspects), the Immigration and Naturalization Service, the Passport Office, the so-called anti-subversive committees in Congress, and the military services. The Army itself has admitted that in the late 1960s it had 1,200 agents doing the field work for a large staff which operated a dossier bank of 25 million "personalities." This was a good deal of the work I did during my tour of duty in the Counter Intelligence Corps in the early 1950s.

I trust it might be fair to guess that if anyone ever took the trouble to tabulate all the millions of persons on file in the millions of dossiers in all these branches of government, over half the citizens of America are in some kind of file for some kind of irrelevant reason. Add to this the millions more who are on file in state and local intelligence offices and the threat to the health of our free society is self-evident.

In testimony before the Senate in 1971, Burt Neuborne, an attorney for the ACLU, stated it this way: "The chilling effect of pervasive surveillance will inevitably destroy any society's capacity for dissent, non-conformity and heterodoxy. Subtract those elements from a libertarian democracy and you have to-talitarianism."

The existing method for undertaking any such surveillance under law or by executive action should be ended and the laws changed to make it unlawful for whatever reason by anyone, government or private.

Those who plead the need of such power for national defense purposes fail to note that even with wiretapping we still are required to spend $80 billion on national defense. And those who maintain that our law enforcement sector needs this power to combat the Mafia, Cosa Nostra, or organized crime are only repeating the usual incantation against a specter which still remains even though they have been using wiretapping for years.

Fourth Amendment protections against unreasonable search and seizure gave some degree of safety to Americans before the technological revolution. But with today's profusion of sophisticated photographic and electronic devices for bugging and wiretapping, a pervasive sense of being watched can stifle the spontaneity without which a free society can slide into a police state mentality.

Efforts by the Nixon administration to conduct carte blanche electronic surveillance are intolerable. A number of clear-cut measures must be enacted to protect against any such actions by future administrations. No surveillance should ever be undertaken without a warrant, which should be granted only after sworn testimony from government officials that probable cause exists that the proposed surveillance will uncover specific evidence of a specific crime. The warrant would authorize surveillance for a limited length of time. If material thus obtained does not produce evidence for use in a criminal action, all such material must be destroyed.

Furthermore, the military must get completely out of the business of snooping on civilians, and all their intelligence dossiers now in existence must be destroyed. All data collection on persons engaged in lawful political activity, no matter how controversial, must be absolutely prohibited. The same ban must be strictly applied to the current practice of storing (and, too often, disseminating) hearsay, anonymous, derogatory information about individuals. As I said earlier, the careless dissemination of arrest records is a practice which can fence a person off from society; strict limitations must be placed on their use. Furthermore, a statute of limitations must be enacted regarding the use of arrest records and other information so citizens can make a fresh start in a social sense, just as bankruptcy proceedings permit persons to make a fresh start in their economic lives. Without such a procedure, as Neuborne noted in his Senate testimony, "There is no escape from our past; no opportunity for a fresh start. As surely as the scarlet letter was once branded on the flesh, our computers now impose an electronic brand upon us."

There are still other safeguards which must be enacted to maintain a free and open society against the surveillance menace. Every person about whom personal data is being stored by the government, or by such organizations as credit bureaus, must be notified of that fact and permitted to check his dossier for accuracy. Individuals must have the right to challenge the veracity of material in their dossiers. They must also have the right to challenge dissemination of material in their dossiers to anyone or any agency, meaning they must be notified whenever anyone is seeking information from their dossiers. When procedural safeguards are violated, individuals will be able to recover damages.

Unfortunately, the democracy-emasculating practices of secrecy are by no means limited in government to the executive branch. While deploring the executive's penchant for secrecy, Congress abets the system by docilely honoring the executive classification of documents and retaining such data behind its closed committee doors. Only on rare occasions is such information "leaked" to the press or otherwise passed along to the public.

At the same time, Congress continues to employ its own

questionable devices of secret floor sessions, closed committee and conference committee hearings, self-censored hearing transcripts, and unrecorded operations. Individual committees, in the main, are permitted to establish their own secrecy rules and are free to conduct either open or closed proceedings as they choose. Also, unrecordable voice votes are still used as an excuse by some committees to avoid full disclosure as intended by the Legislative Reorganization Act of 1970.

So, Congress also is guilty of blatantly disregarding the public's right to know. Surely, if Congress is to carry out its role as the representative body of the people, it must erase all remaining evidences of secrecy in its own conduct and serve as a conduit to the public for whatever information is made available to it.

It is not enough, we have learned, for the people to have faith in their government; those in government, at all levels, must demonstrate their faith in the people as well. The people must be made a part of the decision-making process. To this end, a people's platform must demand information and officials must realize their duty to tear down the repressive walls of secrecy wherever they exist. To do otherwise is to demonstrate a basic mistrust in the collective wisdom of the people and a frightening lack of confidence in our democratic form of government.

Afterword

Still, if we were to begin
now to more than talk of
the need for change . . . and
think hard about the kind of
society we want, there might
be time enough.

—*Robert Dahl*

WHAT HAS BEEN PRESENTED HERE obviously is not a political "platform" in the traditional sense, nor has it attempted to touch upon every major issue or suggest specific solutions for each of the myriad of social, economic, and political problems confronting America today. What has been set forth, however, is my own formulation of what I believe to be a rising popular grass-roots movement that must be finally brought together, summarized, and circulated for revision and ratification by the people.

Make no mistake about it. A people's platform *is* being formed. It is developing out of the people's needs and frustrations, their hopes and aspirations. Indeed, the people are demanding it so vigorously and with such growing unanimity that it can no longer be stifled or deterred. Not everyone, of course, calls it a "platform." Some say they want a "reordering

252

of priorities" or "a better deal." Others ask for a "piece of the action" or just "a chance to be heard." But call it what you will, it is the basis for a platform, because it means the people are seeking a change. Not merely a change of leaders or administrations or political labels—the people want a change in direction. And they want it now.

For too long, the people have been shunted aside while the nation has see-sawed between the liberals' philosophy that seemingly believes all our ills can be cured by more spending and more government and the conservatives' preoccupation with the military, private interests, and less government.

Democrat or Republican, it has made no difference. Each has proved unequal to the task of meeting the needs of the people because, either out of fear or a well-intentioned but misguided sense of paternalism, neither has been willing to trust the people (or their own programs?) enough to share their confidence, seek their counsel, or provide them with a meaningful role in determining their own destinies. With this in mind, I have tried to single out problem areas in our national life which best illustrate these failings, and, when possible, I have suggested how these might be corrected and improved upon through the use of citizen power.

Citizen power goes beyond the sloganeering of "power to the people," which to many implies mob government (or lack of it) from the streets. To the contrary, citizen power to me means *responsible* participation by an *enlightened* public in a democratic society which is operated in the people's interests, by their direction, and with their consent.

The foundation of any true and workable people's platform, therefore, must rely heavily upon the development of highly visible and viable public-interest constituencies to serve as power bases for the citizen.

All the people want is a chance to be participating citizens and to share in the immense power and wealth of this nation, to have a voice and a hand in the making of decisions and the implementation of policies, and to achieve a reasonable measure of control over their individual lives and national aspirations.

It is with a view toward achieving these ends that this book was conceived and is dedicated. In the foregoing chapters, I have tried in some way to serve as a conduit between the people and the "establishment," to help pass the word along that a people's platform is in the making and that citizen power is on the rise.

Now it is my hope that much of what has been discussed and proposed here will be given urgent consideration, especially by the two major political parties. If the yearning for a platform truly representing the people's will is not soon to be recognized and heeded, but is to continue being glossed over by meaningless platitudes, I foresee the eventual demise of both parties as useless to the people (already well underway) and even to the state or, at the least, a continued polarization and deep alienation throughout the society. Either way, the parties, along with the people, will be the losers. In the words of Thomas Jefferson:

> The will of the people is the only legitimate foundation of any government . . .

Appendixes

The Declaration of Independence

WHEN in the Course of human events, it becomes necessary for one people to dissolve the political bands which have connected them with another, and to assume among the Powers of the earth, the separate and equal station to which the Laws of Nature and of Nature's God entitle them, a decent respect to the opinions of mankind requires that they should declare the causes which impel them to the separation.

We hold these truths to be self-evident, that all men are created equal, that they are endowed by their Creator with certain unalienable Rights, that among these are Life, Liberty and the pursuit of Happiness. That to secure these rights, Governments are instituted among Men, deriving their just powers from the consent of the governed, That whenever any Form of Government becomes destructive of these ends, it is the Right of the People to alter or to abolish it, and to institute new Government, laying its foundation on such principles and organizing its powers in such form, as to them shall seem most likely to effect their Safety and Happiness. Prudence, indeed, will dictate that Governments long established should not be changed for light and transient causes; and accordingly all experience hath shown, that mankind are more disposed to suffer, while evils are sufferable, than to right themselves by abolishing the forms to which they are accustomed. But when a long train of abuses and usurpations, pursuing invariably the same Object evinces a design to reduce them under absolute Despotism, it is their right, it is their duty, to throw off such Government, and to provide new Guards for their future security. Such has been the patient sufferance of these Colonies; and such is now the necessity which constrains them to alter their former Systems of Government. The history of the present King of Great Britain is a history of repeated injuries and usurpations, all having in direct object the establishment of an absolute Tyranny over these States. To prove this, let Facts be submitted to a candid world.

He has refused his Assent to Laws, the most wholesome and necessary for the public good.

He has forbidden his Governors to pass Laws of immediate and pressing importance, unless suspended in their operation till his Assent should be obtained; and when so suspended, he has utterly neglected to attend to them.

He has refused to pass other Laws for the accommodation of large districts of people, unless those people would relinquish the right of Representation in the Legislature, a right inestimable to them and formidable to tyrants only.

He has called together legislative bodies at places unusual, uncomfortable, and distant from the depository of their Public Records, for the sole purpose of fatiguing them into compliance with his measures.

He has dissolved Representative Houses repeatedly, for opposing with manly firmness his invasions on the rights of the people.

He has refused for a long time, after such dissolutions, to cause others to be elected; whereby the Legislative powers, incapable of Annihilation, have returned to the People at large for their exercise; the State remaining in the mean time exposed to all the dangers of invasion from without, and convulsions within.

He has endeavoured to prevent the population of these States; for that purpose obstructing the Laws of Naturalization of Foreigners; refusing to pass others to encourage their migration hither, and raising the conditions of new Appropriations of Lands.

He has obstructed the Administration of Justice, by refusing his Assent to Laws for establishing Judiciary Powers.

He has made Judges dependent on his Will alone, for the tenure of their offices, and the amount and payment of their salaries.

He has erected a multitude of New Offices, and sent hither swarms of Officers to harass our People, and eat out their substance.

He has kept among us, in times of peace, Standing Armies without the Consent of our legislatures.

He has affected to render the Military independent of and superior to the Civil Power.

He has combined with others to subject us to a jurisdiction foreign to our constitution, and unacknowledged by our laws; giving his Assent to their acts of pretended legislation:

For quartering large bodies of armed troops among us:

For protecting them, by a mock Trial, from Punishment for any

Murders which they should commit on the Inhabitants of these States:

For cutting off our Trade with all parts of the world:

For imposing taxes on us without our Consent:

For depriving us in many cases, of the benefits of Trial by Jury:

For transporting us beyond Seas to be tried for pretended offences:

For abolishing the free System of English Laws in a neighbouring Province, establishing therein an Arbitrary government, and enlarging its Boundaries so as to render it at once an example and fit instrument for introducing the same absolute rule into these Colonies:

For taking away our Charters, abolishing our most valuable Laws, and altering fundamentally the Forms of our Governments:

For suspending our own Legislatures, and declaring themselves invested with Power to legislate for us in all cases whatsoever.

He has abdicated Government here, by declaring us out of his Protection and waging War against us.

He has plundered our seas, ravaged our Coasts, burnt our towns, and destroyed the lives of our people.

He is at this time transporting large armies of foreign mercenaries to compleat the works of death, desolation and tyranny, already begun with circumstances of Cruelty & perfidy scarcely paralleled in the most barbarous ages, and totally unworthy the Head of a civilized nation.

He has constrained our fellow Citizens taken Captive on the high Seas to bear Arms against their Country, to become the executioners of their friends and Brethren, or to fall themselves by their Hands.

He has excited domestic insurrections amongst us, and has endeavoured to bring on the inhabitants of our frontiers, the merciless Indian Savages, whose known rule of warfare, is an undistinguished destruction of all ages, sexes and conditions.

In every stage of these Oppressions We have Petitioned for Redress in the most humble terms: Our repeated Petitions have been answered only by repeated injury. A Prince, whose character is thus marked by every act which may define a Tyrant, is unfit to be the ruler of a free People.

Nor have We been wanting in attention to our British brethern. We have warned them from time to time of attempts by their legislature to extend an unwarrantable jurisdiction over us. We have reminded them of the circumstances of our emigration and settlement here. We have appealed to their native justice and magnanimity, and we have conjured them by the ties of our common kindred to disavow these usurpations, which, would inevitably interrupt our connections and correspondence. They too have been deaf to the voice of justice and of consanguinity. We must, therefore, acquiesce in the necessity, which denounces our Separation, and hold them, as we hold the rest of mankind, Enemies in War, in Peace Friends.

We, therefore, the Representatives of the United States of America, in General Congress, Assembled, appealing to the Supreme Judge of the world for the rectitude of our intentions, do, in the Name, and by Authority of the good People of these Colonies, solemnly publish and declare, That these United Colonies are, and of Right ought to be Free and Independent States; that they are Absolved from all Allegiance to the British Crown, and that all political connection between them and the State of Great Britain, is and ought to be totally dissolved; and that as Free and Independent States, they have full Power to levy War, conclude Peace, contract Alliances, establish Commerce and to do all other Acts and Things which Independent States may of right do. And for the support of this Declaration, with a firm reliance on the Protection of Divine Providence, we mutually pledge to each other our Lives, our Fortunes and our sacred honor.

The Bill of Rights (The First Ten Amendments to the Constitution)

Amendment I

Congress shall make no law respecting an establishment of religion, or prohibiting the free exercise thereof; or abridging the freedom of speech, or of the press; or the right of the people peaceably to assemble, and to petition the Government for a redress of grievances.

Amendment II

A well regulated Militia, being necessary to the security of a free State, the right of the people to keep and bear Arms, shall not be infringed.

Amendment III

No Soldier shall, in time of peace be quartered in any house, without the consent of the Owner, nor in time of war, but in a manner to be prescribed by law.

Amendment IV

The right of the people to be secure in their persons, houses, papers, and effects, against unreasonable searches and seizures, shall not be violated, and no Warrants shall issue, but upon probable cause, supported by Oath or affirmation, and particularly describing the place to be searched, and the persons or things to be seized.

Amendment V

No person shall be held to answer for a capital, or otherwise infamous crime, unless on a presentment or indictment of a Grand Jury, except in cases arising in the land or naval forces, or in the Militia, when in actual service in time of War or public danger; nor shall any person be subject for the same offenses to be twice put in jeopardy of life or limb; nor shall be compelled in any criminal case to be a witness against himself, nor be deprived of life, liberty, or property, without due process of law; nor shall private property be taken for public use, without just compensation.

Amendment VI

In all criminal prosecutions, the accused shall enjoy the right to a speedy and public trial, by an impartial jury of the State and district wherein the crime shall have been committed, which district shall have been previously ascertained by law, and to be informed of the nature and cause of the accusation; to be confronted with the witnesses against him; to have compulsory process for obtaining witnesses in his favor, and to have the Assistance of Counsel for his defence.

Amendment VII

In suits at common law, where the value in controversy shall exceed twenty dollars, the right of trial by jury shall be preserved, and no fact tried by a jury, shall be otherwise re-examined in any Court of the United States, than according to the rules of the common law.

Amendment VIII

Excessive bail shall not be required, nor excessive fines imposed, nor cruel and unusual punishments inflicted.

Amendment IX

The enumeration in the Constitution, of certain rights, shall not be construed to deny or disparage others retained by the people.

Amendment X

The powers not delegated to the United States by the Constitution, nor prohibited by it to the States, are reserved to the States respectively, or to the people.

Populist Party Platform

The first national convention of the "People's Party" was held at Omaha, on July 2, 1892. C. H. Ellington, of Georgia, was the temporary chairman, and H. L. Loucks, of South Dakota, the permanent president. The platform, reported and adopted on July 4, was as follows.

ASSEMBLED UPON the 116th anniversary of the Declaration of Independence, the People's party of America, in their first national convention, invoking upon their action the blessing of Almighty God, puts forth, in the name and on behalf of the people of this country, the following preamble and declaration of principles:

The conditions which surround us best justify our cooperation: we meet in the midst of a nation brought to the verge of moral, political, and material ruin. Corruption dominates the ballot-box, the legislature, the Congress, and touches even the ermine of the bench. The people are demoralized; most of the States have been compelled to isolate the voters at the polling-places to prevent universal intimidation or bribery. The newspapers are largely subsidized or muzzled; public opinion silenced; business prostrated; our homes covered with mortgages; labor impoverished; and the land concentrating in the hands of the capitalists. The urban workmen are denied the right of organization for self-protection; imported pauperized labor beats down their wages; a hireling standing army, unrecognized by our laws, is established to shoot them down, and they are rapidly degenerating into European conditions. The fruits of the toil of millions are boldly stolen to build up colossal fortunes for a few, unprecedented in the history of mankind; and the possessors of these, in turn, despise the republic and endanger liberty. From the same prolific womb of governmental injustice we breed the two great classes of tramps and millionaires.

The national power to create money is appropriated to enrich bond-holders; a vast public debt, payable in legal tender currency, has been funded into gold-bearing bonds, thereby adding millions to the burdens of the people. Silver, which has been accepted as coin since the dawn of history, has been demonetized to add to the purchasing power of gold by decreasing the value of all forms of property as well as human labor; and the supply of currency is purposely abridged to fatten usurers, bankrupt enterprise, and enslave industry. A vast conspiracy against mankind has been organized on two continents and it is rapidly taking possession of the world. If not met and overthrown at once, it forebodes terrible social convulsions, the destruction of civilization, or the establishment of an absolute despotism.

We have witnessed for more than a quarter of a century the struggles of the two great political parties for power and plunder, while grievous wrongs have been inflicted upon the suffering people.

We charge that the controlling influences dominating both these parties have permitted the existing dreadful conditions to develop without serious effort to prevent or restrain them. Neither do they now promise us any substantial report. They have agreed together to ignore in the campaign every issue but one. They propose to drown the outcries of a plundered people with the uproar of a sham battle over the tariff, so that capitalists, corporations, national banks, rings, trusts, watered stock, the demonetization of silver, and the oppressions of the usurers may all be lost sight of. They propose to sacrifice our homes, lives, and children on the altar of mammon; to destroy the multitude in order to secure corruption funds from the millionaires.

Assembled on the anniversary of the birthday of the nation, and filled with the spirit of the grand general chief who established our independence, we seek to restore the government of the Republic to the hands of the "plain people," with whose class it originated. We assert our purposes to be identical with the purposes of the National Constitution, "to form a more perfect union and establish justice, insure domestic tranquillity, provide for the common defense, promote the general welfare, and secure the blessings of liberty for ourselves and our posterity." We declare that this republic can only endure as a free government while built upon the love of the whole people for each other and for the nation; that it cannot be pinned together by bayonets; that the civil war is over, and that every passion and resentment which grew out of it must die with it; and that we must be in fact, as we are in name, one united brotherhood of freemen.

Our country finds itself confronted by conditions for which there is no precedent in the history of the world; our annual agricultural productions amount to billions of dollars in value, which must, within a few weeks or months, be exchanged for billions of dollars of commodities consumed in their production; the existing currency supply is wholly inadequate to make this exchange; the results are falling prices, the formation of combines and rings, the impoverishment of the producing class. We pledge ourselves, if given power, we will labor to correct these evils by wise and reasonable legislation, in accordance with the terms of our platform. We believe that the powers of government—in other words, of the people—should be expanded (as in the case of the postal service) as rapidly and as far as the good sense of an intelligent people and the teachings of experience shall justify, to the end that oppression, injustice, and poverty shall eventually cease in the land.

While our sympathies as a party of reform are naturally upon the side of every proposition which will tend to make men intelligent, virtuous, and temperate, we nevertheless regard these questions—important as they are—as secondary to the great issues now pressing for solution, and upon which not only our individual prosperity but the very existence of free institutions depends; and we ask all men to first help us to determine whether we are to have a republic to administer before we differ as to the conditions upon which it is to be administered; believing that the forces of reform this day organized will never cease to move forward until every wrong is remedied, and equal rights and equal privileges securely established for all the men and women of this country.

We declare, therefore,—

First. That the union of the labor forces of the United States this day consummated shall be permanent and perpetual; may its spirit enter all hearts for the salvation of the republic and the uplifting of mankind!

Second. Wealth belongs to him who creates it, and every dollar taken from industry without an equivalent is robbery. "If any will not work, neither shall he eat." The interests of rural and civic labor are not the same; their enemies are identical.

Third. We believe that the time has come when the railroad corporations will either own the people or the people must own the railroads; and, should the government enter upon the work of owning and managing all railroads, we should favor an amendment to the Constitution by which all persons engaged in the government service shall be placed under a civil service regulation of the most rigid character, so as to prevent the increase of the power of the national administration by the use of such additional government employees.

We demand,—

First, a national currency, safe, sound, and flexible, issued by the general government only, a full legal tender for all debts, public and private, and that, without the use of banking corporations, a just, equitable, and efficient means of distribution direct to the people, at a tax not to exceed two percent per annum, to be provided as set forth in the sub-treasury plan of the Farmers' Alliance, or a better system, also, by payments in discharge of its obligations for public improvements.

(a) We demand free and unlimited coinage of silver and gold at the present legal ratio of sixteen to one.

(b) We demand that the amount of circulating medium be speedily increased to not less than fifty dollars per capita.

(c) We demand a graduated income tax.

(d) We believe that the money of the country should be kept as much as possible in the hands of the people, and hence we demand that all state and national revenues shall be limited to the necessary expenses of the government economically and honestly administered.

(e) We demand that postal savings banks be established by the government for the safe deposit of the earnings of the people and to facilitate exchange.

Second, Transportation. Transportation being a means of exchange and a public necessity, the government should own and operate the railroads in the interest of the people.

(a) The telegraph and telephone, like the post-office system, being a necessity for the transmission of news, should be owned and operated by the government in the interest of the people.

Third, Land. The land, including all the natural sources of wealth, is the heritage of the people, and should not be monopolized for speculative purposes and alien ownership of land should be prohibited. All land now held by railroads and other corporations in excess of their actual needs, and all lands now owned by aliens, should be reclaimed by the government and held for actual settlers only.

Subsequently, the committee on resolutions made a supplementary report, submitting a series of resolutions which it was explained are not to be regarded as a part of the party platform, but as expressive of the opinion of the party, as follows:—

Whereas, Other questions have been presented for our consideration, we hereby submit the following, not as a part of the platform of the People's party, but as resolutions expressive of the sentiment of this convention.

1. Resolved, That we demand a free ballot and a fair count in all elections, and pledge ourselves to secure it to every legal voter without federal intervention, through the adoption by the States of the unperverted Australian or secret ballot system.

2. Resolved, That the revenue derived from a graduated income tax should be applied to the reduction of the burden of taxation now resting upon the domestic industries of this country.

3. Resolved, That we pledge our support to fair and liberal pensions to ex-Union soldiers and sailors.

4. Resolved, That we condemn the fallacy of protecting American labor under the present system, which opens our ports to the pauper and criminal classes of the world, and crowds out our wage-earners; and we denounce the present ineffective laws against contract labor, and demand the further restriction of undesirable immigration.

5. Resolved, That we cordially sympathize with the efforts of organized workingmen to shorten the hours of labor, and demand a rigid enforcement of the existing eight-hour law on government work, and ask that a penalty clause be added to the said law.

6. Resolved, That we regard the maintenance of a large standing army of mercenaries, known as the Pinkerton system, as a menace to our liberties, and we demand its abolition; and we condemn the recent invasion of the Territory of Wyoming by the hired assassins of plutocracy, assisted by federal officials.

7. Resolved, That we commend to the favorable consideration of the people and the reform press the legislative system known as the initiative and referendum.

8. Resolved, That we favor a constitutional provision limiting the office of the President and Vice-President to one term, and providing for the election of senators of the United States by a direct vote of the people.

9. Resolved, That we oppose any subsidy or national aid to any private corporation for any purpose.

General James B. Weaver, of Iowa, was nominated for President. The vote stood:

Whole number of votes	1263
Necessary for a choice	632
James B. Weaver, Iowa	995
James H. Kyle, South Dakota	265
Mann Page, Virginia	1
Leland Stanford, Calif.	1
—— Norton	1

For Vice-President, James G. Field, of Virginia, was nominated. The vote was as follows:

Whole number of votes	1287
Necessary for a choice	644
James G. Field, Virginia	733
Ben S. Terrell, Texas	554

The representation in this convention was irregular, as may be seen from the fact that Texas cast 60 votes, New York 59, Pennsylvania 21, Massachusetts 28, Illinois 83, and North Dakota 25.

Laws for Citizens
to Make Waves By

NORMALLY the Attorney General is authorized to file suits to enforce federally created rights. However, in the situations listed below any citizen who has been injured may sue and enforce federal rights. These statutes have been gathered together for the first time and demonstrate how effectively a citizen may enforce his own interests if he has a usable vehicle. All a citizen needs to do to enforce these statutes is to uncover a violation of his rights and retain a good lawyer to represent him. The lawyer's fee normally can be paid out of the fine or recovery granted by the Court. Thus, you should not have to pay anything other than a few small court costs, such as a filing fee, out of your own pocket. If a lawyer insists upon a retainer before proceeding, try to find another lawyer who is willing to represent you on a contingent fee basis (the lawyer's fee comes out of your award). For example, if you have been the victim of job discrimination because of your age, sex, color, nationality, or religion, you are entitled to compensation and your lawyer's bills are paid for by the discriminator.

STATUTES SPECIFICALLY AUTHORIZING CITIZEN SUITS

7 U.S.C. Secs. 2561–2569.   The owner of a unique plant variety is protected from infringement and may sue anyone who attempts to sell or reproduce the plant variety.

12 U.S.C. Sec. 1723a (e).   Gives individual right to sue for actual damages and punitive damages and injunction for illegal use of names "Federal National Mortgage Association" and "Government National Mortgage Association" unless set up in accordance with the terms of the statute.

12 U.S.C. Sec. 1749bbb–11.   Gives claimant right to sue upon disallowance of any claims under National Insurance Development Program or upon refusal of claimant to accept amount allowed.

12 U.S.C. Sec. 1975–76.   Gives individual right to sue and recover three times amount of damages, cost of suit, and attorney's fees if individual sustains damages covered under Section 1972. Such damages include a bank's refusal to extend credit, lease or sell property, or refuse to extend service by requiring the customer to meet certain requirements, such as taking out another loan, buy additional property, or use additional services from the bank. Customer also has the right to sue if he is refused service by a bank because he has dealt with that bank's competitor.

15 U.S.C. Secs. 15, 26.   Gives right to recovery of treble damages by persons injured by violation of antitrust laws. Confers right to private injunctive relief (except against common carriers) to those threatened by loss or damage as a result of violation of antitrust laws including price fixing, discrimination in price, service or facilities, or agreements suppressing competition.

15 U.S.C. Sec. 72.   Recovery of treble damages by persons injured by importation or sale of articles at less than market value or wholesale prices.

15 U.S.C. Sec. 77i.   Allows any person aggrieved by an order of the Securities and Exchange Commission to obtain a review of the SEC order by the U.S. Court of Appeals.

15 U.S.C. Sec. 77l.   Suit authorized under Securities Act of 1933, by purchaser of security against a seller who has used the mail or interstate communications when the seller did not have SEC approval.

15 U.S.C. Sec. 77ppp.   Entitles indenture holder to institute a suit against trustees to enforce payment of principal and interest on or after due date.

15 U.S.C. Sec. 77www.   Authorizes a civil suit for statements filed with the SEC that are false or misleading as to a material fact or omissions of any material fact required or necessary to make the statement not misleading.

15 U.S.C. Sec. 78i.   Provides for civil suit for any person who purchases or sells any security at a price affected by illegal manipulations of security prices against any person who willfully participated in an illegal act.

15 U.S.C. Sec. 78r.   Right to civil suit by any person affected adversely by over the counter transactions against any person who makes misleading statements in reports, registration statement application or documents about the stock.

15 U.S.C. Sec. 79p.   Same as 78r in regard to Utility Holding Companies.

15 U.S.C. Sec. 80a–35b.   Right of civil action for security holder against investment advisor or affiliated person if the investment company has committed a breach of fiduciary duty.

15 U.S.C. 298b, c.   Right of competitors, customers, subsequent purchasers, or jewelry trade association to sue for injunctive relief for violations, in-

cluding falsely marked gold or silver goods or goods manufactured there-from.

15 U.S.C. Sec. 1071b. Persons are entitled to civil action when they are dissatisfied with decisions of the Commissioner of Patents or the Trademark Trial and Appeal Board.

15 U.S.C. 1114. Registrant of a trademark is entitled to civil suit against anyone who infringes on the use of the trademark.

15 U.S.C. 1120. Any person who procures registration in the Patent Office by false or fraudulent means is liable in a civil action by a person injured for any damages sustained as a result of the fraudulent action.

15 U.S.C. Sec. 1640. Civil action provided when creditor fails to disclose consumer credit cost pursuant to Truth in Lending Act.

15 U.S.C. Secs. 1681n, 1681o. Action is provided for consumer under Fair Credit Reporting Act against consumer reporting agency or user of information for willful or negligent noncompliance with the requirements of the Act, including the reporting of obsolete information and failing to provide a consumer with a copy if requested.

15 U.S.C. Sec. 1709. Under Interstate Land Sales Full Disclosure Act, suit is authorized for a person acquiring a lot in a subdivision covered by a statement of record against the developer or his agent for an untrue statement or omission to state a material fact. Civil suit also authorized against any developer or agent who sells in violation of any of the prohibitions relating to sale or lease of lots in subdivisions contained in Sec. 1703 or by means of a property report containing an untrue statement or an omission of a material fact.

17 U.S.C. Sec. 101. Infringement proceedings can be brought by copyright proprietor for violation of his copyright.

18 U.S.C. Sec. 1964. Under Organized Crime Control Act of 1970, a treble damage action is provided for persons injured in their business or property as a result of a violation of provisions prohibiting racketeering activities.

18 U.S.C. Sec. 2520. Any person whose wire or oral communication is intercepted, disclosed, or used in violation of the law has a civil cause of action for actual and punitive damages.

23 U.S.C. Sec. 502. Requires the Secretary of Transportation to be assured by state highway departments that persons forced to relocate due to Federal Highway construction will be reimbursed, assisted in relocating and that equivalent dwellings will be made available. *Hanley v. Volpe* (D.C. Wisc. 1969) 305 F Supp 977 ruled that persons who had been displaced or would be displaced could bring class action to enforce compliance.

26 U.S.C. Secs. 7421 and 7422. Taxpayers are generally restricted from suing to stop payment of taxes. Suits may be entertained, however, after the tax has been paid and claims for refunds have been submitted. Suits are brought against the Government by individual taxpayer.

26 U.S.C. 7426. Provides that civil actions may be brought against the United States in a district court by any person other than the person against whom the tax is assessed who claims an interest or levy in property he feels has been wrongfully levied for tax purposes.

29 U.S.C. Sec. 160 (f). Any person aggrieved by a final order of the National Labor Relations Board granting or denying the relief sought may obtain review of the Board's order in the U.S. Court of Appeals.

29 U.S.C. Sec. 185. Any person who is a party to a collective bargaining agreement may sue his employer or his union for any breach of the agreement or deprivation of his rights under the contract.

29 U.S.C. Sec. 187. Authorization for suit by one injured in his business or property resulting from unlawful activities including forcing an employer to join a labor union or employer organization or agreeing to "blacklist" people or products or establish a secondary boycott or to strike as a means of resolving a work jurisdiction dispute.

29 U.S.C. Sec. 216. Action provided for employees against employers who violate sections on minimum wages or maximum hours for unpaid minimum wages, unpaid overtime compensation, and an additional equal amount as liquidated damages.

29 U.S.C. Sec. 308. Any participant in an employee welfare or pension plan may bring a civil action against any administrator of such plan who refuses to provide such participant with a description of the plan or an annual report covering all contributions, benefits paid, statement and description of assets and liabilities, salaries, fees, and commissions charged to the plan.

29 U.S.C. Sec. 412. Any member of a labor organization may bring a civil action against that labor organization for infringement of his rights to nominate candidates for union office, to vote in all union elections, to attend and fully participate in union meetings, to meet with other union members, to express any views or opinions, to vote by secret ballot on rates of local dues and fees, or to sue to enforce these rights.

29 U.S.C. Sec. 481. Any candidate for union office may bring a civil action against that labor organization to compel it to comply with all reasonable requests to distribute campaign literature, to refrain from discriminating among candidates with respect to the use of membership lists, and to inspect within 30 days prior to the election a list containing the names and last known addresses of all union members if they are

subject to a collective bargaining agreement that requires union membership as a condition of employment.

29 U.S.C. Sec. 501.　Any union member may bring a civil action if his union refuses to do so to secure an accounting or recover damages for misuse of union funds or property or for violations of a union officer's fiduciary duty to his union.

29 U.S.C. Sec. 626.　Authorization for any aggrieved person to bring a civil action for legal or equitable relief pertaining to age discrimination in employment. Such right terminates upon commencement of an action by the Secretary of Labor.

29 U.S.C. Sec. 660 (a).　Any person adversely affected or aggrieved by an order of the Occupational Safety and Health Committee or the Secretary of Labor under the Occupational Health and Safety Act may file a civil action to overturn that order in the United States Court of Appeals.

29 U.S.C. Sec. 662 (d).　Any person in imminent danger of injury may sue the Secretary of Labor to require him to enforce the Health and Safety Act.

30 U.S.C. Sec. 30.　Any person asserting a claim to land patented for mining by another has the right to commence a civil action to determine which party has the lawful right of possession to the land.

30 U.S.C. Sec. 51.　Provides that whenever any person, in the construction of any ditch or canal, injures or damages the possession of any settler on the public domain, the party committing such injury or damage shall be liable to the party injured.

30 U.S.C. Sec. 54.　Liability provided for damages to stock raising or a homestead by mining activities.

31 U.S.C. Sec. 232.　Authorization for private suit in the name of the United States against persons making false claims against the United States.

35 U.S.C. Sec. 146.　Authorizes civil suit by party on appeal of decision by Patent Office denying a patent because the invention interferes with a pending patent.

35 U.S.C. Secs. 281–293.　Remedy of civil action given to a patentee for infringement of his patent.

42 U.S.C. Sec. 233.　Right to civil action against the U.S. for damages of $2,500 or less for personal injury or loss of property resulting from performance of functions by Public Health Service employees or officers.

42 U.S.C. Sec. 1404a.　Any person can sue the United States Housing Authority in federal court just like a private landlord.

42 U.S.C. Sec. 1857H-2. Authorized citizen suits against violators, including the United States and Federal Agencies, of emission standards or limitations under the air pollution control laws, or orders issued by the Administrator or states. Action also provided against Administrator for failure to perform mandatory functions.

42 U.S.C. Secs. 1981–1982. Authorizes suits by minority citizen to prevent interference with his right to make a contact, inherit, purchase, lease, or sell any property.

42 U.S.C. Secs. 1983, 1985. Civil action provided for deprivation of civil rights. Action for damages against one or more conspirators in a conspiracy to deprive person of civil rights. Action for damages for neglect to prevent the commission of such a conspiracy in the event person had power to prevent or aid in preventing same.

42 U.S.C. Sec. 2000a-3. Civil action provided for injunctive relief by aggrieved person for violation of prohibition against discrimination or segregation in places of public accommodation.

42 U.S.C. Sec. 2000b-2. Right of any person to sue for or obtain relief against discrimination in public facilities.

42 U.S.C. Sec. 2000c-8. Right of any person to sue for or obtain relief against discrimination in public education.

42 U.S.C. Sec. 2000e-5. Persons aggrieved may file charges with the Equal Employment Opportunity Commission against a person violating the equal opportunity law. If voluntary compliance cannot be obtained by the Commission, the aggrieved person may bring a civil action.

42 U.S.C. Sec. 3612. Provides right for civil action for enforcement of fair housing laws by any person who claims injury resulting from discriminatory housing practices. Civil action must follow compliance with complaint procedure proscribed in 42 U.S.C. Sec. 3610.

45 U.S.C. Sec. 547. An employee or his authorized representative can sue the Rail Passenger Service Corporation (AMTRAK) in appropriate District Court for violation of an existing labor agreement.

49 U.S.C. Sec. 16. If the Interstate Commerce Commission finds a violation of a statute by a common carrier and the common carrier does not pay damages as ordered, persons complaining can bring suit in U.S. District Court for damages.

49 U.S.C. Sec. 304a. Motor carriers, if abiding by appropriate procedures, can sue the U.S. for recovery of overcharges.

49 U.S.C. Sec. 908. Persons injured on a common carrier (by water) can complain to the Interstate Commerce Commission or bring suit for full amount of damages sustained.

49 U.S.C. Sec. 1540. Authorizes suit by War Risk Insurance claimants against the U.S. in District Court if disagreement arises between the U.S. and claimant concerning settlement of claims.

50 U.S.C. Sec. 793 (a). Any person aggrieved by the findings of the Subversive Activities Control Board declaring that person to be a member of a communist organization may obtain review of that finding in the U.S. Court of Appeals.

50 U.S.C. Sec. 813 (a) and 821 (a). Any person arrested on grounds that he will probably engage in or conspire to engage in acts of espionage or sabotage may seek his release in a United States Court.

50 U.S.C. App. Sec. 459 (d). Any person inducted into the Armed Forces and who is forced to leave a permanent job and who seeks reemployment within 90 days of his discharge (or release from hospitalization) and remains qualified for his job or a similar job with like seniority, status and pay or who is being denied advancement because of his reserve obligations may sue in a federal court to regain his job with all rights and benefits as if he were on furlough from his job.

50 U.S.C. App. Sec. 590. Any person may file a civil action while in the military service or within six months thereafter to secure relief from any obligation incurred prior to the period of military service and a court may grant the following relief: With respect to mortgages or installment contracts for the purchase of real estate or for other obligations, liabilities or taxes, the Court may stay the enforcement of such obligation during the period of the person's military service and set a new schedule for payment.

50 U.S.C. App. Sec. 1191 (e) and 1218 (a). Any contractor or subcontractor aggrieved by an order of the Renegotiation Board determining the amount of excessive profits on a defense contract may petition the Tax Court and then the U.S. Court of Appeals for redetermination.

50 U.S.C. App. Sec. 2296 (a). Any person from whom property is taken by the federal government except through judicial proceedings for condemnation may bring a civil action to determine the value of the property seized.

In addition to the statutes listed above, there are statutes which involve the public in the enforcement of a congressional act by making provision either for outright compensation to an informer or by making allowance for a share of the fine recovered to be turned over to the person supplying the information that leads to the conviction. Examples of statutes that provide for payment of compensation to informers are:

18 U.S.C. Sec. 1751. Concerning a presidential assassination, kidnapping, and assault.
19 U.S.C. Sec. 1619. Dealing with enforcement of customs and navigation laws.
21 U.S.C. Sec. 886. Pertaining to drug abuse prevention and control.
22 U.S.C. Sec. 401. Involving illegal exportation of war materials.

There also exists a general "Mandamus" statute, i.e., a statute authorizing a citizen to bring an action against a federal official to require that official to do an act required by law. However, the statute has long been held to apply only to ministerial acts which do not require the exercise of discretion. A revolutionary development would be a simple statute authorizing anyone with a substantial interest (financial or social) to bring a civil action to enforce any statute, rule, or regulation adopted by the Congress or promulgated by any federal agency. The standing of citizens would have to be stated carefully to prevent judicial frustration of the goal, and criminal actions would have to be excluded because of the potential for abuse. However, it should be possible to design a statute that would permit private citizens to enforce all federal laws, even if the Justice Department or the agency involved does not want to proceed because of financial or political problems. One major cost of such a system would be the loss of control by the government over the development of the law. In some respects this should be a welcome change from governmental inaction, favoritism, or special interest control. However, it will also result in a patchwork development of the law which could reduce the effectiveness of a statutory scheme.

In any case, if such a statute were proposed, it must contain a provision for the payment of reasonable attorney's fees. If this section is left out, the cost of litigation would seriously limit the statute's impact. If included, the result would be a flood of new young public interest law firms, each litigating in a certain subject area and financing their actions out of the hides of those who violate federal law.

Sample Neighborhood Incorporation Paper

IN MOST CASES, state law regulates the creation of a corporation and those laws vary from state to state. Many states have enacted a uniform corporation law and a model of the Articles of Incorporation necessary under the uniform corporation law is set forth below. If you wish to incorporate a group and limit your legal liability for debts you should visit with a public service lawyer.

ARTICLES OF INCORPORATION

OF

_____

To: The Recorder of Deeds

City _____, State _____

We, the undersigned natural persons of the age of twenty-one years or more, acting as incorporators of a corporation adopt the following Articles of Incorporation for such corporation pursuant to the Nonprofit Corporation Act:

FIRST: The name of the corporation is:

SECOND: The period of duration is: ninety-nine years.

THIRD: The purpose or purposes for the corporation is:

FOURTH: A statement as to whether or not the corporation is to have members:

FIFTH: The corporation is to be divided into _____ class (or classes) of members. The designation of each class of members, the qualifications and rights of the members of each class and conferring, limiting, or denying the right to vote are as follows:

SIXTH: A statement as to the maner in which directors shall be elected or appointed, if the directors of any of them are not to be elected or appointed by one or more classes of members, or that the manner of such election or appointment of such directors shall be provided in the bylaws:

SEVENTH: Provisions for the regulation of the internal affairs of the corporation, including provisions for distribution of assets on dissolution or final liquidation:

EIGHTH: The address, including street and number, of its initial registered office is:

and the name of its initial registered agent at such address is:

NINTH: The number of directors constituting the initial board of directors is three (or more) and the names and addresses, including street and number, of the persons who are to serve as the initial directors until the first annual meeting or until their successors be elected and qualified are:

NAME   ADDRESS

TENTH: The name and address, including street and number, of each incorporator is:

NAME   ADDRESS

Date _____

I, _____, a Notary Public, hereby certify that on the
_____ day of _____, 19____ personally ap-
peared before me _____(names of incorporators)_____, who signed the
foregoing document as incorporators, and that the statements therein
contained are true.

(Notary Seal)

                                        _____

                                        Notary Public

BYLAWS

OF

_____

The following 11 paragraphs constitute the official bylaws of ____
_____, a non-profit corporation.

1. The Corporation shall have 3 directors.
2. The directors shall meet at the call of the President who shall
also be Chairman of the Board of Directors.
3. The yearly meeting of the Board of Directors shall be held on
_____(date)_____ in _____(city, state)_____.
4. The directors of the Corporation need not reside in _____
_____(city, state)_____.
5. The directors shall have the power to amend, alter, or repeal
these bylaws or adopt new ones.
6. Directors shall be appointed by the President of the Corporation
for a period of ____ years.

7. Directors shall be subject to removal by a majority vote of the Board of Directors.

8. All vacancies in the Board of Directors shall be filled by the President of the Corporation.

9. The Board of Directors shall appoint a 2 man committee, one of which shall be the Chairman of the Board of Directors, to operate the Corporation and the aforesaid Committee shall exercise all of the powers of the Board of Directors.

10. The Board of Directors shall elect the officers of the Corporation at their yearly meeting.

11. If the Corporation shall be dissolved, the assets of the Corporation, after all debts are paid, shall be donated to a non-profit corporation with the same or similar goals.

The above bylaws have been duly enacted by the Director of _____
_____.

_____
President

Model Constitutional Amendment for Initiative and Referendum

JOINT RESOLUTION

Proposing an amendment to the Constitution of the United States with respect to the proposal and enactment of laws and the proposal and adoption of amendments to the Constitution by popular vote of the people of the United States.

Resolved by the Senate and House of Representatives of the United States of America in Congress assembled (two-thirds of each House concurring therein), That the following article is proposed as an amendment to the Constitution of the United States, which shall be valid to all intents and purposes as part of the Constitution if ratified by the legislatures of three-fourths of the several States or by conventions in three-fourths of the several States within 7 years after its submission to the States for ratification:

ARTICLE ———

"Section 1. Notwithstanding the provisions of section 1 of article I and the provisions of article V of this Constitution, the people of the United States shall have power to exercise the powers set forth in this article.

"Sec. 2. The people of the United States may propose the enactment of a law, including a law repealing or amending a law of the United States, by signing petitions setting forth the text of the law proposed to be enacted. The enactment of a law is proposed on the date on which the signatures of three percent or more of the people of the United States who are qualified by law to vote for electors of the President and Vice President are contained in petitions setting forth the proposed law.

"Sec. 3. The people of the United States may propose the adoption of an amendment to this Constitution by signing petitions setting forth the text of the amendment so proposed. An amendment to this Constitution is proposed when the signatures of six percent or more of the people of the United States who are qualified by law to vote for electors of the President and Vice President are contained in petitions setting forth the proposed amendment.

"Sec. 4. The President shall determine on the first day of September of each year whether the enactment of any law or the adoption of any amendment to this Constitution has been proposed under this article within the preceding 12 months. If he determines that any law or amendment to this Constitution has been proposed he shall publish his determination and the text of the law or amendment proposed. The Congress shall provide by law a means of determining annually the number of the people of the United States who are qualified by law to vote for electors of the President and Vice President.

"Sec. 5. An election shall be held on the first Tuesday after the first Monday in November, or on such other date as the Congress may set by law, of each year in which the President determines, under section 4 of this article, that the people of the United States have proposed the enactment of a law or adoption of an amendment to the Constitution under this article. At such election, the people of the United States who are qualified by law to vote for electors of the President and Vice President shall be entitled to vote on the question of whether the proposed law shall be enacted or whether the proposed amendment shall be adopted. If a majority of the people casting votes on the question approve the enactment of the proposed law or the adoption of the proposed amendment, that law is enacted, or that amendment is adopted, and the law enacted or amendment adopted will take effect thirty days after the date on which the election was held at which it was approved by such majority or on such later date as may be set forth in such law or amendment.

"Sec. 6. Any law enacted by the people of the United States under this article shall be a law of the United States the same as any other statute law of the United States, except that repeal or amendment of such law shall require a subsequent enactment by the people under this article or a statute law approved by at least two-thirds of the members of each House of the Congress. No law, the enactment of which is forbidden the Congress by this Constitution or any amendment thereof, may be enacted by the people of the United States under this article.

"Sec. 7. The Congress shall have power to enforce this article by appropriate legislation."

Constitutional Amendment for the Single Tax

JOINT RESOLUTION

Proposing an amendment to the Constitution of the United States prohibiting the imposition and collection of any tax by the United States except a tax on personal income.

Resolved that the following article is proposed as an amendment to the Constitution of the United States, which shall be valid to all intents and purposes as part of the Constitution if ratified by the legislatures of three-fourths of the several States, or by conventions in three-fourths of the several States, within 7 years after its submission to the States for ratification:

ARTICLE _____

"Section 1. The Congress shall make no law imposing a tax other than a law imposing a tax on the gross income of individuals.

"Sec. 2. Liability for tax under any law of the United States in effect on the date of ratification of this article of amendment, other than a tax imposed under the authority of the sixteenth article of amendment to this Constitution, shall terminate on the date of the first anniversary of that ratification except for liability for taxes incurred prior to the date of that anniversary.

"Sec. 3. The Congress shall have powers to enforce this article by appropriate legislation."

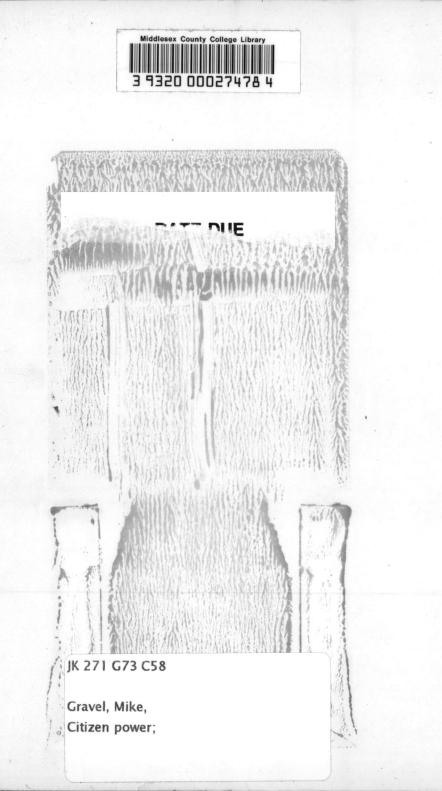